Advance Praise

Herbert Jacobsen's study on the Gospel of Mark reflects a deep plunge into the depths of this Gospel, exploring its ideas and characters, especially Mark and Peter, and ultimately our Lord's most vital question to the apostles and all humankind, "Who do you say I am?" Jacobsen's many years as a professor and pastor enable him to gather up the theological strands of Mark and lay them out in ways we can understand.

C. Hassell Bullock, PhD

Franklin S. Dyrness Professor of Biblical Studies Emeritus
Wheaton College (Illinois)

Academically sound. Devotionally penetrating.

Herb Jacobsen's presentation of the Gospel of Mark probes the question most essential to Jesus' ministry: "Who do you say that I am?" Jesus' disciples follow his journey from village carpenter—to healer and teacher—to someone with authority—to the crucified and risen Christ, the Son of God. In doing so, they discover not only who Jesus is but who they can become as well.

Mark's Gospel—good news—*tells us about Peter's struggle to understand and believe, culminating in his repentance and coming to faith in a living Jesus. In the process, Peter learned what it means to be not just a disciple, but a representative of Jesus, carrying the good news to the heart of a self-obsessed world in Rome. This makes the Gospel of Mark not just a strung-together collection of Jesus events but a book that compels us on the same journey. Mark ends his gospel abruptly, with astonishment at the empty tomb. Like Peter, it prompts a personal response. Who do we say that Jesus is? How do we finish His story in the world where we live?*

Rev. Dr. Paul H. Wright

President, Jerusal

The product of a lifetime of patient listening to, and careful interaction with, the text of Gospel of Mark, Dr. Herbert Jacobsen's book is not your typical Bible commentary. In essence, it is a piece of Biblical theology which distinguishes itself both by its uniqueness and its freshness. The book organizes the fast-paced narrative of Mark into a drama whose unfolding reveals before our eyes, in clear terms, the identity of Jesus, the Son of God. Its masterful thematic exposition of the text draws from it insights that enrich theological understanding and strengthen the believer's faith. These features of Dr. Jacobsen's commentary draw the reader in and keep him captive until the last page of his fascinating text.

Dieumeme Noelliste, PhD
Professor of Theological Ethics
Denver Seminary

If you have been fortunate to hear the sermons and lectures of my friend, Pastor Herb Jacobsen, you are then aware of his verbal skills, a master manipulator of words and vocabulary. He writes as he speaks, with simplicity and clarity. In his examination of Mark's Gospel, he stakes a claim that this Gospel is not inferior to its brethren, but rather its equal, using thought and logic that corresponds to Rabbinical and Talmudic theory. Softly, steadily, and securely, this skilled storyteller and orator offers the reader the joy of new discoveries through the telling of Mark's Gospel.

Rabbi Johanan Bickhardt
Temple Israel of the Poconos
Stroudsburg, Pennsylvania

The author of this book is an NYU-trained scholar and a lifelong pastor with a successful parish ministry. These two roles have impelled him to look at biblical texts with a scrutinizing eye of truth and a searching mind of salvation. In Who Am I?, Dr. Jacobsen takes us on a journey into the forest of Mark's Gospel, a text that is dense with tall trees as well as narrow paths, which are intermittently hidden by thickets and bushes from the view of casual readers.

Dr. Jacobsen has provided instruction on this premise for nearly fifty years, including eight years ago when I, as the Dean of the Center for Studies of the Biblical World of the Korea Baptist Convention, invited Dr. Jacobsen to lead a weeklong seminar in biblical research for a group of Korean pastors in Seoul, Korea. I was his translator. His choice of studying Mark was well received by the attendees. It has been a privilege to have an ongoing dialogue with Dr. Jacobsen over the years as his ideas took shape and developed into the text you now have before you.

I am confident that this book will equip pastors, seminary students, and laypeople alike to better understand the depth of the text as they dig more deeply into the salvation soil of the Gospel.

SeJin Koh, PhD

Senior pastor, Seoul Union Church, Seoul, Korea

Former Director of Robert C. Cooley Center for Early Christianity, Gordon-Conwell Theological Seminary (Charlotte, North Carolina)

Former president, Asia United Theological University, Korea

Former president, Jerusalem University College, Israel

PhD in Near Eastern Archaeology, University of Chicago

As a fisherman, my dad knows what it is like to fish all night long (and catch nothing). To be fair, he is not alone, and while this experience is not necessary to understanding the Gospel of Mark through the eyes of Peter, it certainly helps. Where do you find someone—a professor, teacher, evangelist, pastor, and even a fisherman—who has lived the word shared in Mark's Gospel?

Dad graciously taught Mark in my home to some brothers and sisters from my local church. When teaching in person, he brings you into the story—into the process of learning and experiencing the material. He enables you to become your own best teacher (this is one reason why I tell others he is the best teacher I've ever had). I trust this book, with the help of the Holy Spirit, will do the same for you.

Kevin Jacobsen (son)

I have had the privilege of calling Herb Jacobsen: Dad, coach, professor, and friend. In each of these roles he has demonstrated a love of Christ and of others. He has taught me to do the same.

I remember the first time he taught a class on Mark outside of the academic world. His passion for the message Mark brings to all of us was remarkable, even for a young child. I am confident that you will experience that same passion through this book as he shares the message of Christ through the life of Peter.

Cathie Vitro (daughter)

Who Am I?

A PASTORAL COMMENTARY ON

the Gospel of Mark

Who Am I?

Exploring Peter's Relationship with the Christ

Dear Michael
God bless you
Herb Jacobsen

DR. HERBERT K. JACOBSEN

ISBN: 979-8-218-09217-7 (Print)

ISBN: 979-8-218-09218-4 (Ebook)

Cover Design: Style-Matters.com

Cover Imagery: Storm clouds and rain above the Sea of Galilee in Israel, Shutterstock/Alexander Turovsky

CONTENTS

Preface

I am nearing the final days of my professional career. Throughout my time, both at Wheaton College and in pastoral ministry, I have been fortunate enough to be able to share this perspective on Mark's Gospel. Yet, until now, I have not shared this perspective through the written text. This book is my attempt to communicate what I believe to be an accurate and fair measure to understanding the *good news* from Mark.

There are at least three unique features to this perspective:

1. It benefits from a literary understanding first shared with me by my colleague at Wheaton, Dr. Gilbert Bilezikian, that views the text in the genre of a Greek tragedy.
2. There is an inherent and intended double entendre for the reader to engage in the story at several key moments.
3. I have benefited from a pastoral vantage point into the very real struggles of individuals and families within congregational life.

Mark's Gospel provides true comfort to people in their time of need. More will be said about each of these factors within the text. There is also a fourth feature to this perspective that I find to be among the most profound.

My hope is that the reader will view this work as more than a scholarly effort. In fact, it is not written with the level of theological scholarship as to be subject to detailed scrutiny. That being said, there is a career of scholarship invested in the text. Rather, my hope is that this reading will engage the heart in a thoughtful manner.

In the beginning, it is important for the reader to be reminded of how, when, and why Mark committed this story to writing. There were several vectors converging from political, social, economic, and developmental influences. We will start there, even as if the story had already begun.

Mark is an evangelistic and pastoral presentation of the Gospel calling on its readers to have faith. When Jesus begins his ministry, he declares, "The time has come. The kingdom of God has come near. Repent and believe the good news."

I believe repentance and faith provide access into the kingdom of God. Yet, when teaching the Gospel of Mark, I found that more people treated it as a travelogue or a biography of Jesus rather than an evangelistic document.

Take, for example, Everett Harrison, professor of New Testament at Fuller Seminary. In his introduction to the New Testament he identifies the first major section of Mark (1:14–9:50) as "The Galilean Ministry." Under that heading, he provides titles for twenty-four narratives. The first five of them are listed as follows, and the others are identified with similar brevity:

1. Jesus' Proclamation and the Calling of Helpers (1:14–20)
2. A Sabbath in Capernaum (1:21–38)
3. A Circuit through Galilee (1:39–45)
4. Opposition from Scribes and Pharisees (2:1–3:6)
5. Popularity with the Multitude: The Choice of Helpers (3:7–21)

The second major section (10:1–16:8) he titles "The Ministry in Judea and Jerusalem." This section covers the remainder of the Gospel of Mark with thirteen narratives.

Harrison is not wrong in listing the narratives. These are in the text. In explaining the purpose of Mark he first laments Mark has failed to declare an explicit purpose for his writing. Then he argues that attention to the text makes it evident that the story of Jesus is the "Gospel." In so doing, he appears to understand Mark as a biography of Jesus traced through two major geographical districts.

Harrison is an excellent scholar, yet his outline of Mark leaves me puzzled. The headings follow in a similar mundane list that holds no corresponding theological or human value. Such a mutilation of the text seems to miss the underlying *good news*.

The author I have found most helpful in understanding the text of Mark is William Lane. In his commentary, *The Gospel According to Mark*, he offers similar analysis to Harrison.

His first section (1:14–3:6) is called "The Initial Phase of the Galilean Ministry." Harrison had five subheadings for this section; Lane has eight. Then Lane switches to "Later Phases of the Ministry in Galilee," (3:7–6:13) with seven subsections.

A more recently published introduction to the New Testament (Carson 2005) done by D. A. Carson and Douglas J. Moo offers similar categories: "First Part of the Galilean Ministry" (1:16–36), "Second Part of the Galilean Ministry" (3:13–5:43), and then "The Concluding Phase of the Galilean Ministry" (6:7–8:26).

A yet more recent commentary on Mark (Stein 2008) is by Robert H. Stein, graduate of Princeton and professor at Bethel Seminary and at Southern Baptist Theological Seminary. He sees the document as focusing on "the historical biography/narrative of Jesus Christ" and therefore provides an outline by asking first, "Who Is This Jesus?" and eventually lapses into a similar listing of events found in Harrison—some lists with fourteen subpoints, others with twelve or thirteen. His commentary is well worth the reading.

My initial quarrel with these approaches is the lack of a reasonable order of events that can be memorized by a student learning the structure of the Gospel. Imagine the frustration of the student who needs to remember twenty-four (or ten, twelve, or fifteen) narratives in sequence without a thread that ties them together. Geography (Galilee) may be true, it is not helpful.

I wanted the students in my classes on Mark to have a better outline—something they could easily memorize and something that would challenge them to have faith.

A subsequent quarrel, one that comes many years later, is from my years as a minister. There is a profound difference between a lecture and a sermon. Early interpretations of Mark identify him as writing down Peter's sermon. This would suggest and maybe entail an evangelistic effort on Mark's part rather that the scholarly historical account. None of the aforementioned approaches is written like a sermon.

It took decades for me to reach the point I am at in my life now. I have three children and a number of grandchildren who have heard me speak often of the substance of faith. Many of them have actually heard my explanations of Mark. Now my wife and I have been blessed with several great-grandchildren. A major concern is that they all find in Mark the challenge that I believe can guide them on their way in life.

Allow me to fill in a few details from my own journey in understanding Mark. Along the way, I will offer a word of thanks to a few of the many people who have had a significant part in shaping my thoughts.

I begin with the frustration of years ago. Requiring a student to memorize a list of narratives is not helpful. I turned to my colleague at Wheaton College, Gilbert Bilezikian, for help. He began by repeating the frustrations I had experienced. He had them too. Then he suggested reading Mark as a dialogue, a drama, even a Greek tragedy. Bilezikian had just finished his doctoral dissertation on Mark using Aristotle's *Poetics* as guide for interpretation. Unfortunately, for me, I was not familiar with his dissertation at the time (published under the title "The Liberated Gospel" in 1977). Nonetheless, I followed his advice and found it quite helpful.

At about the same time Bilezikian published his thesis, Alec McGowen, a British actor, took the Gospel of Mark to the stage in England in 1978. McGowen merely recited the book of Mark, and hundreds came to hear the recitation. Later, some of his protégés would take the work to America where Bilezikian and I, along with our wives, heard the dramatic recitation. It was spellbinding. It had the appeal of a good drama and of a good sermon.

My outline of Mark fell into five sections, each with a specified purpose. Each section typically had three to five subsections and sometimes a subsection would have three to five stories to make its point. I have tried to identify them accordingly.

The outline was my vision for interpreting, teaching, and preaching from Mark. I am indebted to the many students who took my classes. They provided wonderful feedback on the significance of the outline. It was a privilege to present the basic thoughts to several Bible study groups. They, too, provided helpful feedback. To these I must add summer camps, confirmation classes, and churches.

Each time a class concluded, I gained insight and support for the outline. I also found more questions. The lack of a clear statement of purpose in Mark caused me to struggle with what that purpose might be. I struggled with the question, "For whom should I be writing this material?" And, "Why?" Clearly, my concern was not a commentary similar to so many of them in the marketplace.

I had begun in frustration and then found a vision. In time, I also found a structure for that vision. Unfortunately, I still lacked a clear understanding of Mark's intended audience. This was the last piece of my puzzle.

A few years ago, a trusted friend, SeJin Koh, asked if I would teach a group of forty or so ministers at a minister's retreat in Korea. He would translate. Then he asked what I would like to teach. I offered Mark. I believe he was a little skeptical, yet he agreed. As the class was about to begin, some of the students wanted to know of my background for a class on Mark. My education was more in theology than in exegesis. So, in all honesty, they were wondering if they would be wasting their time even before the class started. The class ended without even one student dropping out, and with a request to repeat the class at another time. There was even a request to publish the material in both Korean and English.

What did I learn? I learned that Mark was written for people just like those ministers in South Korea. The people of South Korea face a constant threat from North Korea. This is not unlike the threat that the church in Rome faced when Peter was executed. They did not need a lecture; they needed comfort and encouragement. This is Mark's Gospel.

I have a word to share with my colleagues in academia. A few years ago, I had the opportunity to share a later draft of my work on Mark with my New Testament professor, David L. Beckman. He was living with his wife in a retirement home in Colorado. I visited him as often as I could and frequently would talk with him on the phone. He had been to my home when I was still an undergraduate; my parents and I had great admiration for him. I wanted him to know what I was doing and to get his perspective on the change I proposed in interpreting Mark.

At the dinner table, he and I sat with some of his friends. He introduced me to them as one of his former students—an introduction he had made several times before. Then he turned to his friends and said he had taught Mark many times over his lifetime and that I had written a book on Mark. Without stopping, he added, "I finally understand what Mark is about."

That was a breathtaking moment for me. My professor liked what he had read. I needed no more response than that. I still take joy from his comment. He is gone now, and so is his beloved wife. We saw each other a few more times over the next few years, and each time was a blessing.

I share this story because I feel there are many of my colleagues, and perhaps many other scholars teaching the New Testament, who might have the same reaction he had. I hope so. I do not think that the exegetical work done by my colleagues is likely to change very much. I hope, however, that their orientations can shift from innocuous geographical markers and serial listings of story after story to something much more substantive.

As I have completed this work, I have come to understand what is perhaps the fourth unique feature of viewing Mark from the perspective of *good news*. I encourage the reader to consider Peter's sermon from the Day of Pentecost (Acts 2:14–41). The evangelistic impact from that sermon is the beginning of the Church. In much the same manner (and outline), the Gospel of Mark gives testimony, Peter's testimony, to Jesus as the Christ. His testimony is a call to repentance. Specifically, it is Peter's call to repentance. I share this with you up front, and look forward to our dialogue as you read the *good news* of Jesus according to Mark.

INTRODUCTION
Golden Palaces

Today, parents name their sons Paul...
—Merrill C. Tenney

Political, social, economic, and developmental influences converged in Rome to persecute its people under the authoritarian guidance of one person: Nero. There are several parallels throughout history, including travesties in Uganda, Romania, Armenia, Stalinist Russia, and Nazi Germany during just the twentieth century. The persecution for many subjects of Rome was inhuman, especially those professing this newfound faith in the Nazarene as the Son of God. Women and children were fed to lions in front of thousands in the Colosseum. Other believers were used as torches, burned alive along the roadside just to light the way. In the midst of this first-century torture, even the Apostles Peter and Paul were killed. All this at the hands of Caesar, the evil emperor Nero.

This is the historical context for the writing of Mark's Gospel. It does not come simply from a thoughtful reflection on the teachings of Jesus. Nor does it come about as a political campaign intended to persuade others. It is written in the crucible of oppression. It is written only a few decades following the life, death, and resurrection of Jesus. And it bears witness to the Christ when faith is challenged by human atrocity—*the* Christ, who demonstrates true kingship.

Peter and Paul had each come to Rome proclaiming that Jesus is that Christ. Their presence, bolstered by overwhelming acceptance, created within Rome what some may have considered a social uprising. Scores of Jews were acknowledging the Messiah. Even Gentiles were recognizing this new king. Such disturbance threatened Caesar's authority.

Nero was so offended at the perceived threat to his rule by Peter and Paul that he had them both thrown into prison. Even in prison, they continued to profess the good news. They converted several to the Christian faith, further angering Nero. This social disruption was growing. John Foxe, one of the earliest chroniclers of Christian martyrdom, explains simply, "Having been nine months in prison, and after being scourged, he [Peter] was crucified with his head down. It is related that he himself chose this painful posture because he did not think he was worthy to suffer in the same manner as the Lord." [1]

The persecution under Nero in AD 64 was beyond brutal. The city of Rome itself was set on fire. Nero blamed the Christians. He sentenced many of them to death. Many scholars have speculated that Nero's intense hostility stemmed from his own psyche—projecting blame onto innocents in a vain effort to deny personal responsibility. Perhaps Nero himself set the city ablaze. Stories have been told that Nero merely watched the city burn as he callously played his violin to the carnage. As emperor, he fancied himself the premier ruler and builder of all human civilization. Perhaps Nero simply wanted to rebuild the city.

Fear was everywhere. Believers bore the brunt of Nero's rage. Even those Roman citizens who felt it was possible that the Christians might be guilty of something believed that the ruthless torture was excessive. "For it was felt that they were being sacrificed to one man's brutality [Nero] rather than to the national interest." [2]

The infant church was struggling. And Peter was its *rock*. He had previously witnessed similar hostility toward the innocent.

---

1 John Foxe, *Foxe's Christian Martyrs of the World*, 33.

2 Quotation from Tacitus in *The Gospel according to Mark* (William Lane, page 14).

In his own fear, he had once (actually, three times!) denied his faith. This time around, Peter was resolved to hold fast to the truth. By his calm disposition, he gave strength to all who struggled through the suffering. His behavior gave further testimony to the good news of God's salvation, causing the Church to grow even more quickly in the face of persecution and adversity.

When Peter was killed, the newfound faith seemed in peril. Believers may well have asked, "Who will comfort us now? Who will preach the good news?" Some may have focused on their own needs: "What will happen to me? Will I survive this carnage?" Others may have doubted the value of this faith that seemed to bring judgment, suffering, and death. It was a critical moment in the development of the Church.

Peter's death was personally difficult for the young congregation in Rome. Peter, an Apostle for the worldwide Church, was their pastor. It was through Peter they had come to know Jesus as Lord. With his death, the church had lost its leader.

Following Peter's death, the church sought ways to keep his presence known. Peter had not written his testimony. John Mark, whom Peter trusted fully, was asked to write down Peter's sermons. According to Eusebius, "Mark, having become the interpreter of Peter, wrote down accurately whatever he remembered of the things said and done by the Lord, but not in order." [3] Mark adapted what he knew from Peter to meet the needs of the people in the church in Rome. It is Mark's writing flowing from the apostolic authority of Peter, who was witness to the Christ.

Mark records many stories of Jesus, especially those that intersect with the experience of Peter. He did not include every story he knew. Eventually, the stories he did share would explain the passion of Peter to proclaim, "Jesus is Lord." They also offer a reason why Peter was so calm under the threat of his own

---

3 Quotation from Eusebius in *The Gospel according to Mark* (William Lane, page 8).

torture. These are the stories that Mark selected. They would bring comfort to the young church in its time of trial. Mark himself had learned the same comfort with Peter as his mentor.

Mark is telling more than the story of Jesus. He is also telling the story of the Church. Surely influenced heavily from Peter's vantage point, Mark brings his own experiences and insights into the spread of the Gospel throughout the Roman Empire.

The story of the Church, however, does not begin in Rome. That story begins in Jerusalem, a few decades earlier, with Peter's proclamation of the Gospel on Pentecost. It may be worth noting that scholars have long recognized Mark's Gospel to have been written after AD 64 (when Rome burned). Some have speculated it was written perhaps as late as AD 70 (when Jerusalem was destroyed by the Roman General Titus). If that were the case, the suffering is even greater, as Christians would find refuge neither in Rome nor in Jerusalem.

After the resurrection, Jesus instructed the disciples to remain in Jerusalem. Jesus himself would ascend into the presence of God the Father. Yet he promised the coming of the comforter, the Holy Spirit, to be with his disciples.

On the day of Pentecost, ten days after the ascension, those gathered in Jerusalem heard the sound of a violent blowing wind. They saw what looked like tongues of fire descend onto the disciples. Everyone heard the disciples speak in their own native language. How can this be? I admit, Hagar and I sometimes wonder if a Norwegian were there. *Uff da!*

Peter explained that this moment fulfilled what the Prophet Joel had said about God pouring out his Spirit in the last days. He then boldly proclaims Jesus of Nazareth, whom they witnessed crucified on a cross, to be risen from the dead. This Jesus is the One whom God has made Lord and Christ.

The appropriate response to the sacrificial love of God was to repent and put faith in Jesus as the long-awaited Messiah. The crowd listened as Peter explained all that was witnessed at Pentecost, quoting from the Prophet Joel and from David in the Psalms. In the crowd were people from many countries, including citizens from Rome. About three thousand people responded to Peter's message that day, acknowledging Jesus as the Christ.

From Pentecost to the moment of his own death, Peter continued to bear witness to the Christ. He traveled throughout Jerusalem, Judea, Samaria reaching out to the Jewish population, and then, even to the Gentiles. He moved toward Rome, which was recognized as the capital city for the civilized world. There, he became pastor to the people who came to know Jesus as Savior and Lord.

While it is important, and relevant, to know the historical events in the life of Jesus (and the Church), the story of faith is greater than a mere collection of facts or even stories. Mark knows what the people of Rome need to hear.

Mark begins the Gospel with the baptism by John the Baptist. He avoids any mention of the birth or childhood of Jesus. He proceeds to share selected stories of Jesus, primarily as if viewing Jesus' life through Peter's eyes. Mark concludes with the Passion narrative, ending with the crucifixion. He does not tell the story of the resurrection. A full understanding of Mark's Gospel must account for the absence of these stories. The reasons for this omission are central to the themes developed in the chapters to come.

Mark similarly wants to ensure that the congregation in Rome is comforted. Toward that end, he is sharing the testimony of his mentor, Peter. Yet, Mark's Gospel is not a complete story about Peter either. The Gospel message transcends the story of any one individual.

Mark places Peter near the beginning of the story and at the ending. Immediately following the brief narrative of Jesus' baptism, Jesus calls his first four disciples. Simon (whom Jesus will later rename Peter) together with his brother, Andrew, are the first two Jesus calls to become disciples. James and John are next.

Near the end of the Gospel, Peter is the last disciple to be mentioned by name. This final portion of the Gospel compares the trial of Jesus before the authorities with a "trial" of Peter before people with no legal standing.

Between these references to Peter, Mark focuses on Peter's role more than any of the other disciples. Peter speaks on behalf of the disciples. He is in a more intimate group that includes James and John. Peter as well as the other disciples witness the power of Jesus to heal those who were blind, deaf, dumb, lame, possessed by an alien spirit, or even dead. He also demonstrates his ability to calm a troubled sea. Eventually, Peter's hope will embrace Jesus' anointing to "heal" the nation—liberating it from Roman dominion and restoring Jewish independence and sovereignty.

Throughout the text, Peter's relationship with Jesus plays a central role in his revelation of good news. Their relationship depicts both the epiphany and confusion that results from experiencing God. Mark identifies the moments when Peter seems to understand just who it is who has called him; only to be followed by many more moments that show Peter's inexplicable ignorance. Perhaps, Mark is giving the reader a hint as to the way many of us relate to God, and to the Christ.

Mark's reference to Peter's experiences as a disciple traces the foundational development of Peter's spiritual life. To some extent, it suggests a reason why Peter would eventually feel unworthy of being crucified in the same manner as his Lord. The people of Rome would recognize how Peter's thoughts about suffering had become so important to him. In all likelihood, Peter would have mentioned his personal failings as a disciple directly to Mark. He especially struggled with understanding why the righteous suffer. Mark makes it a point to record Peter's thoughts and actions on this matter. Later, as a witness to the resurrection, Peter would begin to understand the significance of suffering in light of God's mercy. From this perspective, suffering gives birth to hope.

In Peter's first epistle, Peter refers to Mark as his son. This expression reveals the intimate and trusting relationship between the Apostle, Peter, and the younger follower of Jesus, Mark. The church in Rome recognized that Peter trusted Mark. It is likely for this reason that they called upon Mark to write down Peter's sermons. The written Gospel is one way for Peter's message to endure and his presence to be felt.

Mark is well chosen. He has proven capable of writing more than the story of Jesus or the story of Peter. He has documented the Gospel that spawned the Church. Indeed, he is eminently qualified. More than the interpreter for Peter, Mark also worked alongside the Apostle Paul.

It is in connection with Paul we learn that Mark, also known also as "John Mark," is a cousin of Barnabas. Barnabas recommended that Mark, likely a young adult at the time, accompany Paul on the first missionary journey. Mark handled the journey well when Barnabas appears to be the leader of the group. When Paul appears to become the leader, Mark left the team and went home. This caused a rift between Mark and Paul. When Barnabas and Paul talked about a second missionary journey, Paul refused let Mark on the team. Paul went one way and Barnabas took Mark in another.

Years later, the rift seems to have mended, as Paul speaks of Mark as a great help to him in the ministry. Mark becomes the faithful helper while Paul is a "prisoner" of Christ Jesus—likely in Rome. In the end, Paul, like Peter, expresses confidence in Mark.

We may assume Mark benefited substantially from his relationship to Paul, even as his Gospel demonstrates he had learned much from Peter. Paul often spoke of himself as a person who originally sought to destroy the Christian faith. By the grace of God, Paul became an Apostle of Christ. In terms of preaching, Paul emphasized the crucifixion, which he knew was a stumbling block for Jews and foolishness to Gentiles. In the crucifixion, Paul saw the wisdom of God.

For Mark, the crucifixion demonstrates both the loving wisdom of God as well as the foolishness of those who reject salvation. Remember, Mark ends the Gospel with the crucifixion. The reader is left to question why the "good news" concludes with the hero's death.

In contrast with Peter's story, we do know how Paul got to Rome. It was on an appeal to Caesar regarding a legal matter. Paul had been charged with a crime by some Jews in Jerusalem who were unable to prove their case. Paul surmised it was because he had preached the resurrection of the dead. In any case, after two years there was still no resolution to the charges. Paul, as a Roman citizen, appealed his case to Caesar. He arrived in Rome when Emperor Nero was engaged in a despotic and riotous lifestyle.

I want to share a personal story from Nero's golden palace that greatly affected all who were there. Merrill Tenney, together with my group of students, was on a guided tour of Nero's enormous palace: the Domus Aurea. Retired at the time, Dr. Tenney was a New Testament scholar and former Dean of the Wheaton College Graduate School.

At that time, the palace had been partially excavated allowing the group to catch a glimpse of Nero's accomplishments. One of the excavated rooms was a spectacular octagonal dining room. The room boasted a waterfall on one side. The flow of water turned a large round table in the center of the room. The emperor and his guests sat at the table as it turned, bringing food of various kinds to where each of them sat. On the opposing side was the vomitorium—allowing guests to empty their stomachs into the stream as it flowed out of the palace. Then they might return to the dining room for more food. Each additional side had an adjoining room of significance and purpose.

One side room provided for an orchestra to entertain the guests. This room was separated visually from the octagonal room hiding Nero's guests from the musicians. The guide similarly explained the purpose of each room. One was for matters of state. The emperor was informed when matters were awaiting his decision. When ready, Nero excused himself to pass judgment.

The class stood in this room set aside for judgment. Their beloved teacher listened to the guide explain its purpose. When the guide finished, Tenney suggested that perhaps this was where the Apostle Paul stood before Nero to have his case adjudicated. If so, Paul would have talked about the righteousness of God, a Savior who died for the world and the resurrection of the Savior from the dead—these were things Paul believed in deeply and for which he felt he might have been charged. The Gospel message shared in the inner sanctum of the emperor's palace.

None of this made much sense to Nero. Perhaps Caesar simply halted the conversation reminding Paul that it was he who was on trial. As such, Paul should be aware of the power Nero wielded. Paul should humble himself before Nero, perhaps satisfying Nero with a bribe. Nero had the power of life and death and was willing to use that power as he wished. If allowed to speak, Paul might have countered declaring Nero had no power unless it had been granted from above. The scene was a clash of two prominent people: Paul and Nero.

Ultimately, Nero sentenced Paul to death. Dr. Tenney paused, reflecting briefly on the grandeur of Nero's golden palace in which they stood, and the decadent lifestyle Nero celebrated. He closed his remarks with these words: "In his day, Nero may have had what seemed like unlimited power. Today, parents name their sons Paul and their dogs Nero."

Silence fell upon the room.

Dr. Tenney walked back to his place in the group. Others began to realize the meaning of what they had just observed. It was a value statement about life, about good character, about different perspectives on what is truly valuable—wealth, power, and service. A person of good and noble character will have many friends. A man of evil intent, many enemies, even if he rises to the position of Caesar. Those who sit around the luxurious table offer nothing to it. They will walk away at the first sign of adversity.

The story Dr. Tenney shared mirrors the purpose found in the Gospel of Mark. In the Jewish tradition, the significance of a good character and the warning against being a fool had come centuries earlier in the book of Proverbs:

> The fear of the Lord is the beginning of knowledge,
> but fools despise knowledge and wisdom.
> —Proverbs 1:7

Both Paul and Peter knew this life lesson and practiced it. Both were strong in their Jewish faith, and both were men of good character and great courage.

Interestingly, the writer of Proverbs illustrates this principle, warning specifically against those who benefit at the expense of others. "Stay away from them, they are swift to shed blood," the writer warns, and then explains their true predicament: "These men lie in wait for their own blood; they waylay only themselves" (Proverbs 1:15–18).

Another significant theme in Mark concerns the character development of Peter. His story moves from being called to follow Jesus, to becoming an observer, to being reprimanded, to swearing his allegiance, to being ashamed of himself. There are also subplots for other disciples.

The primary story in Mark concerns Jesus. The first verse alone affirms his purpose, "The beginning of the Gospel of Jesus Christ, the Son of God" (Mark 1:1). With Jesus in mind, it is tempting to read Mark as a biography. Note, however, the "biography" provided by Mark does not cover Jesus' birth nor include any resurrection appearances—as written, Mark is not a biography.

In other interpretations, Mark has been described as a "passion narrative with a long introduction." After all, Mark records Jesus saying, "The Son of Man did not come to be served, but to serve, and to give his life as a ransom for many" (Mark 10:45). The crucifixion is in Jerusalem in the province of Judea far away from Galilee in the north where the earlier events in Jesus' life take place. These earlier stories fill in partially the background of Jesus' life, especially those prior to Jesus asking his disciple in Caesarea Philippi, "Who do people say that I am?" (Mark 8:27). This inquiry, "Who am I," is the central question of the entire gospel. However, those stories carry virtually no reference to a crucifixion and very little reference to suffering. Mark records the story of Caesarea halfway through his Gospel and the balance of his work is punctuated with suffering.

Hence, it is important to note the Gospel of Mark truly is a Passion narrative. I would add that the stories in the early chapters are critical to the *good news* Mark wishes to present. Therefore, a mere listing of these stories without understanding how they function in the Gospel would be misleading. What takes place with the disciples in Galilee is connected directly to the theme of Jesus as the Savior.

We have identified the historical context for Mark to write his Gospel: including a lengthy understanding of the persecution under Nero. We have identified key themes that are intertwined throughout the text: Peter's character, the person of Jesus, and the development of the Church. I would be remiss if I did not at least mention the importance of understanding the context of the land.

For nearly fifty years, I have served as a member of the board at Jerusalem University College. Through the school, I have had opportunity to read Scripture within the very settings in which these stories occurred. I encourage every reader to consider how valuable it is to walk the shores of Galilee when reading of Jesus calming the seas; to look upon the Holy City from the Mount of Olives; and to see the life that flourishes in the wilderness. The perspective that follows is informed by each context.

Finally, for Mark, the *good news* centers on the crucifixion.

It is presented with the promise of a resurrection, and a greater promise to sit at the table with Jesus in his golden palace. Although familiar with the resurrection, Mark tells only of the crucifixion. Indeed, it is the victory in the crucifixion that makes the Gospel according to Mark profoundly *good news.* This is the beginning of the Gospel of Jesus Christ.

UNDERSTANDING THE GOSPEL OF MARK

The Literary Structure of the Gospel: Who Am I?

Prologue	**In the Beginning**	**1:1–13**
Act 1	**Who Is This?**	**1:14–4:41**
	Announcing the Kingdom	*1:14–20*
	Catching the Crowds	*1:21–45*
	Meeting Defenders of the Faith	*2:1–3:6*
	There's One in Every Family	*3:7–35*
	Privilege for the Disciples	*4:1–41*
Act 2	**Isn't This the Carpenter?**	**5:1–6:6a**
	Witness of Legion	*5:1–20*
	Witness of Jairus and a Woman of Faith	*5:21–43*
	Witness from Home	*6:1–6a*
Act 3	**"Who Do People Say I Am?"**	**6:6b–9:29**
	Setting: Disciples Heal / John Beheaded	*6:6b–6:32*
	Four Stories: Feeding Five Thousand; Walk on Water; Confronting Pharisees; Two Miracles	*6:33–7:37*
	Four Stories: Feeding Four Thousand; Rejecting Pharisees; No Bread in the Boat; Healing a Blind Man Twice	*8:1–26*
	Jesus Question: Who Do People Say I Am?	*8:27–30*
	Son of Man Must Be Killed	*8:31–9:1*
	"This Is My Son, Whom I Love"	*9:2–13*
	Disciples Unable to Heal	*9:14–29*

Act 4	**Why the Son of Man Must Be Killed**	**9:30–13:37**
	Teaching the Disciples	*9:30–9:50*
	Individual Ethics: Hardness of Heart *Purpose of the Law* *The Son of Man Came to Serve*	*10:1–52*
	Triumphal Entry	*11:1–11*
	Social Ethics: Religious Corruption *Four Questions*	*11:12–12:44*
	God's Redemption of the Created Order	*13:1–37*
Act 5	**Are You the Christ?**	**14:1–16:8**
	Setting: Anointed for Burial	*14:1–9*
	Plotting the Betrayal of Jesus	*14:10–11*
	The Last Supper: Transforming Passover	*14:12–26*
	Gethsemane: Thy Will Be Done	*14:27–52*
	Human Judgment: Religious Trial of Jesus *Social Trial of Peter* *Political Trial of Jesus*	*14:53–15:20*
	Crucifixion: Good News!	*15:21–47*
	Transformation: The Empty Tomb	*16:1–8*
Epilogue	**Who Do You Say That I Am?**	

PROLOGUE TO THE GOSPEL

In the Beginning (1:1–13)

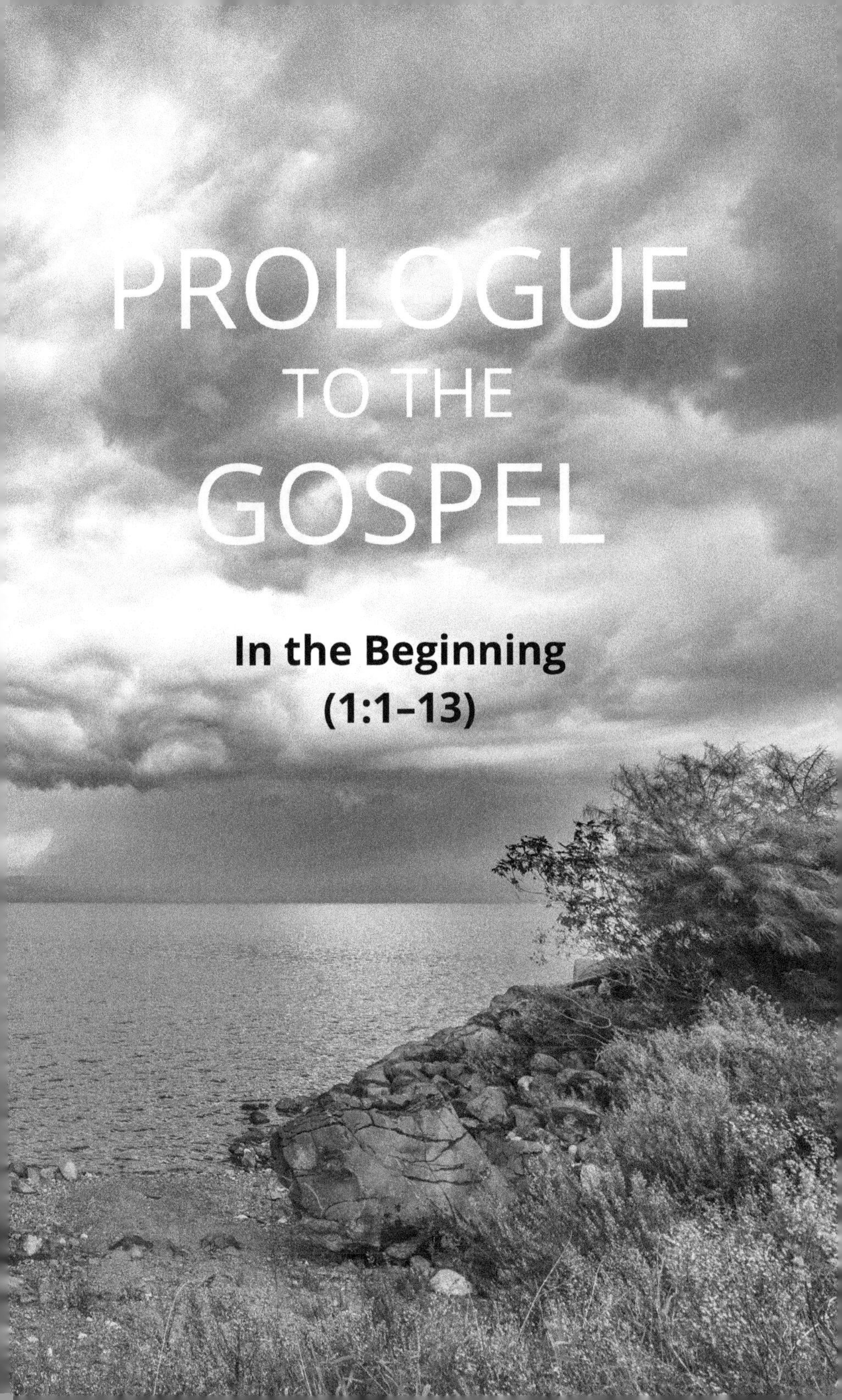

In the Beginning (1:1–13)

You are my Son, whom I love; with you I am well pleased.
—Mark 1:11

1 *The beginning of the Gospel of Jesus Christ, the Son*
of God.

2 *It is written in Isaiah the prophet: "I will send my mes-*
senger ahead of you, who will prepare your way" — 3 *"a*
voice of one calling in the desert, 'Prepare the way for the
Lord, make straight paths for him.'"

4 *And so John came, baptizing in the desert region and*
preaching a baptism of repentance for the forgiveness of
sins. 5 *The whole Judean countryside and all the people*
in Jerusalem went out to him. Confessing their sins, they
were baptized by him in the Jordan River. 6 *John wore*
clothing made of camel's hair, with a leather belt around
his waist, and he ate locusts and wild honey. 7 *And this*
was his message: "After me will come one more powerful
than I, the thongs of whose sandals I am not worthy to
stoop down and untie. 8 *I baptize you with water, but he*
will baptize you with the Holy Spirit."

9 *At that time Jesus came from Nazareth in Galilee and*
was baptized by John in the Jordan. 10 *As Jesus was coming*

up out of the water, he saw heaven being torn open and the Spirit descending on him like a dove. [11]*And a voice came from heaven: "You are my Son, whom I love; with you I am well pleased."*

[12]*At once the Spirit sent him out into the desert,* [13]*and he was in the desert forty days, being tempted by Satan. He was with the wild animals, and angels attended him.*

It is the year AD 64 and the city of Rome is on fire for nearly a week. A large portion of the city is destroyed. This is not the only fire during this decade. Under Nero, the Roman Church is subjected to what is called the First General Persecution of Christians. Nero orders the Christians to be hunted down, captured, and slain. Some of them become human "torches" whom Nero orders to be burned on poles to illumine the night. Others are dressed in animal skins and attacked by wild animals. "To the lions with the Christians," could be heard in the streets. Among those killed are the Apostle Paul, who authored much of the New Testament, and the Apostle Peter, who was pastor to the church in Rome.

There is another fire burning in the hearts of the believers: a fire of devotion and love. They secretly gather in the catacombs to celebrate their faith. They sing; they pray; they worship. This fire burns warmly without consuming. It is fueled by the God that called Moses, the God of Abraham, Isaac, and Jacob. It is Jesus, whom they love.

Amid the persecution and the secret worship there is a student of both Peter and Paul who sets about to write down words of comfort and encouragement. His name is Mark.

The words of comfort came from Peter's sermons to the congregation in Rome as well as his letters to other believers. Peter had written, "Praise be to the God and Father of our Lord Jesus Christ! In his great mercy he has given us a new birth into a living hope through the resurrection of Jesus Christ from the dead, and into an inheritance that can never perish, spoil or fade" (I Peter 1:3–4). The good news about Jesus comes from a sovereign God and includes a guaranteed inheritance.

As Peter's protégé, Mark opens his Gospel in similar style. He calls attention to Jesus as the Son of God, and reminds his listeners that God has good news for them. He writes, "The beginning of the Gospel of Jesus Christ, the Son of God." The *Good News* is from God, through Jesus, and for all his readers, including us today.

Given his relationship to Peter, it is fitting for him to begin by honoring Peter with this introduction of Jesus. What follows is a series of statements all related to Jesus: a prophecy from Isaiah, a description of John the Baptist, the baptism of Jesus, and the temptation of Jesus in the wilderness. Mark uses each of these statements to construct a framework for the Gospel he is about to present. Individually, the statements do not appear well developed. Together, they form a coherent prologue providing the two major themes that characterize the entire Gospel story.

Before identifying these or other themes that permeate throughout the text, it is important to identify what is not included. There are several parts of the stories of Jesus, Peter, and the Church that seem to be omitted. Let us examine a few.

For example, only one prophecy is mentioned. Were there not other prophecies worthy of consideration? People familiar with Matthew's Gospel know there were several other prophecies to consider. Mark uses only one.

Likewise, is there more to the story of John the Baptist? Of course, and all the other Gospel writers have more to say about John the Baptist. However, Mark records no dialogue between Jesus and John.

The statement about Jesus and the Tempter is also brief. We know from other accounts that there is significant and substantial dialogue between Jesus and the Tempter. Mark does not provide any of that dialogue. Hence, readers familiar with the life of Jesus from the other Gospels often round out the framework Mark provides with details from the other three Gospels. Mark's brevity is intentional. He is sharing an insight that does not require the dialogue of Jesus and Satan.

Mark has his own story to tell. This story is one grounded in the Apostle Peter's perspective on the Passion of Jesus. It is informed by the interests and experiences of the church at Rome. Reading the stories told by other Gospel writers into Mark's Gospel may have a place. Unfortunately, most of the time it distracts, causing us to miss what is right before us. The dialogue Mark does include involves Jesus with a variety of witnesses, and especially Peter. Consider a brief comparison of Mark with the other evangelists.

Mark begins telling the story of Jesus by identifying it as "Gospel," or "good news." This is different from all three of the other Gospels and it is significant. All four Gospels present the story of Jesus as good news—only Mark uses the word Gospel to describe the story. Notice in the brief comparisons below what themes with are presented by each of the other Gospel writers.

MATTHEW'S GOSPEL

- Matthew calls Jesus, "son of David" (Matthew 1:1). King David. He continues to emphasize the theme of royalty as he presents a lineage of Jesus from Abraham to King David to Joseph. His interests are in Jesus as the promised Messiah (King) who would sit on the throne of David.
- Wise men come looking for the King of the Jews because they have seen his natal star. The Prophets spoke of the place of his birth in Bethlehem, David's city. The hostility from Herod, who believes himself to be on the brink of being dethroned, requires Joseph and Mary to escape with Jesus to Egypt. This fulfills the prophecy that calls "my son out of Egypt."
- When Matthew eventually begins the ministry of Jesus, he relates details with regard to John the Baptist's

diet and dress as well as the warning John gives to the Pharisees and Sadducees about impending judgment upon them.

- Matthew records the baptism of Jesus. He includes John's response that it is Jesus who ought to be baptizing him.
- In terms of the temptations, Matthew identifies three of them used by the devil. Matthew also presents Jesus rebuking Satan with responses quoting prophecy to each.

LUKE'S GOSPEL

- Luke writes at a time when the story of Jesus is already well-known. His effort is to provide an orderly account of the human interaction of Jesus with various individuals in Jesus' life.
- He includes the story of the birth of John the Baptist. While he is still in his mother's womb, Mary, the mother of Jesus, comes to visit her cousin, Elizabeth. Although still in the womb, John recognizes the presence of Jesus.
- He reminds us Jesus is a child born of a humble woman, Mary, to whom the angel of the Lord said, "Greetings, you who are highly favored" (Luke 1:28). She responds with a song of praise that Luke also includes.
- He tells us of a visit from shepherds to whom angels spoke.
- He tells of Jesus' visit to the temple and the witnesses of Simeon and Anna.
- Before Jesus' ministry begins with the baptism, Luke tells a story of Jesus as a twelve-year-old engaging the rulers of the Jews in the temple courts. That story concludes with Jesus telling Joseph and Mary that he was in his Father's house.
- Luke's narrative is replete with personal reactions of people to Jesus. Eventually, he tells of Jesus' baptism in a similar manner to Matthew's account, with added

teaching on ethical behavior. The temptation stories also parallel Matthew.

JOHN'S GOSPEL

- In the Gospel of John, the theme emphasizes Jesus' deity. Jesus is the Word identified with God and made flesh (John 1:1, 2, and 14). This is substantially different from Matthew, Mark, and Luke as John focuses on the eternal aspects of Jesus as person.
- The extensive similarity in the text of Matthew, Mark, and Luke results in these three as being referred to as synoptic Gospels. Collectively, they may be viewed as having a common literary source and largely centered in Galilee. In contrast, John offers little regarding Jesus' ministry in Galilee. Instead, he concentrates on a handful of "miracles," some teaching sessions, and Jesus' experiences in Jerusalem and Judea.
- John has no lineage for Jesus. This is not as significant for John's purpose. Jesus is the Word that becomes flesh. He is God.
- John has no references to prophetic voices. Nor does he refer to Jesus' baptism or temptation. Even John the Baptist is merely described as "a man sent from God to bear witness to the light even though he was not the light" (John 1:6–8).
- John the Baptist introduces Andrew and one other disciple to Jesus with the words: "Look, the lamb of God!" (John 1:36). Then Andrew goes to tell his brother Peter, "We have found the Messiah" (John 1:41).

Mark's theme is different from the other three Gospels. Virtually none of this material is in Mark. There are no setup comments about his kingly lineage (Matthew and Luke), no birth narratives (Matthew and Luke), no family history (Matthew and Luke), no angelic visitations to the parents of

Jesus (Matthew and Luke), no apparent grand themes regarding his relationship to God or to the creation (John). Mark does mention one prophecy, a few statements about John the Baptist, little about Jesus' baptism, and little of his temptation.

Mark calls his message Gospel. It is not just any "*good news*." It is the ultimate *Good News*! Although, as noted, he does not anchor his story with Joseph (Matthew) or Mary (Luke) or with a genealogy, Mark is aware there is a prophetic foreshadowing. The Prophets foretold his coming would be announced by a voice calling in the desert. Mark refers to Isaiah (Isaiah 52:7–10) as the Prophet, yet the quotation also has references to other passages (Exodus 23:20 and Malachi 3:1; 4:5). The reference signifies the coming of a singularly great person called "the Lord."

Perhaps from some perspective it would have been helpful if Mark had included a glossary of all the prophetic references to the significance of Jesus. Such is not the case. A glossary would detract from Mark's mission of sharing *good news*. However, the reference to the "voice in the desert" makes it clear that the story of Jesus does not "start" with Jesus' life; it has a start and significance long before Jesus' ministry begins and long before his birth. Prophets of old anticipated this good news.

Along the way, Mark addresses John the Baptist's diet and dress. Unlike Matthew and Luke, he leaves out any dialogue between Jesus and John. Further, he ignores the conversation between Jesus and the tempter. In spite of the brevity of the prologue, we find in Mark two comments not in the other three Gospels. When Jesus was tempted, Mark tells us he was with the wild animals. This is significant enough for Mark to include, and we will discuss it below. Then notice again, only Mark uses the word "Gospel." Clearly this promises to be especially significant! And this is where we begin.

For believers under Roman persecution, this beginning will remind them that the believer starts with the good news of who God is and what God has done for them. Good news does not originate from human imagination. Murderous threats from those persecuting the Church hold no power to overcome it.

The first two words Mark uses are: "The beginning." It sounds as though this is intended to be nothing more than a way to start the story Mark is telling. However, upon reflection we may wonder if Mark has another reason for starting this way. Is he suggesting a foundational principle, a framework, for understanding reality? If he is, the reference is very subtle and not without merit.

Consider parallels for this foundational interpretation in Genesis: "In the beginning God created ..." (Genesis 1:1) and again in the Gospel According to John: "In the beginning was the Word and the Word was with God and the Word was God" (John 1:1). Perhaps Mark intends for the "Gospel" to provide meaning throughout all of creation from the very beginning. Or is there something more? There is a sense in which Mark is suggesting a hidden principle that has existed since before creation: a good news that is God's ultimate purpose for his creation.

There is a Mishna that claims, "The world was not made except for the Messiah." [1] If this is Mark's perspective, he need only note the Prophets of old had some sense of it. The prophecy from Isaiah is sufficient for this purpose. Further, it introduces us to John the Baptist, the Prophet who will be the voice in the desert preparing the way for the Lord.

In contrast to the little said prophetically, much is said about John the Baptist, notably his diet and dress. He eats locusts and wild honey; he wears clothing made of camel's hair with only a leather belt around his waist—an ultimately simple man. And the whole Judean countryside went out to him to confess their sins and be baptized. What he said to them we do not know, and how he confronted the religious leaders and the politicians is also left unsaid, at least for the moment.

1 Alfred Edersheim, *The Life and Times of Jesus the Messiah.*

John the Baptist is an unusually dedicated person. The details of his diet and dress are sufficient to identify his commitment. He is not caught up with the glamour of society, whatever that glamour might be. He is singularly dedicated to calling people to repentance. Large crowds of people respond to his message. It would be nice to know more about him. In Mark's Gospel, he is merely the "voice in the desert" anticipated by the Prophets. Yet, there is a richness to his character that goes beyond worldly valuation.

Those familiar with Jewish prophecy, including those in Rome who had been present during Pentecost, would recognize a parallel between John the Baptist and Elijah. Both John and Elijah were dedicated to the mission God called them to fulfill. Both prefer doing the will of God effectively while living in the desert without any personal pretense.

Mark concludes his brief discussion of John's personal assessment and a prophetic message. The assessment: "After me will come one more powerful than I, the thongs of whose sandals I am unworthy to stoop down and untie," and the promise, "He will baptize with the Holy Spirit."

This picture of John the Baptist, like the references to the Prophets before him, echoes "the beginning" as something far more than the mere beginning of a story. There is a quality which suggests that the Gospel has its origins much earlier than "the beginning." The promise also serves as an encouragement to those suffering under Roman authority.

One more powerful and worthy than John will come. He is Lord: a ruler whose might, power, and authority could compete victoriously with Caesar as Moses confronted Pharaoh. Further, this suggests Jesus is part of a divine plan from the beginning and the one through whom the ultimate meaning of all creation will be revealed. If so, this Gospel certainly is *good news*.

Personally, this is the heart of the message that I have sought to share with family and friends, students, and parishioners throughout my ministry. More so, it is my most fervent hope for my children, grandchildren, and now great-grandchildren. God loves you. For no other purpose, Jesus set out before the creation of the world to live and die so that you may be in fellowship with God: Father, Son, and Holy Spirit.

Preparing the way for the Lord meant calling people to repent. John called everyone to repent. The citizens of Jerusalem and Judea came to him confessing their sins. The text has no mention of any of the sins or, for that matter, any one person among them. Presumably, they carried a guilty conscience prompting them to repent. Perhaps also, they held a hope for self-determination, to be rid of the Roman occupation. If the God who liberated their ancestors from Egyptian rule would act again, this time on their behalf, they would gladly repent.

The religious faith of those baptized by John would encourage them to remember the wrongs for which they were responsible. If they wanted forgiveness from God, they would need to ask forgiveness from each other. If they had a sense of history that a new "exodus" or a new deliverer were needed to escape Roman occupation, they may well have anticipated a new Moses. So, they went to John, the prophetic herald of God calling for repentance.

Jesus, the presumptive hero of this tragedy, also comes to be baptized by John. Yet, there is something different in his coming. While others "went" to John, the text has a different tone upon Jesus' arrival. Jesus is said to have "come" from Nazareth. This change in verb usage suggests Jesus' arrival was not necessary to have his sins forgiven. Rather, his baptism demonstrated how he identifies with his people in anticipation of his own destiny to "serve" them (Mark 10:45).

The implication is that Jesus' story is a revelation with foundational significance from the very beginning of creation. Jesus' baptism is unique. The citizens "went" when called. Jesus "came" on his own. He came because he is the One who can provide everyone else with the truth they seek, and the life God intended.

Parenthetically, the difference in usage between these two words (*went* and *came*) may supply an answer to a troubling question for many concerning the baptism of Jesus. Why is he baptized? Do not the Bible and the Church teach he is "without sin" (2 Corinthians 5:21; I Peter 2:22; and I John 3:5) and, therefore not in need of repentance, confession and baptism? No simple answer given here will suffice for those who wish a detailed study of the subject. Mark does not provide much for us to examine either, yet the following may offer a plausible explanation.

At the conclusion of Jesus' baptism Mark reports an affirmation of Jesus in a unique fashion. There is a voice from Heaven and a visual image of a dove descending upon him. No other person experienced such affirmation. It is as though others being baptized will need to be cleansed again and again.

The presence of the voice affirming Jesus reveals his intimate relationship with God: "This is my Son whom I love!"

Jesus joins the ones being baptized as a willing participant in their community. This is part of his overall identification with all creation.

The perspective on baptism suggests there are at least two elements in John's baptism: turning away from sin and turning resolutely toward God. The latter is more important. When sin is present it is impossible to turn completely toward God. Sin is focused on self. Often, we find ourselves seeking more to avoid punishment than to be truly forgiven.

Martin Luther put it this way: "A Christian who is truly contrite seeks and loves to pay penalties for his sins."[2] Unfortunately, once we claim to be forgiven, we typically forget about the consequences.

At this point it is probably best for the reader to consider a longer study on the effects of sin and the meaning of baptism than this text intends. For our purposes, it is sufficient to

---

2 Tappert, *Selected Writings of Martin Luther,* 55.

identify that there is a difference between the contrite heart seeking God's forgiveness versus the basic human need seeking acceptance of any kind. There is much greater value for the creation in the former, and even greater value in the relationship that Jesus has with the Father. Jesus had no need for contrition. He has an intimate relationship with the Father. His baptism demonstrates the love of God in a manner that invites all creation into that relationship.

The people of Judea, like all sinners, recognized the barrier sin places on any intimate relationship. There is merit, of course, in a sinner's repentance. There is also a blindness caused by sin. One result of this blindness is that we often misread even our own motives for either sinning or seeking forgiveness. Like a child facing punishment for misbehaving, it will be easier to avoid the punishment if one confesses. With sins against God (are not all sins against God?) it is not the love of God but the fear of retribution that motivates many of our pleas for forgiveness. This implies that the repentance of the citizens of Judea, though highly valuable, will stand in need of repetition throughout life unless there is one who, without sin, can turn fully toward God and make his baptism available to others. The same is true for us.

In this light, Jesus' baptism identifies him with the people whose life he shares. At the same time, the voice from Heaven announces the fullness of his relationship with his Father. Jesus' baptism is an affirmation of the ultimate goodness of creation and the original purpose for the creation to remain in harmony with the loving and gracious creator. His baptism also affirms the ministry of John the Baptist, the clarion voice calling in the desert.

The prologue concludes with Jesus being driven into the desert and tempted by Satan. This stands in direct contrast to the voice coming down from Heaven. There is a battle being waged through Jesus' presence—and Satan is well aware of who Jesus is.

Mark does not provide the details of the temptations like the other Gospels (see Matthew 4:1–11 and Luke 4:1–13). We do not need those details. Satan's presence is enough. It is a foreboding reminder of the battle between good and evil. This is a universal struggle. Perhaps, this highlights the importance of Mark's first words, "In the beginning," as a reference to the beginning of all creation, and not simply the start of the story. If so, we should not be naive about the temptation of Jesus by thinking once it is successfully overcome in the desert that the temptations are over. We should anticipate Satan ambushing Jesus challenging his efforts, and ours as believers, when we least expect it.

This is an important distinction. The temptations are ongoing. Many of us face similar situations. Our temptations are not overcome once. They must be battled every day. Jesus, by defeating Satan in the desert, models for us the importance of relying on God's Word, every day, as that is how he was victorious. This theme returns in even greater glory as we gain a better understanding of the Gospel.

One additional element in this section deserves special mention. For all that Mark excludes from the temptation narratives, there is one thing he includes that is unmentioned in the other Gospel accounts: Jesus was "with the wild animals." The most likely reason is that the people in Rome would identify this comment with their experience of Nero's reign of terror. Being with wild animals would be readily understood as a reference to persecution. Jesus being among the wild animals would most likely be considered a comfort to those who were being persecuted, knowing that their Savior experienced similar horrors as he began his ministry.

Mark closes the prologue reporting that angels attend Jesus. In the context of suffering for righteousness, God provides a source of heavenly comfort. This is not only for Jesus. It is available for all who embrace the Gospel. For people in Rome, the heroic example of Peter's testimony at his crucifixion would be most notable. Even in the midst of suffering, God has already provided comfort.

PERSPECTIVE ON THE PROLOGUE

The prologue consists of five statements. Each statement holds intrinsic value. However, the value increases exponentially with the recognition of two important concepts that serve as dual perspectives holding the entire Gospel together; namely, the integration of Spirit and desert.

Spirit permeates Mark's Gospel. John the Baptist anticipates the Spirit's coming with the coming of Jesus. It is the Spirit that descends upon Jesus. The Spirit also drives Jesus into the desert where he is tempted. Implied by the use of "Spirit" is the providence of God exemplified in Jesus' life as well as through Christ to the entire creation. The Spirit is the force of God in the world. It is reminiscent of the Spirit that hovers over the waters at creation (Genesis 1:2). It is the Spirit that leads Prophets to speak (II Peter 1:20). It is the Spirit that calls people to the truth and empowers them to the right (Psalm 51:11). It is the Spirit that comes upon Jesus and is the very same Spirit with which he alone is able to bless and baptize.

The word "desert" stands in direct contrast to the use of Spirit. Such a contrast may seem to contradict the providence of God. It does not. The Isaiah prophesy talks about a desert, John is the voice in the desert, Jesus comes to John (at the Jordan River near Jericho, as it flows through the desert) to be baptized, and the Spirit drives Jesus into the desert. Indeed, the desert represents the barren wasteland of a life without God. It is into this desert that God intervenes by sending his son—that is the heart of "good news."

A word of explanation is in order for the benefit of readers who might not be familiar with the landscape. This deals especially with the references to desert. For many readers the word *desert* signifies rolling hills of sand and a complete absence of water, a Sahara. Such is not the case, however, in the land east of Jerusalem. A preferable word might have been *wilderness*. Indeed, this word is used in some translations. The wilderness is not a desert. In a desert, life is impossible because water is not available; whereas in a wilderness, life is possible as some water is available. In the wilderness, life simply doesn't thrive. This is the land into which Jesus is led to be tempted.

Subtly, this theme affirms life as the gift of God in creation while recognizing that sin keeps life from flourishing. In terms of the grand theme of *good news*, Mark defines our lives as wilderness no matter how good our lives may appear. Life outside of a relationship with God is destined for frustration.

Perhaps poetically, Mark wants the readers to understand this life in terms of locusts and wild honey—no matter what quality of food may sit on their tables. Fortunately, from before the creation of the world, God purposed to make known his will in Christ when the time reached its fulfillment (Ephesians 1:4–10; I Peter 1:20; and Galatians 4:4). With Jesus there is a new Spirit blowing and the wilderness will blossom with the crocus (Isaiah 35:1, 2). This is the *good news*.

If Mark has creation in mind when he uses the word "beginning," it seems appropriate to say creation was intended to flourish—and that it would do so only as centered in God. Sin is a barrier to that relationship. The good news is that the "center" of all creation, the Spirit of all creation, the reason for creation, its heart and soul, is now about to be revealed. To quote Psalm 1, the tree "which yields its fruit in season and whose leaf does not wither" has come, and, "whatever he does prospers."

It is no wonder that Mark records the voice from Heaven at Jesus' baptism saying, "You are my Son!" This quotation from an enthronement Psalm (Psalm 2) promises a rich inheritance to the Son, namely, the nations of the world. It also includes a word of warning to the kings of this world, a word which those with a Jewish heritage living under Roman authority might have recognized.

Serve the Lord with fear and rejoice with trembling.
Kiss the Son, lest he be angry, and you be destroyed
in your way, for his wrath can flare up in a moment.
Blessed are all who take refuge in him.
—Psalm 2:11–12

As seems appropriate, we will take seriously the notion that the opening words of the Gospel reflect the words of Genesis and parallel the prologue in John. These words offer a foundational perspective for life in the wilderness. They introduce a new paradigm to interpret life. [3]

Look again at the first sentence: "The beginning of the Gospel of Jesus Christ the Son of God." With Jesus from before the creation, comes the plan of God for blessing, healing, and fruitfulness. With Jesus comes the fulfillment of the created order. This is the ultimate good news, the Gospel.

How better to call attention to the story of Jesus than with a provocative opening sentence. With what words could Mark have begun that would have been as grand or more impressive, more subtle and more pregnant with meaning than these? Each word carries significance.

- "The beginning..." The start of a story? Maybe something similar to, "Once upon a time?" Not really! A reference to something larger than life, like, "In the beginning God created?" Better!
- "...of the Gospel..." A story with a nice ending? A reference to a "news flash" similar to a banner headline in a newspaper? A new word for a specific historical person

3 I suspect that these thoughts might be confusing for some. I admit, they are filled with the history of my experience in academic and pastoral roles—and I often mix the content of these experiences. Yet, these thoughts are central to understanding the love of God expressed in Mark's Gospel. For that reason, I emphasize even the smaller details of the text. My grandkids might say, "This is Papa being Papa!"

revealed through selected events in his life? "Gospel"—a fulfilled life, a great word.

- "...of Jesus Christ, the Son of God." A "Savior?" The "Anointed?" A name? A title? A destiny? A Son? The Messiah?

If this truly is the first "sentence," it is an opening "sentence" without a verb. For some these words are the title selected by Mark for his story of Jesus. Maybe so, although we see it as eye-catching, majestic, and impressive, containing a thought of its own: *Good News* for all creation!

My hope at this point in the text is that the reader is beginning to understand the simple complexity of Mark's Gospel. As a theologian, I have often witnessed the paradoxical manner in which God cares for his creation. There is no stronger display than how God uses suffering to bring joy—a theme repeated throughout history and exemplified in the Gospel message. As we continue through the five acts of Mark's Gospel, there will be several opportunities for the reader to interact directly with the text. Some invitations will be simple. Others may be subtle and complex. Each is a call to relationship.

ACT ONE

Who Is This?
(1:14–4:41)

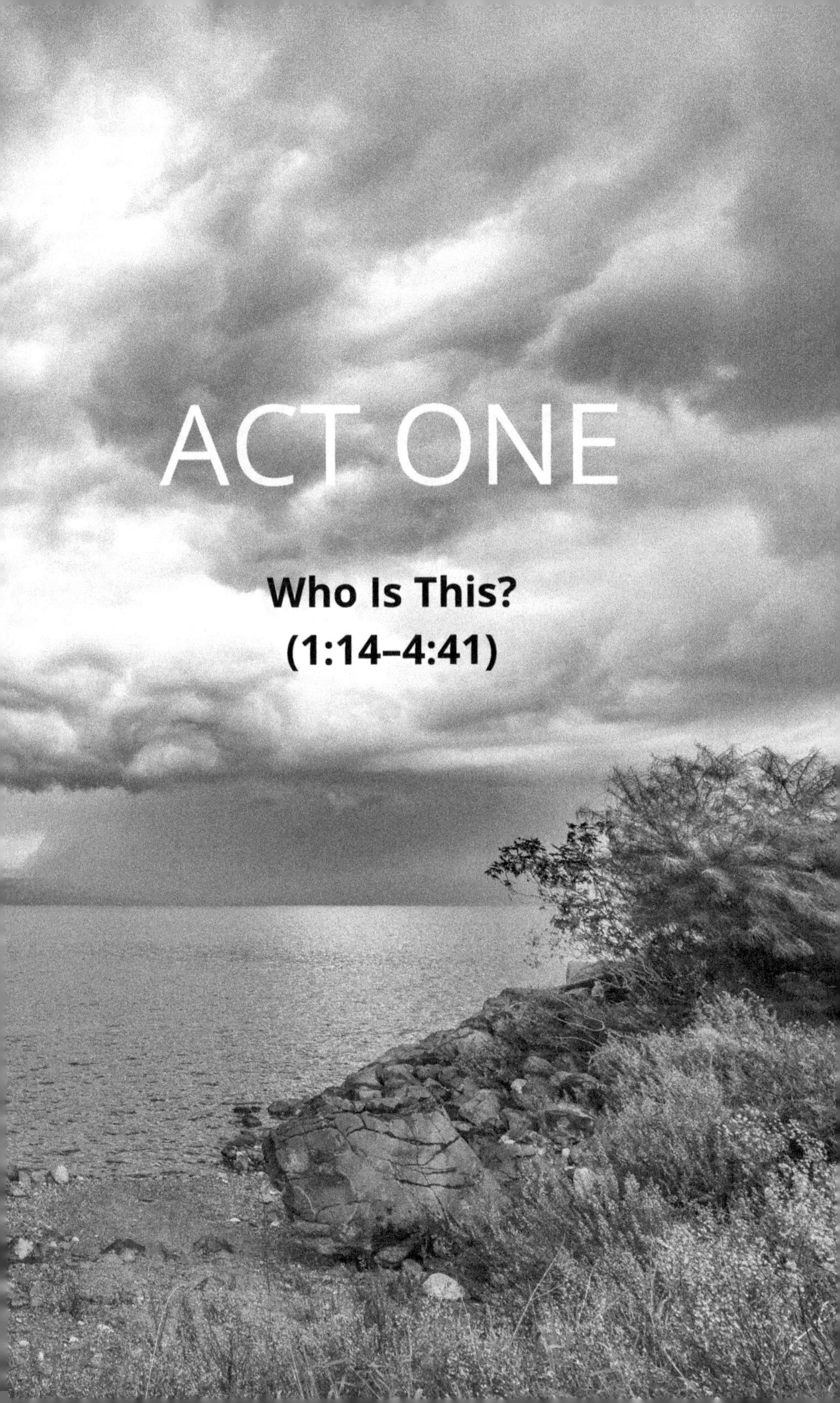

Announcing the Kingdom (1:14–20)

THE TIME HAS COME

Jesus begins his ministry in Galilee after John the Baptist, the forerunner, is no longer part of the story. By informing us that John is in prison, Mark opens the door for the "one more powerful than John" to be revealed. For the people in Rome, John's imprisonment would be understood from their own situation. Jesus' announcement of a new kingdom to begin his mission affirmed what Peter had done for them in proclaiming new life with Jesus as the Christ.

> [14] *After John was put in prison, Jesus went into Galilee, proclaiming the good news of God.* [15] *"The time has come," he said. "The kingdom of God has come near. Repent and believe the good news!"*

Like several of the comments in the prologue, these comments are brief. They could easily have been expanded to include a reference to the Lamb of God which the Gospel of John provides or either of the two lineages provided in Matthew and Luke respectively.

From the Jewish perspective, God had promised an heir to Abraham, Isaac, and Jacob, an heir through whom the world would be blessed. That promise was renewed to David in terms of a son to sit on his throne forever. Mark does not get caught up in any of these references to earlier Jewish life and thought. We may be sure that those with a Jewish background who joined the church in Rome might have focused on this promise. After all, the disciples were caught up in it even after the resurrection.

Instead, Jesus announces the basis for the good news with two simple declarations: "The time has come" and "The kingdom of God is near." These two declarations foreshadow a major change in human society effecting the entire world. This is the good news from God who orchestrates the events.

First, consider the phrase that the time has come. Jesus is beginning his ministry and will bring it to its proper conclusion. This phrase suggests that the world has been waiting. And now, a plan from the ages is unfolding.

The reference to the kingdom of God, especially in the mind of those in the Roman church, implies a rule and authority second to none. This is especially true if those who are explaining the kingdom come from a Jewish background. This is the Lord of Heaven and earth. Caesar cannot control him, and neither can the Roman senate. The religious authorities in Jerusalem cannot contain him. In fact, there is nothing in all creation that is above him.

To say the kingdom is near, or at hand, is partly prophetic. It will have immediate relevance as soon as Jesus exercises his authority. Not even the demons can stand against him. The kingdom is the power of God that can overcome all obstacles: healing those with diseases, comforting those in prison, and bringing joy to those who trust in God.

For those who will participate in the change there are two correlating commands: repent and believe the good news. In calling for repentance, Jesus links his message to that of his forerunner, John the Baptist, who likewise called upon people to repent.

Calling for repentance also identifies Jesus as the "Lord" whom John proclaimed would baptize with the Spirit. At this stage in the story, repenting and believing have little by way of explanation. Repent from what? Believe in what? The commands will be made clearer as we gain more information about Jesus and his disciples.

The declaration on the nearness of God's kingdom promises a change in human history as we know it, a confrontation that challenges human understanding. The promise is greater than simply restoring the kingdom of David (I Chronicles 17:11–14). This kingdom will be of God. And as God is greater than David, the kingdom will also be greater. The change is epic. It requires new thinking that can only come through a new revelation from God. Even after the resurrection, the disciples have difficulty perceiving the nature of this new kingdom (Acts 1:6–8).

If we borrow from sources other than Mark, we find the "kingdom of God" anticipates profoundly new realities, among them: new birth, new life, a new Jerusalem, a new earth, a new Heaven. It will be a place where lions lie down with young lambs and where wars cease to the ends of the earth. It heralds a new day, one without any crippling sins or demonic interference, one with beauty, peace, and prosperity.

Mark anticipates these new realities with his observation that the Spirit of God will invade the wilderness of human existence. Life will become what it was originally created to be and perhaps even better. We may add, most importantly, that the new kingdom is available even in those places where wilderness seems strongest. Examples of this will come much later in the story. For now, notice that the story of John the Baptist has become the story of the Spirit "driving Jesus into the wilderness."

After the announced themes, Mark informs us that Jesus selects several disciples to witness what he teaches and does. As the good news progresses, Mark will let us know what they are thinking. According to the Evangelist Luke, their witness from the time of John's baptism to the resurrection is crucial (Acts 1:15–22). Luke notwithstanding, their witness will be valuable for us as readers as we learn from both their observations and our own.

THE DISCIPLES ARE CALLED

> *16 As Jesus walked beside the Sea of Galilee, he saw Simon and his brother Andrew casting a net into the lake, for they were fishermen. 17 "Come follow me," Jesus said, "and I will make you fishers of men." 18 At once they left their nets and followed him.*
>
> *19 When he had gone a little farther, he saw James the Son of Zebedee and his brother John in a boat, preparing their nets. 20 Without delay he called them, and they left their father Zebedee in the boat with the hired men and followed him.*

Jesus walks along the shore of the Sea of Galilee calling some fishermen to follow him. The readiness of Simon, Andrew, James, and John to follow Jesus is impressive. Mark does not give us any background to them and so Mark emphasizes the immediacy of their response. In the fourth Gospel we learn that Andrew and one other disciple, likely the same John as in this passage, had previously followed John the Baptist as John's disciples (John 1:35–42). They switch over to Jesus at the invitation of John the Baptist. Then Andrew's first act is to call his brother Peter to join them in following Jesus.

This background implies they may have had a prior agreement for his call, one that was understood by their families and likely, the other workers left in the boat. In any case, their response indicates the authority of Jesus and their commitment to him. Notice also that of all the disciples, Simon is mentioned first. The name "Simon" is given him by his parents. Jesus gives him the name of "Petros," which is Greek and translated "Cephas" in Aramaic, "Rock" in English, and "Peter" by common usage. Petros is not merely a name, it is a calling.

These four will become devoted learners of all that Jesus wishes to teach them, even though at times it will seem as though they are not even able to stay awake, let alone pay attention. Jesus begins their study with a statement of their purpose: "I will make you fishers of men." Pay no more attention to them than that, at least for now. They are called, they are designated as witnesses, they will be nurtured, and they have a purpose: fishers of men. Among them Peter will have a central role.

Initially, the disciples observe Jesus interacting with people facing various needs, which Jesus is able to remedy. The crowds gathering around Jesus watch what is happening and express their amazement. As students of Jesus learning what it means to be fishers of people, the disciples pay careful attention to the reactions of crowds as Jesus introduces himself them. In the second lesson, the disciples witness the reaction of religious leaders of the community represented by scribes and Pharisees. The third lesson provides a perspective from Jesus' family. In the last lesson, the disciples receive private instruction and, for the first time in Mark's Gospel, tell us what they think.

The stage is set. The disciples are in place for lessons on becoming fishermen. They witness firsthand the work of Jesus. They are informed that a new kingdom is coming, a kingdom greater than any the world has ever known, the kingdom of God.

In this section we are given insight as to how people first respond to the ministry of Jesus: his authority, his message, and his actions. With each witness, there will be growth evident throughout the text. We will pay closer attention to the development among the disciples, especially Peter, as they are closest to Jesus throughout his ministry.

It is at this point that I want to share a personal comment. To the readers of Mark's Gospel: you will have opportunity, similar to that of the disciples and the crowds, to respond in many ways to Jesus. At times, you may be impressed. You may find yourself questioning either Jesus or those who respond to him. You may find yourself embracing Jesus even if you do not yet know who he is. I encourage you to consider your interactions with Jesus throughout the text.

Catching the Crowds (1:21–45)

Filled with Compassion, Jesus reached out his hand...
—Mark 1:41

FISHING 101: THE FIRST LESSON FOR THE DISCIPLES

Jesus introduces his ministry in the public arena by teaching in a synagogue in Capernaum on the north shore of the Sea of Galilee, Peter's hometown. In all likelihood, the story in the synagogue takes place very near where the disciples left their boats to follow Jesus. Capernaum boasts today of its ancient heritage, a beautiful synagogue of white limestone, a small harbor, and what archeologists identify as Peter's house between the two. A modern church stands above the house so that visitors may worship there or merely have a perspective of his humble home from above the ruins.

21 They went to Capernaum, and when the Sabbath came, Jesus went into the synagogue and began to teach. 22 The people were amazed at his teaching, because he taught them as one who had authority, not as the teachers of the law. 23 Just then a man in their synagogue who was possessed by an impure spirit cried out, 24 "What do you want with us, Jesus of Nazareth? Have you come to destroy us? I know who you are—the Holy One of God!"

25 “Be quiet!” said Jesus sternly. “Come out of him!” 26 The
impure spirit shook the man violently and came out of
him with a shriek.

27 The people were all so amazed that they asked each
other, “What is this? A new teaching—and with author-
ity! He even gives orders to impure spirits and they obey
him.” 28 News about him spread quickly over the whole
region of Galilee.

29 As soon as they left the synagogue, they went with James
and John to the home of Simon and Andrew. 30 Simon’s
mother-in-law was in bed with a fever, and they imme-
diately told Jesus about her. 31 So he went to her, took her
hand and helped her up. The fever left her, and she began
to wait on them.

32 That evening after sunset the people brought to Jesus all
the sick and demon-possessed. 33 The whole town gathered
at the door, 34 and Jesus healed many who had various
diseases. He also drove out many demons, but he would
not let the demons speak because they knew who he was.

35 Very early in the morning, while it was still dark, Jesus
got up, left the house and went off to a solitary place, where
he prayed. 36 Simon and his companions went to look
for him, 37 and when they found him, they exclaimed:
“Everyone is looking for you!”

38 Jesus replied, “Let us go somewhere else—to the nearby
villages—so I can preach there also. That is why I have
come.” 39 So he traveled throughout Galilee, preaching in
their synagogues and driving out demons.

40 A man with leprosy came to him and begged him on his knees, "If you are willing, you can make me clean."

41 Jesus was indignant. He reached out his hand and touched the man. "I am willing," he said. "Be clean!"
42 Immediately the leprosy left him, and he was cleansed.

43 Jesus sent him away at once with a strong warning: 44
"See that you don't tell this to anyone. But go, show yourself to the priest and offer the sacrifices that Moses commanded for your cleansing, as a testimony to them." 45
Instead he went out and began to talk freely, spreading the news. As a result, Jesus could no longer enter a town openly but stayed outside in lonely places. Yet the people still came to him from everywhere.

Mark tells us very little about the Scripture being read and nothing of Jesus' teaching. Perhaps Jesus read from the scroll of Isaiah (see: Luke 4:18–19) which Jesus used in the synagogue in Nazareth.

> The Spirit of the Lord is upon me because he has anointed me to preach good news to the poor. He has sent me to proclaim freedom for the prisoners and recovery of sight for the blind, to release the oppressed, to proclaim the year of the Lord's favor.
> —Isaiah 61:1, 2

Instead, Mark tells us of the impression Jesus had on the worshippers—they were amazed at the authority with which Jesus taught. First impressions can make a big difference and the first impression Jesus makes from his teaching in a synagogue is very positive. What follows next may have appeared even more amazing to them.

As though in answer to the amazement of the crowd at his teaching, one man identifies the authority of Jesus with an astounding declaration: "[He is] Jesus of Nazareth—the Holy One of God" (1:24b).

Mark calls this man someone who is possessed and controlled by an evil spirit. The man needs to be set free and Jesus obliges. By itself this is a marvelous story. In terms of Jesus' pledge to make the disciples into fishers of men, it is an even more powerful and compelling drama. This is the first illustration of what Jesus may have meant when he called the fishermen to follow him. One fish caught! That might be exciting—although Jesus has a different purpose.

There are at least two relevant references in the Prophets that identify the role of divine deliverance to be of fisherman hauling out evil as one would take fish from the sea.

Consider the following judgment oracle against those who oppressed the community on Mount Samaria: "The sovereign Lord has sworn by his holiness: 'The time will surely come when you will be taken away with hooks, the last of you with fishhooks...'" (Amos 4:2).

A similar image shows up in the Prophet Jeremiah. The people who had forsaken the Lord were under judgment from God. "I will send for fishermen," declares the Lord, "and they will catch them... My eyes are on all their ways, they are not hidden from me, nor is their sin concealed from my eyes..." (Jeremiah 16:16–17).

Whether the Christians in Rome, in particular those with a Jewish background, would know of these passages about deliverance by fishermen is unknown. Perhaps only Peter and Mark were aware of them. Either could have used the prophetic remarks to interpret what Jesus meant by fishers of men as judgments against the evil that was demonizing people in the "wilderness."

If this is true, when Jesus calls his disciples to become fishers of men, he is anticipating something more. He understands that setting the oppressed free begins with removing that which inhibits them from living a full life. The frequent explanation of "fishers of men" in terms of "saving people from a sinful world" may need to change. It is not that people are themselves evil. Rather, it seems more that people live in an environment of sin, as if they are immersed in sinful waters. From this perspective, the people must be "fished" out of those waters, and into waters that are pure and holy, free from sin.

Jesus commands the evil spirit to be silent and to leave the man. The evil spirit, with a shrieking protest, obeys. What an incredible first impression! Those gathered in the synagogue are impressed and eager to tell the story to anyone who might listen. They immediately begin to ask what is happening, amazed at the authority. Mark is silent regarding the responses of the disciples or the formerly demon-possessed man. This is evidence of the universal struggle that goes well beyond catching a single fish.

There is an important observation about the crowd: not one among the people in the synagogue, neither from the crowds nor the man set free, is called to follow Jesus in the same manner as the disciples. They have no name or face to identify them, no promise of training to become fishers of men themselves. They are just the "crowds," ordinary people able to be impressed by events they observe. To be sure, among them are individuals with personal concerns for health and well-being who will benefit from the one called Jesus should he bring them relief.

Mark continues his "first impression" stories with four more like the first. It is clear that Jesus is indeed setting people free by rooting out the evil. The very next story takes place in Peter's house. A fever leaves Peter's mother-in-law unable to fulfill the customary role of hospitality. When Jesus takes her hand, the fever leaves her and she is free to serve her guests graciously. This is the second healing Jesus performs.

Mark explains the astounding response that night following her healing. After sunset the people brought all those infected with diseases to him. The crowds are awed. Jesus is popular.

Wherever he goes, crowds surround him pressing in on every side. They bring the sick and the lame and he heals many.

It is significant to notice that the reference to healing many (1: 34) does not imply there were some that went unhealed. The reference is to "the many" and all were made whole. This is good news, no more sickness, at least temporarily.

Jesus is teaching his disciples how to fish. These healing stories highlight several lessons. First, Jesus has the authority (from God) to perform the healings. Second, the woman healed has a purpose, to be hospitable to others. She must be made clean before she is able to fulfill that role—perhaps foreshadowing that Jesus will need to be prepared for his role of service. Third, everyone who knows they are sick will seek to become made well.

In was an impressive evening. Early the next morning Jesus left Peter's house and went off to a place of solitude where he prayed. Mark offers no record of the prayer itself. We may imagine Jesus gave thanks for all that had happened and continued praying for those who were healed, for the disciples, and for the crowds. The disciples, led by Peter, went looking for him. They recognized the eagerness of the crowds to embrace Jesus, so when they found Jesus they joyfully exclaimed, "Everyone is looking for you!" (1:37).

Abruptly Jesus announces his purpose to preach in other towns and villages throughout Galilee. In one of them they encounter a leper begging to be clean. With a simple spoken word, "Be clean," the leprosy is gone from his body. Freed from his leprosy, the leper cannot contain his gratitude even when told to do so. His public thankfulness to God prevents Jesus from openly entering any city.

These narratives move rapidly from one story to another. Four of the five result in healing. You can be sure the disciples were impressed with what they saw. Mark does not reveal their reactions—at least not yet. He merely tells us what the disciples witnessed: a man set free from an evil spirit, the response of

Peter's mother-in-law, a time alone for prayer, the town's people in the evening, the joy of the leper. More importantly, Mark acknowledges the amazement of the crowds.

The crowds have a desire to see Jesus. They are amazed at the benefits some receive through his healings. Remember, the crowds have no call to follow Jesus. They are not learning, as are the disciples, how to be fishers of men. They do not even understand the significance of the authority they witness. And Jesus does not teach them. They are merely amazed.

As this section comes to a close, Mark gives us the reaction of Jesus. He is filled with compassion. [1] This is important as it reveals a motive for healing the sick. We hear of it only in the story of the leper, yet it permeates the entire section with the crowds.

The motive for *good news* is found in compassion. This is the role of the Spirit of God in the wilderness to help life prosper. It is this motive which wields authority over the demons and all that is unhealthy.

In the prologue, we are given the basic plot to the story, as one might find in a playbill. We have the benefit of the testimony from John the Baptist: Jesus is more powerful and far more worthy. Jesus baptizes with the Spirit. He has a divine testimony, "You are my Son whom I love." Having put away the playbill, we are now watching the drama unfold.

This is what we have witnessed thus far. Jesus has been identified as "the Holy One of God." Ironically, this identification is from the demon. The demon continues to recognize Jesus as the one who has "come to destroy us [the demons]."

This is the first designation of Jesus since the lesson began. The fact that this identification comes from the demon should give us pause. The crowds and the disciples would certainly have

---

1 The NIV reads, "filled with compassion." The New English Bible uses "in warm indignation." For a discussion of these variations, read *The Gospel According to Mark* (William Lane, pages 84–86).

recognized that the demon is not trustworthy. Demonic intention is to deceive, destroy, and devour. Therefore, even though the demon rightly identifies Jesus as the Holy One of God, it is not to be trusted. Jesus commands the demon to be silent.

The crowds are left with a question: what is this authority that he [Jesus] is able to command demons and heal the sick. Mark does not, at this point, provide much more information.

If Mark had wished, he might have added a commentary such as is given by James: "Even the demons believe in God, and they shudder" (James 2:19). Mark chooses to leave us waiting.

We can confidently affirm that people respond to Jesus with awe and amazement. In that way, we are very much like the crowds. Like them, we have no means for making further judgment. We are not called to be disciples or to learn at his side. As a result, our judgment of Jesus as the Holy One needs to be suspended until more evidence is gathered.

As I reflect on my career as professor and pastor, I recall many moments in which others, including those close to me, have struggled with their "demons." One in the midst of the struggle is very much aware of how long that time might last. I am familiar with at least one mental health professional who would read no further in Mark's Gospel—claiming that it is not sufficient to simply command the demon to leave. This colleague found the story to be one of a false hope—healing by a single command. I believe there is reason to read further, as did the crowds, who were asking by what authority Jesus acted. If, as I suspect, it is by God's authority, then surely he is capable of healing by his very word.

As Mark continues, the crowds will remain in the story. We will often see their awe and amazement. Although at times the crowds may turn hostile, their identification of Jesus remains rather shallow throughout. Mark continues by revealing how other groups respond to Jesus. In the next section, Mark turns attention to how the religious leaders respond to the compassionate act of Jesus healing a paralytic.

Meeting Defenders of The Faith

(2:1–3:6)

Jesus is angry and deeply distressed at their stubborn hearts
—Mark 3:5

FISHING 201: PARALYZED

Turning from the individuals who are healed and the astonishment of the crowds, Mark calls our attention to some of the religious leaders in the society: namely, Pharisees and Sadducees. Each group has an interest in what will help the Jewish society. Given the acclaim Jesus has already received from the crowds, how will he be received by civic leaders. Both of these groups are steeped in the knowledge of Torah and of Jewish history, as well as prophetic words about a coming Messiah. We would expect from them a helpful comment on Jesus. So, what do they say about Jesus? Is he a person of prophetic promise? Is he "the Holy One of God?"

> *2 A few days later, when Jesus again entered Capernaum, the people heard that he had come home. [2] They gathered in such large numbers that there was no room left, not even outside the door, and he preached the word to them. [3] Some men came, bringing to him a paralyzed man, carried by four of them. [4] Since they could not get him to Jesus because of the crowd, they made an opening*

> *in the roof above Jesus by digging through it and then lowered the mat the man was lying on. [5] When Jesus saw their faith, he said to the paralyzed man, "Son, your sins are forgiven."*
>
> *[6] Now some teachers of the law were sitting there, thinking to themselves, [7] "Why does this fellow talk like that? He's blaspheming! Who can forgive sins but God alone?"*
>
> *[8] Immediately Jesus knew in his spirit that this was what they were thinking in their hearts, and he said to them, "Why are you thinking these things? [9] Which is easier: to say to this paralyzed man, 'Your sins are forgiven,' or to say, 'Get up, take your mat and walk'? [10] But I want you to know that the Son of Man has authority on earth to forgive sins." So, he said to the man, [11] "I tell you, get up, take your mat and go home." [12] He got up, took his mat and walked out in full view of them all. This amazed everyone and they praised God, saying, "We have never seen anything like this!"*

For the paralytic and for many others, this is a most encouraging story. In contrast, the religious leaders find the story is unsettling. These are the guardians of the society. They have an ear for religious teaching that conflicts with Jewish tradition and faith. The leaders stir with questions until Jesus puts them on the horns of a dilemma, paralyzing their ability to respond. What is easier for them, to forgive sins or to command the paralytic to walk? They are unable to answer.

The story does not dwell on their paralysis nor on the paralytic. Mark is revealing aspects of Jesus' authority for the reader to interpret. Will the religious leaders accept his authority? What do we, as readers, think?

In terms of the structure of the narrative, notice first that the paralytic is unable to navigate on his own. Four friends bring him to Jesus. The paralytic must have been grateful and certainly pleased with their kindness and determination. Yet, as the story eventually reveals, he has a significant reason to be anxious about seeing Jesus. He carries a private burden, his sin.

We had no idea the paralytic had any sin and Mark never reveals to us what it might have been. In fact, up to this point in the Gospel there is little mention of sin. Only in connection with John the Baptist who had preached repentance for the forgiveness of sins have we heard it.

The mention of sin in the paralytic's story comes as a surprise. We have already seen that Jesus heals people with health issues. With this story, the disciples learn Jesus has authority to deal with sin. Even more, the recognition of the paralytic's undisclosed sin implies Jesus is aware of that which we think is hidden.

This thing called "sin" prevents life from flourishing. It underscores the need for a qualified fisherman to enter the wilderness and deal with the underlying realities. Most of all, it underscores Jesus as the one with the authority to forgive sin and make things right.

In addition, we observe Jesus recognizes faith in people. Jesus seems to have knowledge of those who trust in God as well as of those needing forgiveness. When Jesus pronounces forgiveness, he honors the unspoken faith of the friends concerned about the paralytic, and he honors the deeper prayer from the paralytic.

Parenthetically, Mark does not confirm any connection between the sin and the paralysis, although there might have been one. Often, as a pastor, I have met with people who struggle with various physical ailments. The mere presence of a physical malady is not a direct indication that any one of them was dealing with a particular sin. For a better understanding, we might consider the story of Job, who suffered more for his faithfulness than for sin. We often put far too much a burden on our understanding of God's grace when we evaluate it by an undesirable physical condition.

Notice, the pronouncement of pardon for sin troubles the teachers of the law. They charge Jesus with blasphemy. Confronted by their critical spirit, Jesus challenges them with a dilemma. Which is easier, to forgive sin or to say to the paralytic, "Rise and walk?" The dilemma *paralyzes* the religious leaders. They are unable to forgive the paralytic (they are not in the seat of judgment) or to heal his paralysis (they are mere mortals). Certainly, had the paralytic sinned against one of them, that person could offer forgiveness. It does not appear in Mark that such is the case.

The religious leaders have no answer for Jesus. They remain silent. Since they are unable to answer Jesus' dilemma, why do they prefer to hang onto the charge of blasphemy? I believe this gives us a clue into how the religious leaders are responding. Their power in the social structure is as challenged by Jesus' authority as that of the demon earlier.

The paralytic stands up and walks away, and everyone is amazed. This amazement is no doubt especially true for the paralytic and his friends. Can you imagine their delight at the paralytic's healing? Did they even realize that Jesus had forgiven the paralytic man's sin? Do not forget the teachers of the law. They, too, were taken back by what they saw and heard. They could have remained silent and grateful to God as was the crowd. Instead, they persist in skepticism while the crowd, in contrast, praises God.

We need to mention the reference to "Son of Man," which is used to identify the authority by which Jesus heals the paralytic. It does not necessarily identify Jesus with the "Holy One of God." The religious leaders seem to be more concerned about Jesus' claim to be able to forgive sin. Yet, it is a second identification of Jesus.

In the end, the crowds predictably are awestruck. They have never seen anything like it. One would suspect they are speaking about the healing of the paralytic or possibly the forgiveness of sins. However, they might have thought of the stymied religious leaders as well.

THE ADDITION OF A DISCIPLE

> *13 Once again Jesus went out beside the lake. A large crowd came to him, and he began to teach them. 14 As he walked along, he saw Levi son of Alphaeus sitting at the tax collector's booth. "Follow me," Jesus told him, and Levi got up and followed him.*
>
> *15 While Jesus was having dinner at Levi's house, many tax collectors and sinners were eating with him and his disciples, for there were many who followed him. 16 When the teachers of the law who were Pharisees saw him eating with the sinners and tax collectors, they asked his disciples: "Why does he eat with tax collectors and sinners?"*
>
> *17 On hearing this, Jesus said to them, "It is not the healthy who need a doctor, but the sick. I have not come to call the righteous, but sinners."*

It would appear that the story of Levi, [2] like the story of the paralytic, is a foil for including another opinion from the religious leaders. Earlier, the leaders questioned the authority to forgive sin, neglecting, to be sure, to question by what authority Jesus healed the paralytic. Now they question Jesus' choice of companions noting that one of the "tax collectors" is called to be a disciple. In terms of vocation, the tax collector has a job

2 Levi is identified in Mark as the "son of Alphaeus." In the Gospel of Matthew, Matthew is called the "son of Alphaeus." Matthew is also referred to as the "tax collector" among the list of disciples in Matthew 10:10.

often identified by the religious leaders as sinful. Eating with tax collectors and sinners is unacceptable to the leaders in their understanding of righteousness. In terms of drama, Mark's focus in both cases is on the Pharisees' assessment of Jesus and on their growing antagonism toward him.

Two additional items from this story require attention. Unlike the previous narrative which does not name the paralytic, this one names the tax collector, Levi. This naming is likely to emphasize that he joins the band of disciples as a "fisherman." He is known to us as Matthew. Mark could be reminding us of the unique character of the disciples. It might well be that Peter and Levi often clashed as one was actually a fisherman and the other the tax collector from Peter's territory—who likely collected tax on the fish that Peter caught. Mark does not give us a clue and Levi's story is not told. In any case, Levi is a disciple and he and Peter must get along as members of the same team.

The second item concerns the need for a doctor. Could society itself be sick? Is Jesus criticizing the religious leaders for failing to recognize the sickness in society—and their responsibility to deal with it? Tax collectors, known for being somewhat unscrupulous, may be among the deplorables of society. Isn't it fair to expect the religious leaders to display a greater moral ethic than simply criticizing others? Indeed, Jesus expects them to be aware of their own failures.

Mark continues with two more illustrations of the growing hostility.

A TIME FOR FASTING

> [18] *Now John's disciples and the Pharisees were fasting. Some people came and asked Jesus, "How is it that John's disciples and the disciples of the Pharisees are fasting, but yours are not?"*
>
> [19] *Jesus answered, "How can the guests of the bridegroom fast*

while he is with them? They cannot, so long as they have him
with them. [20] *But the time will come when the bridegroom*
will be taken from them, and on that day they will fast.

[21] *"No one sews a patch of unshrunk cloth on an old*
garment. Otherwise, the new piece will pull away from
the old, making the tear worse. [22] *And no one pours new*
wine into old wineskins. Otherwise, the wine will burst
the skins, and both the wine and the wineskins will be
ruined. No, they pour new wine into new wineskins."

SABBATH MADE FOR MAN

[23] *One Sabbath Jesus was going through the grainfields,*
and as his disciples walked along, they began to pick some
heads of grain. [24] *The Pharisees said to him, "Look, why*
are they doing what is unlawful on the Sabbath?"

[25] *He answered, "Have you never read what David did*
when he and his companions were hungry and in need?
[26] *In the days of Abiathar the high priest, he entered the*
house of God and ate the consecrated bread, which is
lawful only for priests to eat. And he also gave some to
his companions."

[27] *Then he said to them, "The Sabbath was made for man,*
not man for the Sabbath. [28] *So the Son of Man is Lord*
even of the Sabbath."

Both of these illustrations reveal the determination of the Pharisees to find something with which they can discredit Jesus. Jesus handles himself well. He offers justification for the celebration of his disciples and a correction regarding the reason for the Sabbath. It would have been quite inappropriate either to mourn while the bridegroom was present, or to treat the Sabbath as a bondage. The rest from labor is intended by God to benefit human beings.

In both cases the Pharisees are requiring Jesus to abide by their interpretation of the law and the rules *they* establish. To them, it is about their own authority. One wonders how often maintaining a status quo sacrifices a better alternative. The final story in this selection continues the narrative of Pharisaic hostility but it also includes the opinion of Jesus on them.

THE WITHERED HAND

> ***3** Another time Jesus went into the synagogue, and a man with a shriveled hand was there. 2 Some of them were looking for a reason to accuse Jesus, so they watched him closely to see if he would heal him on the Sabbath. 3 Jesus said to the man with the shriveled hand, "Stand up in front of everyone."*
>
> *4 Then Jesus asked them, "Which is lawful on the Sabbath: to do good or to do evil, to save life or to kill?" But they remained silent.*
>
> *5 He looked around at them in anger and, deeply distressed at their stubborn hearts, said to the man, "Stretch out your hand." He stretched it out, and his hand was completely restored. 6 Then the Pharisees went out and began to plot with the Herodians how they might kill Jesus.*

Notice, for the second time, we have five narratives with a single purpose: on this occasion, to reveal the thoughts and intentions of the religious leaders. Not only are they unwilling to give Jesus a hearing, they do not realize how far out of step they are with their own teachings. They rush to judgment rather than deal with the challenges Jesus gives them. Eventually, they are so challenged by his authority that they align themselves with one of their political adversaries, the Herodians, in search of a way to execute him.

I want to add a thought about the Pharisees of today. Even religious institutions, in fact, every religious institution, is itself part of the wilderness. For my own part, as ordained in the Evangelical Covenant Church, I am aware that the rules we set forth as a denomination come from human authority—even as much as we try diligently to be faithful to God's leading. I am reminded of how many are driven away from the Church because of the Church's own inability to show compassion. The good news Mark introduces begins with the authority of who Jesus is.

The Pharisees are profoundly uncomfortable with Jesus' teachings and his actions. How sad for them! Even more, how sad for us the readers! Had they commended Jesus in some fashion, it would have been much to our delight. Imagine what the crowds would have been able to say, "This Jesus is approved by the authorities, and we have been doubly blessed, by Jesus and by them!" Unfortunately, this is not what happens in the story when the Spirit enters the wilderness. The hostility is real.

The crowds, even without the sanction of the leaders, praise God for what they see. They still do not understand all that Jesus says or does. Yet, they like him. They see what he does, and they know he cares for them. He teaches them to rejoice, to be of good cheer, to do good to each other, and to cherish the Sabbath—knowing it was made for them. Would that the religious leaders cared as much for the "common" person as Jesus cared!

The people of Rome would readily accept the witness of the crowds. They, too, would be amazed. They might even easily dismiss the intolerance and hostilities of the religious leaders. From their own experience with civic leaders, identifying with Jesus is likely easier than siding with the authorities.

The disciples witness all of this. They say nothing. While

they have been with Jesus the entire time and have witnessed all that has taken place, Mark does not even tell us their opinion. We do not know what they think of the crowds, the religious leaders, or Jesus. Even their feelings about Levi joining the group are not mentioned. Soon Mark will reveal their opinion of Jesus.

The narrative about the leaders concludes by letting us know how Jesus feels about them. Jesus is angry with them and their stubbornness of heart. They are unwilling to give God praise, unable to recognize God's compassion (whether it is in healing the paralytic or the man with the shriveled hand), and unaware of their own condition. Jesus' reaction to the religious leaders is opposite from the compassion Jesus had for the man with leprosy. He is indignant. The disciples witness his reaction in both cases.

What has Mark accomplished by telling us the story so far? Minimally, we may say he wants us to be grateful for those who are healed. We sit in awe of the one who heals. Perhaps Mark is pushing his readers to develop sensitivity to basic physical needs stemming from hunger, or basic social needs to be accepted and given purpose. There is nothing that says to the disciples *this is what you will do*. And there is nothing yet clarifying the commands to repent and believe.

Mark has not identified Jesus. Instead, Mark has made the identification more difficult. He gave us two statements: "Holy One of God" and "Son of Man." Neither is a reliable identification. The first comes from a demon. The second is challenged by the religious leaders.

Had the leaders of the society given approval of Jesus, they would have helped the crowds, the disciples, and the reader, identify him. Their failure to approve Jesus puts everyone else in a quandary. The good Jesus does cannot be denied. The power by which he does it is not yet confirmed.

Let us make two more observations.

First, the Pharisees are known for their strict observance

of the law. Their observance is not primarily in terms of the temple and the sacrificial system. It is more in terms of personal morality and behavior considered above reproach. Mark presents their rejection of Jesus as an inversion of moral significance. Consider: forgiving sin is a major issue while eating with sinners is not so important. Similarly, fasting is somewhat arbitrary and picking grain even less important. Doing good on the Sabbath should not be a problem. Yet it is in reaction to the least "immoral" of these matters, *Jesus doing good*, that causes the Pharisees to reach their conclusion to kill him. One wonders how many authorities are like them!

Second, notice the pact of the Pharisees with the Herodians. The Pharisees typically have no dealings with Herodians. The Herodians are a political party conspiring with the Roman oppressors of the day. What strange bedfellows we make when we feel threatened. We believe so much that we are in the right that *anything we do* to defend ourselves is acceptable! Is this not a picture of life in the wilderness?

I find that these observations are difficult to accept, yet they are all too common. As a father, grandfather, and great-grandfather, I spend much time in prayer personally seeking to understand, and then asking God to help my children understand. In faith, it is much more important that I wait on God's working in their lives.

We all sin—that is, we all make mistakes. Sometimes it is out of our own love that we cause hurt. Sometimes our pride blinds us to what is plainly seen by everyone else. And sometimes we get upset with others who are doing exactly as they should. Should we, like the Pharisees, rely on our own position and understanding? Should we, as parents, force children to see things as we do? It is better to be humble. Then it is no longer for us to defend ourselves. We are simply called to repent. It is on us to recognize that God is working—with our children, as well as with us. God have mercy.

There's One in Every Family (3:7–35)

"Whoever does God's will is my
brother and sister and mother."
—Mark 3:35

We have come far enough in Mark to detect the unfolding of a pattern in dealing with the theme of the wilderness being invaded by the Spirit. The nature of the wilderness is present in the dilemmas people face until the Spirit drives Jesus into their situations. The reactions of those whom Jesus meets tell us much about them and about the Spirit.

The pattern begins with individuals who are not defined in any way other than their illness, with the notable exception of Peter's mother-in-law. They include a troubled man set free from a demon, Peter's mother-in-law who rises to serve her guests, a leper who is so delighted that he spreads the good news everywhere contrary to Jesus' admonition to be silent, a paralyzed man who walks, and a man with a crippled hand. Others whom he heals spread his fame far and wide. None are mentioned by name. Their stories paint the background for the wilderness.

The pattern continues with the crowds who witness what Jesus does for individuals with awe and astonishment. Filled with excitement, they rejoice at his presence among them, bringing the sick to be healed and proclaiming they have never seen anything like this before. In some measure they may be echoing the reaction of individuals who are healed. In other respects, they are telling us as readers how we react. Again, none of them are identified. Initially, they are a useful barometer informing the readers how to understand what is happening. Mark is presenting *good news* and it is impressive, it is appropriate to be in awe. Follow the reaction of the crowds, even as they shift toward hostility.

The pattern includes opposition to Jesus. The demons know who Jesus is and have no authority over him. He tells them to be silent, and they are. It is significant that the first encounter Jesus has is with a man possessed by a demon. The tempter from the wilderness is not yet done with his temptations. This time it is through a person whose individuality has been overtaken by an alien power. Jesus is tempted to follow the demon's lead rather than the Spirit's guidance. While the ministry has begun, listening to this tempting voice abandons following the Spirit. Jesus commands it, "Be silent." Because it is an alien power he adds, "Come out of the man."

The guardians of the society form a fourth group in the pattern. They do not know what to make of Jesus. Recognizing the reactions of the crowds and the faith of people bringing their friends to Jesus, they are conflicted by what appears to be a great good. Namely the paralytic is healed. This healing, which seems to be a good thing, conflicts with their understanding of God who alone forgives sin. In their fear, they eventually make what appears to be a defense of their faith by collaborating with their political rivals to eliminate Jesus. Jesus is angered by them and their stubbornness.

We have been introduced to the disciples, a small group so far, only five, whose role seems to be watching and learning. Hence from them we have received no reaction. In the very next portion of Mark they will receive private instruction from Jesus regarding the kingdom of God. Then, they will offer a reflection on Jesus. It will become clear that they are not yet ready to answer the central question of the Gospel either for themselves or for us, "Who is this Jesus?" Fortunately, they will do that soon enough.

The one group not yet included is the family of Jesus, his mother and his brothers. They have familial concerns for Jesus, his arduous schedule, his health, his welfare. Mark does not spend much time with them except to remind us that the family which Jesus seeks are those who are devoted to God.

Notice in what follows how Mark presents each of these groups.

[7] Jesus withdrew with his disciples to the lake, and a large crowd from Galilee followed. [8] When they heard about all he was doing, many people came to him from Judea, Jerusalem, Idumea, and the regions across the Jordan and around Tyre and Sidon. [9] Because of the crowd he told his disciples to have a small boat ready for him, to keep the people from crowding him. [10] For he had healed many, so that those with diseases were pushing forward to touch him. [11] Whenever the impure spirits saw him, they fell down before him and cried out, "You are the Son of God." [12] But he gave them strict orders not to tell others about him.

[13] Jesus went up on a mountainside and called to him those he wanted, and they came to him. [14] He appointed twelve that they might be with him and that he might send them out to preach [15] and to have authority to drive out demons. [16] These are the twelve he appointed: Simon (to whom he gave the name Peter), [17] James son of Zebedee and his brother John (to them he gave the name Boanerges, which means "sons of thunder"), [18] Andrew, Philip, Bartholomew, Matthew, Thomas, James son of Alphaeus, Thaddaeus, Simon the Zealot [19] and Judas Iscariot, who betrayed him.

20 Then Jesus entered a house, and again a crowd gath-
ered, so that he and his disciples were not even able to eat.
21 When his family heard about this, they went to take
charge of him, for they said, "He is out of his mind."

22 And the teachers of the law who came down from
Jerusalem said, "He is possessed by Beelzebul! By the
prince of demons he is driving out demons."

23 So Jesus called them over to him and began to speak to
them in parables: "How can Satan drive out Satan? 24 If
a kingdom is divided against itself, that kingdom cannot
stand. 25 If a house is divided against itself, that house cannot
stand. 26 And if Satan opposes himself and is divided, he
cannot stand; his end has come. 27 In fact, no one can enter a
strong man's house without first tying him up. Then he can
plunder the strong man's house. 28 Truly I tell you, people
can be forgiven all their sins and every slander they utter, 29
but whoever blasphemes against the Holy Spirit will never
be forgiven; they are guilty of an eternal sin."

30 He said this because they were saying, "He has an
impure spirit."

31 Then Jesus' mother and brothers arrived. Standing
outside, they sent someone in to call him. 32 A crowd was
sitting around him, and they told him, "Your mother and
brothers are outside looking for you."

33 "Who are my mother and my brothers?" he asked.

34 Then he looked at those seated in a circle around him and
said, "Here are my mother and my brothers! 35 Whoever
does God's will is my brother and sister and mother."

In the case of the crowds, we again see their amazement at what Jesus is able to do. Their numbers have stretched far beyond the borders of Galilee. The crowds are swelling! Jesus' popularity on one occasion is so great that he requests a small boat to escape the crowd pressing in on him. Yet his compassion for them remains strong and unchanged as he continues to heal those with various diseases.

The disciples are merely listed, all twelve. [3] How each one came to be called is not Mark's concern. Likewise, the vocational background is irrelevant to Mark. It is significant that Mark lists Peter first and informs the people of Rome that his name had not always been Peter. With the name change, Jesus gives priority to Peter. He is Petros, Rock, a very dependable person in time of trouble. The church at Rome has been especially privileged to have him in their midst.

Otherwise, all we need to know about the disciples is that they are called, they are learning from Jesus and, eventually, they will be commissioned to preach and cast out evil spirits. It would be appropriate for us as readers to ask what privileged teaching the disciples received. Further, how do they respond to Jesus and the question of his authority? Mark has not yet given us this insight.

The Pharisees continue in their stubborn ways. They freely ascribe to Jesus a malady of his own: he is possessed by the prince of demons. It may be an act of patience and kindness on Jesus' part when he restrains from upbraiding them with strong words. Rather, he tells a parable keeping the door open for them to change their opinion, to repent. Jesus and the Pharisees both know a house divided against itself cannot stand.

In the same breath Jesus speaks cryptically about robbing a strong man and about an unforgivable sin committed against

---

3 In *The Gospel According to Mark*, William Lane suggests that James, the son of Alphaeus, may be the brother of Levi. In this case, the disciples includes three pairs of siblings.

the Holy Spirit. Precisely what sin is unforgivable does not get stated. However, if Jesus is revealing the love of God in healing the sick, then referring to Jesus as demonic likely carries dire consequences. The soul that persists in calling *evil that which is good* and *good that which is evil* builds up a resistance to good that can seldom be overcome.

Instead, if one recognizes the *good* in what Jesus does when he heals the sick, one should acknowledge it as *good* with at least a minimum attitude of amazement. If, by grace, the Holy Spirit calls for repentance, then repent. The reference to the Holy Spirit is most likely informed by the events on Pentecost and later apostolic teaching that would have been familiar to the Christian community in Rome. Remember, it was Peter who gave the sermon at Pentecost, and Mark is telling Peter's narrative of the Christ.

The strong man is Satan whose influence in the world brings chaos, destruction, calamity, and hostility. How the strong man will be bound is not revealed here. Hints at Satan's loss of power and ultimate downfall is in the work of the "fisherman" freeing people from their captivities, from disease, from possession by alien spirits, from dependencies, from paralysis, and from deformity. The work of God is a serious matter. The strongman needs to be bound. He is not to be taken lightly.

There are about three decades of students from Wheaton College who know what comes next. "A Mighty Fortress," perhaps my favorite hymn, acknowledges the strength of Satan. We are unable to defeat him by our own authority. As I am quite sure you have all committed this hymn to memory, I will hold off, for now, on stating by whose authority he is defeated. Jesus is making the point—the strong man is real. In the end, "one little word shall fell him."

Finally, the introduction of Jesus' family seems relevant to our discussion. Surely, his family will be able to help us understand who Jesus is. We hope they will offer insight as to why his ministry is so significant. However, Mark does not let the biological family have much of a central role. They appear to act out of compassion: seeking to bring Jesus home when they believe he is mentally ill, delusional, or working too hard.

There may have been deep concern for Jesus' welfare or there may have been some hostility in their assumption of Jesus' illness (see John 7:1–5). Mark offers no explanation. Jesus himself excludes them with a brush of his hand claiming that those who do the will of God rank higher than they in terms of true spirituality. Perhaps better, Jesus describes a different family in terms of the kingdom of God. (see also John 1:12, 13).

Jesus' conclusion to the matter is challenging. Who are the ones who do the will of God? As Jesus has already explained, they are those who repent and believe. It would appear Mark is inviting his readers into this family.

Aspects of this summary imply it is written from a perspective following the resurrection. The twelve are referred to as "Apostles" as opposed to "disciples." This designation comes into effect after the ascension. Then there is a reference to the Holy Spirit noted above. When Jesus was baptized the Spirit descended upon him as a dove and a voice was heard from Heaven. When the disciples are similarly baptized, the Spirit descends as fire, and they speak in praise of Jesus in a way that people from many lands hear the words in their own native language.

Remember, Mark is not writing a biography. The relevance of his using the word "apostle," for example, is in telling the good news—the twelve are already well-known as Apostles to the audience to whom Mark is writing, the Christians in Rome.

The function of this section seems to highlight the difference between the disciples and the religious leaders. One will become part of the family. The other will conspire to execute Jesus. Between them are the uncommitted individuals, the awe-struck crowds, the concerned biological family members, and the readers of this Gospel.

Privilege for the Disciples (4:1–41)

"Who is this? Even the winds and the waves obey him?"
—Mark 4:41

FISHING 301: LEARNING ABOUT THE KINGDOM

If there is any one group of people who "do the will of God," it is this small group of disciples. The first four of them dropped everything, "leaving their nets" to follow Jesus. Since called to become "fishers of men," Mark has said very little about them. Their numbers have grown to twelve. They have seen and heard a great deal. We don't know what Jesus may have been teaching them aside from what they have witnessed. Have they received any special insight? At this point, Mark turns our attention to some of the privileged teaching on the kingdom of God.

Four parables are given in this, the third and concluding part of what we are calling Act 1. They are designed for the reader to know that the disciples are specifically taught and nurtured by Jesus on all matters of his ministry especially on the kingdom of God. Mark lets us know that in each case they are receiving private instruction.

4 Again Jesus began to teach by the lake. The crowd that gathered around him was so large that he got into a boat and sat in it out on the lake, while all the people were along the shore at the water's edge. 2 He taught them many

things by parables, and in his teaching said: 3 "Listen! A
farmer went out to sow his seed. 4 As he was scattering the
seed, some fell along the path, and the birds came and ate it
up. 5 Some fell on rocky places, where it did not have much
soil. It sprang up quickly, because the soil was shallow. 6
But when the sun came up, the plants were scorched, and
they withered because they had no root. 7 Other seed fell
among thorns, which grew up and choked the plants, so
that they did not bear grain. 8 Still other seed fell on good
soil. It came up, grew and produced a crop, some multiply-
ing thirty, some sixty, some a hundred times."

9 Then Jesus said, "Whoever has ears to hear, let them hear."

10 When he was alone, the Twelve and the others around
him asked him about the parables. 11 He told them, "The
secret of the kingdom of God has been given to you. But to
those on the outside everything is said in parables 12 so that,

"'they may be ever seeing but never perceiving, and ever
hearing but never understanding;otherwise they might
turn and be forgiven!'"

13 Then Jesus said to them, "Don't you understand this
parable? How then will you understand any parable? 14
The farmer sows the word.15 Some people are like seed along
the path, where the word is sown. As soon as they hear it,
Satan comes and takes away the word that was sown in
them. 16 Others, like seed sown on rocky places, hear the
word and at once receive it with joy. 17 But since they have
no root, they last only a short time. When trouble or perse-
cution comes because of the word, they quickly fall away. 18
Still others, like seed sown among thorns, hear the word; 19

but the worries of this life, the deceitfulness of wealth and the desires for other things come in and choke the word, making it unfruitful. [20] *Others, like seed sown on good soil, hear the word, accept it, and produce a crop—some thirty, some sixty, some a hundred times what was sown."*

The first parable is about a sower preparing for a grain harvest by spreading seed seemingly indiscriminately on the ground. The seeds fall on four different types of soil. The first is so hard that some readers might find it difficult to believe that any farmer would even attempt to plant seed there. However, remembering the land, we may have a better understanding. Jesus is in a boat just off the northern shore of the Sea of Galilee, likely near Capernaum. In this region, the rich soil is very capable of yielding an excellent crop. Unfortunately, the soil is also quite deceptive, as there are often rocks hidden just beneath the top layer.

This understanding of the land in this region is important to all four types of soil. Animal tracks are commonly seen in the soil; birds will easily have access to freshly scattered seed; and, since the soil is good for good seed, it is equally good for weeds, thorns, and thistles. Overall, it would be commonly understood that a farmer might scatter his seed exactly in this manner. The parable fits the region just north of the Sea of Galilee.

In the parable Jesus brings together the significance of the soil, the importance of the seed, the threats to a harvest, and finally, the work of the sower. Jesus explains this parable—as if the disciples were incapable of understanding. We are told that the seed is the word and that it produces valuable grain. Regrettably, it can also be lost in a variety of ways. The sower appears to be Jesus and he is generous with the seeds, sowing everywhere. The different ground surfaces are those who hear Jesus' teaching—perhaps referring to the crowds, religious leaders, family, and disciples.

Although Jesus explains the soil—he does not do much to

explain the role of the birds that snatch away the seed or the thorns and thistles that choke out a growing harvest. Consider the demons that Jesus has encountered. The seed is not sown for them. However, they play a role in reducing the harvest. Thorns and thistles may include various mental illnesses. More likely, they refer to people more concerned with their own prestige and power than in caring for others. Like Nero, persecuting believers for self-aggrandizement.

The seed is sown for the crowds. They initially respond to Jesus with amazement as they witness the healing of a man with an unclean spirit and afterward the healing of many others. Mark does not tell us if their commitments run deeper. It is possible that, for some, their trust in Jesus as Lord matures very deeply. It is likely, however, that the people within the crowds have very different reactions, with some blossoming while others wither away. There seems to be a point Jesus is making: commitment to God is fruitful only when the roots are deep in good soil.

The disciples have witnessed Jesus sow the seeds. They have seen the various "soils" on which the seeds have fallen. They do not yet understand, either the parable or what they have witnessed. They ask for an explanation. Jesus provides it, and Mark includes it. That explanation is provided because the parable is also about us. The seed has also fallen on us.

It is one thing to be able to interpret this parable correctly. Seeing the imagery of sower, seed, and soil may prove helpful in many human circumstances. How often do we want to identify others as shallow or choked out by weeds? The parable is not about human situations. Jesus explains: You have been given the secret to the kingdom of God.

Remember from the prologue, the kingdom of God has come into the wilderness so that life may flourish. Regardless of our circumstances, we are called to produce fruit because the kingdom of God is here. It is a call to repent and to believe. Those who understand will hear the word, accept the word, and do what it says.

ADDITIONAL LESSONS ON THE KINGDOM

21 He said to them, "Do you bring in a lamp to put it
under a bowl or a bed? Instead, don't you put it on its
stand? 22 For whatever is hidden is meant to be disclosed,
and whatever is concealed is meant to be brought out into
the open. 23 If anyone has ears to hear, let them hear."

24 "Consider carefully what you hear," he continued. "With
the measure you use, it will be measured to you—and even
more. 25 Whoever has will be given more; whoever does
not have, even what they have will be taken from them."

26 He also said, "This is what the kingdom of God is like.
A man scatters seed on the ground. 27 Night and day,
whether he sleeps or gets up, the seed sprouts and grows,
though he does not know how. 28 All by itself the soil pro-
duces grain—first the stalk, then the head, then the full
kernel in the head. 29 As soon as the grain is ripe, he puts
the sickle to it, because the harvest has come."

30 Again he said, "What shall we say the kingdom of God
is like, or what parable shall we use to describe it? 31 It
is like a mustard seed, which is the smallest of all seeds
on earth. 32 Yet when planted, it grows and becomes the
largest of all garden plants, with such big branches that
the birds can perch in its shade."

33 With many similar parables Jesus spoke the word to
them, as much as they could understand. 34 He did not say
anything to them without using a parable. But when he
was alone with his own disciples, he explained everything.

These three parables, as well as the others Mark references, are each descriptive of the kingdom of God. While Jesus explains them to the disciples, Mark does not include an explanation for the reader. The cloaked message may be an indication of persecution under Nero. This may have been a benefit to the church at Rome. It may also be descriptive of how Jesus taught his message of the kingdom.

How fortunate for the disciples! When alone with Jesus, they receive privileged insight into all that Jesus taught and they have already witnessed what he does. They know his power to heal, to forgive sins, and to drive out demons. They have been chosen to be the good soil on which the seed falls. They know something about the kingdom of God that is at hand.

What is most interesting is discovering how the disciples respond. Jesus is teaching about the kingdom of God. One may assume that the teacher, therefore, knows something about the kingdom. He has some authority—or at least knowledge that supports his capacity to teach. He also acted on behalf of the kingdom. It was more than teaching. He was bearing fruit. On some level, the disciples must have recognized his authority. Pay close attention to the personal response that comes from the disciples. What do they say concerning Jesus?

> 35 *That day when evening came, he said to his disciples,*
> *"Let us go over to the other side."* 36 *Leaving the crowd*
> *behind, they took him along, just as he was, in the boat.*
> *There were also other boats with him.* 37 *A furious squall*
> *came up, and the waves broke over the boat, so that it*
> *was nearly swamped.* 38 *Jesus was in the stern, sleeping*
> *on a cushion. The disciples woke him and said to him,*
> *"Teacher, don't you care if we drown?"*
>
> 39 *He got up, rebuked the wind and said to the waves,*

"Quiet! Be still!" Then the wind died down and it was completely calm.

40 He said to his disciples, "Why are you so afraid? Do you still have no faith?"

41 They were terrified and asked each other, "Who is this? Even the wind and the waves obey him!"

How disappointing! The disciples have all the parables explained and they do not know who Jesus is in relation to the kingdom of God. They saw it all! They heard it all! It was all explained to them. Still, they do not yet know who Jesus truly is. Even Jesus marvels at them (4:40).

Before leaving this part of the narrative, I ask you to consider why Mark may have included these particular stories for the people of Rome. Specifically, why tell the story of the sower? I submit to you the parable of the sower is extremely important in its own right, and in Rome, more so. In Rome, the face of the "sower" is likely Peter. The seed he has sown has fallen on various types of soil. Nero, like Satan, has made repeated efforts to destroy the Christian community. How are these people who are subject to Nero's brutality going to continue their trust in God? They will surely ask themselves if trusting in Jesus is an illusion. They will wonder if the salvation proclaimed by Peter is worth the consequence of dying a brutal death.

Then they read how Jesus spoke of good soil and an abundant harvest from the seed that is sown. They read how Jesus dies alone, betrayed and abandoned by his followers. Included among the deserters is Peter, denying he even knows Jesus. They learn that after the resurrection Peter is reinstated and becomes the seemingly unshakeable "rock" in the face of Nero's persecution. So, when Peter dies, will there be deserters? Will any of them get caught up with other affairs in their lives? These are likely possibilities except for the grace of God. Of those denying Christ will any be like Peter and return to faith? How important is prayer on their behalf? By God's grace, many of the believers in Rome remained faithful despite being subjected to intense persecution.

In addition to those about whom Mark writes, there is another to add to our discussion. Not least among those faithful under persecution is the Apostle Paul, who like Peter, is a mentor to Mark and, again like Peter, a martyr in Rome. Paul writes:

> *I have worked much harder, been in prison more frequently, been flogged more severely, and been exposed to death again and again. Five times I received from the Jews the forty lashes minus one. Three times I was beaten with rods, once I was stoned, three times I was shipwrecked. ... I will boast all the more gladly about my weaknesses, so that Christ's power may rest on me. That is why, for Christ's sake, I delight in my weaknesses, in insults, in hardships, in persecutions, in difficulties (2 Corinthians 11:23–25;12:9, 10).*

Similarly, Peter writes, likely from Rome, to believers in Asia Minor (North Central Turkey) to explain it this way:

> *Dear Friends, do not be surprised at the painful trial you are suffering, as though something strange were happening to you. But rejoice that you participate in the sufferings of Christ, so that you may be overjoyed when his glory is revealed (I Peter 4:12-13).*

One of the joys of teaching is the ability to share peculiar insights that elevate how others may understand situations. Sometimes, the joy is made greater when students realize that such observations apply to their own life as well. Amid persecution, it would generally be expected that the Christian faith might wither away. Such is not the case. In fact, there is a paradoxical effect from the persecution. The followers of Jesus in Rome will increase several times over until, several centuries later, Christianity becomes the official religion of the empire. Perhaps this is why James states, "Consider it pure joy when you face trials of many kinds" (James 1:2).

Mark has now given us five reactions to Jesus. Demons. They can't be trusted, although they identify Jesus as the Holy One of God. Crowds. They are simply in awe of his power. Religious leaders. They seek to kill him, presumably because they find him a threat to their own position. Family. They judge him to be out of his mind. And, now, the disciples. Despite private lessons that explain everything, they are left asking, "Who is this?"

There is at least one more group that has witnessed all of these events: the readers. Do you find yourself identifying Jesus? Is he what you expect—or has his actions and comments confused you at times? Do you identify with one of the other five: Demons? Crowds? Pharisees? Family? Disciples? These are questions that no one else can answer for you. You must determine how you respond to the *good news* of Jesus that Mark is sharing.

PERSPECTIVE ON THE SOWER AND THE SEED

Mark knows the story of Jesus is *good news*. He wishes the reader to identify Jesus based on the leading of the Spirit and the mounting evidence. He does not wish to state the answer directly. We are not told why Mark does this, at least not yet. In his own way, Mark treats the readers much the same as Jesus treats the crowds or the disciples. The readers are observers. In the end the disciples are amazed and overwhelmed with Jesus authority over the forces of nature. Still, the response of the disciples to all they have heard and seen is a question: "Who is this?"

We, like the disciples, witness the healing of a man possessed by an evil spirit. We get to hear both the plea from the evil spirit and Jesus' rebuke. In the opinion of the crowds, this is "awesome!"

On a personal level, we get invited to Peter's house and learn of Peter's mother-in-law. We learn Jesus is concerned with hospitality! We know how the many are healed, and we feel sympathy for the sick, enough to join with their search for Jesus when he retreats from the crowds in their desire to bring him back. We identify with them.

We even appreciate the enthusiasm of the leper who cannot contain his delight. We rejoice with him and his restoration to society. Why Jesus asked him to be silent about his healing, we do not know. We wonder if we could have remained silent about such a blessing. After all, our friends would certainly be asking us how our "leprosy" was cured.

If there had ever been a doubt about how to react initially to Jesus, we had the benefit of the crowds. We know their reaction, they are amazed! We should be too. This is a significant jubilant response in terms of the incredible drama Mark provides even if it is a minimal response. Beyond this awe, we are silent—and in our silence we gather up the stories. We remember Jesus was filled with compassion as he saw the needs around him.

The healing of a paralytic was spectacular. Imagine the determination of the paralytic's friends prompting them to tear open the roof. Were they among the many who had been healed before and hence knew exactly how to help their paralyzed friend? Maybe, but when their friend picked up his mat and walked, we can picture his friends skipping alongside him on the way home shouting, "I told you so!" And then their friend, the paralytic, might be willing to talk about the forgiveness of his sin, a much better result from visiting Jesus than just the ability to walk!

Surprising to us is the reaction of the religious leaders. They certainly could be expected to evaluate Jesus and even to be suspicious of Jesus' claim to forgive sin. When Jesus asked them whether it was easier to forgive sin or to say, "Get up and walk," they should have gotten the point. Jesus had authority to do both, while neither could be done by them nor any other human being. It is only God's authority that can heal and forgive sins. If Jesus did both, why couldn't they see what was plain before their eyes? Were they threatened somehow by Jesus?

It seems these guardians must have been threatened because they eventually project onto Jesus a sinister interpretation, possession by the prince of demons. This is a strange way to respond to Jesus' teachings about the Sabbath and to Jesus' willingness to do good just by speaking to the man with the withered hand. The least they could have done was to be silent like the crowds, especially as they were in a house of worship. Jesus was doing wonderful things, and they could not see them. Why they had to consult with the Herodians makes no sense based on what they saw. This decision on their part and their projection of evil onto Jesus also suggests that the religious leaders felt threatened.

We are not threatened. As Jesus lifted up his disciples as family, he lifts us up. He told the disciples the hidden meaning in his parables and let them witness all he was doing. They were indeed privileged, and we, together with them, are allowed to have some private instruction on one of the parables.

However, we do not hear everything the disciples heard as only one of the parables is explained to us. We know very little about the coming kingdom, and we are not yet ready to embrace Jesus as either the king or a herald of the kingdom. And this is to say nothing of him as Savior or Christ or Son of God. But we are at a point where we can recognize choices.

We can choose to be like the crowds and stay with our personal needs. There may not be anything wrong with their enthusiastic response, although it seems a little immature of them if not taken to another level.

We can choose to be like the religious leaders, and some of the readers of this story will be exactly like them, rejecting the story outright. For many others, the rejection seems presumptive, a far too hasty conclusion. The religious leaders seem to have a major blind spot when it comes to life experiences that lie outside the way they are accustomed to view life. They portray a certain arrogance that prevents them from having the simple joy and wonder of life which we found in the crowds. Further, they offer no explanation for the healing of the paralytic apart from a possible reference to the prince of demons.

Many of us, as readers, would prefer identification with the disciples. Sitting at Jesus' feet seems by itself to be a profound privilege.

In the parable about the sower, the first major instruction Jesus gives to his disciples, Jesus explains that the secret of the kingdom of God is given to them (Mark 4:11). What is this secret?

Jesus says the kingdom of God is like a man scattering seed that sprouts and grows without further attention from the sower (Mark 4:26).

The kingdom of God is also like a small mustard seed that becomes the largest of all garden plants (Mark 4:30). What is the meaning of kingdom?

The last three parables are explained to the disciples but neither the disciples nor Jesus, reveal to the readers exactly what is meant by them. Pointedly, Mark does not tell us either.

We know Jesus will eventually use the disciples in a preaching and healing ministry. He said so. They will need to understand the parables and they will use them in preaching. The disciples have come a long way on the path to becoming fishers of men and women. If they are ready to begin their ministry, we will learn who this Jesus is. Unfortunately, the disciples are not ready for such an assignment. The episode in the boat confirms for us their need for further study. In our case, we are certainly not prepared to proclaim *good news* about the kingdom. We do not even know for sure what the parables about the kingdom mean. We will need to wait for a later discussion on the matter.

Life did not let the disciples sit idly by, nor it does it let us sit by idly either. The disciples found themselves in a boat tossed about by a violent storm. We also face storms that come up unexpectedly. And when the storms come, the storms are frequently very upsetting and often experienced as most severe in the circles in which we feel the most expertise, control, and comfort. It is quite common then to ask in desperation, "Where is God? Doesn't God care about what is happening to us?" Like the disciples, we wonder if the deity is sleeping, or in this case, if Jesus is sleeping. Are the assurances we thought we had as Jesus' friends being suspended? Do the people of Rome agonize over the possibility of their lives being turned upside down?

It is then that Jesus speaks, and the storm subsides. We find ourselves wondering how the disciples, after all they had heard and seen, could ask, "Who is this? Even the wind and the waves obey him?" Yet this is precisely what they ask. We ask it too. Perhaps more often that we care to admit.

We might have expected the disciples to have learned more about Jesus and themselves. Jesus has provided the instruction necessary for the disciples to know that faith holds a higher value than knowledge. As teacher, he has demonstrated patience, extreme patience, with how slowly the disciples (we) learn. He is showing concern for the development and growth of their faith. Just as there is more for the disciples to learn, there is more for us to learn as well.

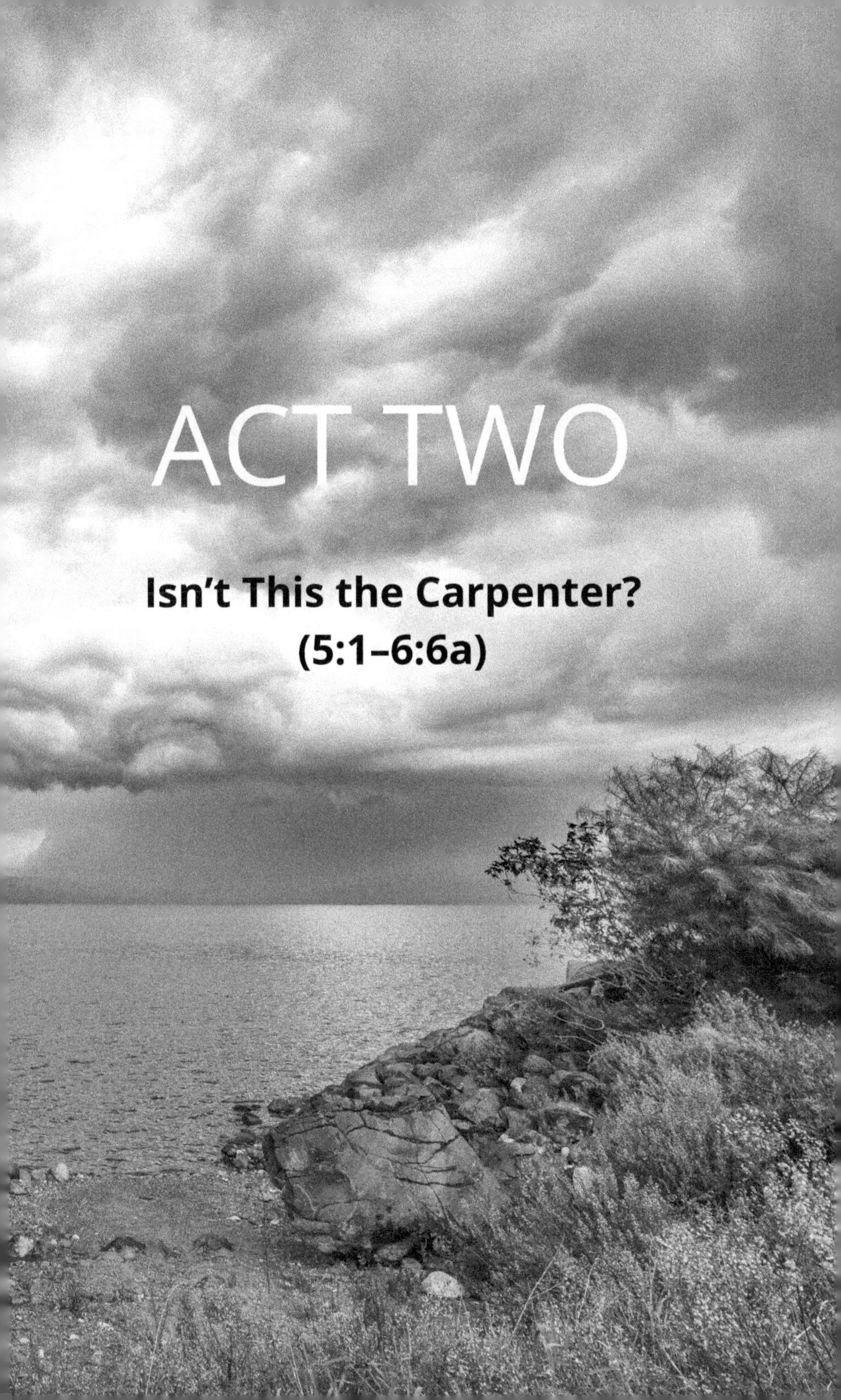

ACT TWO

Isn't This the Carpenter?
(5:1–6:6a)

Witness of Legion (5:1–20)

The conclusion to the previous act is tied to the second act with two items: the trip across the lake and the question "Who is he?"

First, the disciples, together with Jesus, got into a boat with the intention of crossing to the other side of the lake. A storm arose, interrupting the short journey across the lake. There is no indication where they came ashore after the storm. The new chapter indicates that they went across the lake to the region of the Gerasenes.

Second, the previous act ended with a question, "Who is he?" When the new scene comes to a close, it will answer that question from the perspective of the people of Nazareth, the village in which Jesus grew up.

Outside of these similarities this chapter stands on its own. The stories of three people dominate the narrative, two are mentioned by name. This stands in contrast to the previous stories where none are named. Mark identifies no name for the man liberated from the evil spirit, no name for Peter's mother-in-law, no name for the paralytic or his friends, no names for the religious leaders and their accomplices, and no names for Jesus' family members, not even his mother.

Why does Mark provide us with names of people now? Mark is calling attention to them. There is something for us and the disciples to learn, and Mark wants to make sure we notice these individuals. How do they enhance the significance Jesus as a person? We begin with a man called Legion in the region of the Gerasenes.

LEGION IN THE REGION OF THE GERASENES

5 They went across the lake to the region of the Gerasenes.
2 When Jesus got out of the boat, a man with an impure
spirit came from the tombs to meet him. 3 This man lived
in the tombs, and no one could bind him anymore, not
even with a chain. 4 For he had often been chained hand
and foot, but he tore the chains apart and broke the irons
on his feet. No one was strong enough to subdue him. 5
Night and day among the tombs and in the hills, he
would cry out and cut himself with stones.

6 When he saw Jesus from a distance, he ran and fell on his
knees in front of him. 7 He shouted at the top of his voice,
"What do you want with me, Jesus, Son of the Most High
God? In God's name don't torture me!" 8 For Jesus had
said to him, "Come out of this man, you impure spirit!"

9 Then Jesus asked him, "What is your name?"

"My name is Legion," he replied, "for we are many." 10
And he begged Jesus again and again not to send them
out of the area.

11 A large herd of pigs was feeding on the nearby hillside. 12
The demons begged Jesus, "Send us among the pigs; allow
us to go into them." 13 He gave them permission, and the
impure spirits came out and went into the pigs. The herd,
about two thousand in number, rushed down the steep
bank into the lake and were drowned.

14 Those tending the pigs ran off and reported this in the
town and countryside, and the people went out to see

what had happened.[15] *When they came to Jesus, they saw the man who had been possessed by the legion of demons, sitting there, dressed and in his right mind; and they were afraid.* [16] *Those who had seen it told the people what had happened to the demon-possessed man—and told about the pigs as well.* [17] *Then the people began to plead with Jesus to leave their region.*

[18] *As Jesus was getting into the boat, the man who had been demon-possessed begged to go with him.* [19] *Jesus did not let him, but said, "Go home to your own people and tell them how much the Lord has done for you, and how he has had mercy on you."* [20] *So the man went away and began to tell in the Decapolis how much Jesus had done for him. And all the people were amazed.*

This narrative offers a significant deepening of our understanding of the scope of Jesus' ministry. To start, Mark introduces us to a change in scenery to highlight the new focus. Jesus moves from homeland territory near Capernaum on the north shore of Galilee to a place on the eastern shore of the lake. It is a short distance, merely a few miles, and it is a whole new territory.

Mark calls it the region of the Gerasenes. In effect, this crossing of the lake may be considered a border crossing which by today's standard might have require a passport. At that time, however, the entire area was under Roman authority. The political reality of the region began decades earlier (63 BC) under Pompey as a "League of Ten Cities," the Decapolis. By the time of the first century it was likely identified more loosely as Gentile territory. [1]

---

1 In *Greatness, Grace, and Glory,* Paul Wright phrases the issue as follows: "Whether the gospel writers understood the term 'Decapolis' to indicate a geographical region or a political entity is a matter of debate. It is possible that they used the term rather generically for 'eastern gentile regions' of any kind" (Paul Wright, page 178).

The drama begins abruptly. As Jesus arrives on the shore, a man called Legion runs to Jesus. Falling on his knees before Jesus, he immediately calls out, "What do you want with me, Jesus, Son of the Most High God?"

It is not clear how this person knew Jesus unless it is the spirits within him who are calling out. Nor is it clear if the man himself is responsible for the unusual behavior of falling on his knees or if it is the evil spirits with which he wrestles who are responsible. It is further unclear if falling before Jesus is an act of worship or a humble plea for help. What is clear is that this man has an evil spirit which, like the man with the demon whom Jesus met earlier, (Mark 1:21–28) also identifies Jesus with God.

For the second time, Mark gives a clear identification of Jesus with deity and then, compromises it by allowing it to come from a questionable source, the evil spirits. Note also, unlike the man in the first story, this man has a name and eventually he will request to become a disciple.

Mark provides us with a detailed description of the man and his troubled lifestyle. He screams throughout the night, he lives among the tombs, he has super strength, and he cuts himself with rocks, presumably to end his agony. In short, he is not in his right mind. It is what Mark identifies as possession by many spirits and what we might recognize as signs of mental illness.

Jesus asks him his name. "Legion," he answers. Then Jesus frees him from his possession by allowing the spirits to enter a herd of nearby pigs.

The reference to pig herding is significant for at least two reasons. First, it is a further indication Jesus is in Gentile territory. Jewish dietary laws would preclude such an occupation. More importantly, it is an amplification of our understanding of the demons. They have invaded creation with destructive intent. In contrast to Jesus, the demons have no respect for the goodness of creation. They torment people without compassion. When they enter the pigs, the demons are in full control. The resistance they experienced from the human being (who is created in the image of God) is gone. This allows the demons to achieve their goal. The work of evil is not just to cripple, but to destroy.

One wonders if Mark has in mind a perspective given by Peter: "Be self-controlled and alert. Your enemy the devil prowls around like a roaring lion seeking someone to devour. Resist him, ..." (I Peter 5:8–9). This is a powerful story of compassion mingled with a strong suggestion that the evil spirits, lacking any compassion on their part, desire to destroy the man.

The internal struggles of this man must have been profound! The fact that he comes to his right mind is heartwarming. When the owners of the pigs come with the pig herders and the other townspeople, they recognize a power none of them had and one greater than any one of them had experienced. They are the ones who had tried to bind Legion out of their compassion for him. Their work was unsuccessful and so they learned to live with him. In the face of Jesus' superior power to the demons, they are fearful. In one of the saddest requests in the Bible, they ask Jesus to leave. Jesus honors their request.

As Jesus gets into the boat to leave, the man called Legion approaches him again. Unlike the townspeople, Legion is not fearful. His newfound freedom leads him to follow Jesus and prompts him to request becoming a disciple. Clearly, he recognizes Jesus as his "Savior." However, Jesus does not allow him to become a disciple alongside the twelve. Rather, he sends Legion to witness to his family and his hometown to tell them what God had done for him.

Once free from the evil spirits, Legion can be restored to his family and community. The family no longer needs to fear what he might do. Legion no longer needs to live in isolation. It is interesting that Jesus, who commanded the leper to remain silent, tells this man to share his story freely with family and friends and to proclaim his liberation to anyone who will listen.

The story concludes with Jesus going in one direction and Legion in another. Those who remained were all amazed (Mark 5:20). We may assume some surface similarity of this crowd to the ones encountered in Jewish territory but this one also includes many who were afraid of Jesus. After all, they did ask Jesus to leave their territory. Because Jesus leaves them, we get the impression his primary work will be accomplished within Jewish society even if the benefit of his work includes Gentiles.

There is one other observation to suggest. The episode concerning Legion is in an area under Roman control. It has often been suggested that Legion's name is the result of severe trauma likely associated with a Roman legion. [2] For the church in Rome, this story would resonate with their struggles in the empire and might be a comfort to them as Jesus reversed the damage allegedly done to Legion by Roman troops.

JAIRUS, A RULER IN THE SYNAGOGUE, AND A WOMAN OF FAITH

Again, Jesus crosses the lake, this time returning to Jewish territory. Even though, like the region of the Gentiles, it is under Roman occupation, the primary drama in this location has a strong Jewish flavor.

> *21 When Jesus had again crossed over by boat to the other side of the lake, a large crowd gathered around him while he was by the lake. 22 Then one of the synagogue leaders, named Jairus, came, and when he saw Jesus, he fell at his feet. 23 He pleaded earnestly with him, "My little daughter is dying. Please come and put your hands on her so that she will be healed and live." 24 So Jesus went with him.*

---

2 It is tempting to interpret someone with a significant personality disorder and a name such as "Legion" as someone who has suffered significant trauma from the occupying Roman army. A legion is reported to have as many as six thousand soldiers. According to Robert Stein, there is no supporting evidence of trauma. Therefore, the narrative is best understood in reference to multiple demons (Robert Stein, page 255).

*A large crowd followed and pressed around him. 25 And
a woman was there who had been subject to bleeding for
twelve years. 26 She had suffered a great deal under the
care of many doctors and had spent all she had, yet instead
of getting better she grew worse. 27 When she heard about
Jesus, she came up behind him in the crowd and touched
his cloak, 28 because she thought, "If I just touch his clothes,
I will be healed." 29 Immediately her bleeding stopped and
she felt in her body that she was freed from her suffering.*

*30 At once Jesus realized that power had gone out from
him. He turned around in the crowd and asked, "Who
touched my clothes?"*

*31 "You see the people crowding against you," his disciples
answered, "and yet you can ask, 'Who touched me?'"*

*32 But Jesus kept looking around to see who had done
it. 33 Then the woman, knowing what had happened to
her, came and fell at his feet and, trembling with fear,
told him the whole truth. 34 He said to her, "Daughter,
your faith has healed you. Go in peace and be freed from
your suffering."*

*35 While Jesus was still speaking, some people came from
the house of Jairus, the synagogue leader. "Your daughter
is dead," they said. "Why bother the teacher anymore?"*

*36 Overhearing what they said, Jesus told him, "Don't be
afraid; just believe."*

*37 He did not let anyone follow him except Peter, James
and John the brother of James. 38 When they came to the
home of the synagogue leader, Jesus saw a commotion,*

with people crying and wailing loudly.[39] *He went in and said to them, "Why all this commotion and wailing? The child is not dead but asleep."* [40] *But they laughed at him.*

After he put them all out, he took the child's father and mother and the disciples who were with him and went in where the child was. [41] *He took her by the hand and said to her, "Talitha koum!" (which means "Little girl, I say to you, get up!").* [42] *Immediately the girl stood up and began to walk around (she was twelve years old). At this they were completely astonished.* [43] *He gave strict orders not to let anyone know about this and told them to give her something to eat.*

There are two stories here: one centering on a religious leader, Jairus, whose daughter dies, and the other centering on a woman. The two represent opposite ends of social status: Jairus is a "ruler" in the synagogue in Capernaum. The woman is ritually impure. Her issue prevents her from even attending worship in the synagogue. [3] Notice also, the fact that Jairus seeks out Jesus indicates that not all of the religious leaders are hostile to Jesus. His personal situation, a sick and dying daughter at home, makes him desperate. He will risk the scowls and opprobrium of his superiors and peers.

The woman, Mark tells us, has lost a fortune at the hands of the medical community and no one could help her. She, too, is desperate. She intercepts Jesus and Jairus when they are on their

---

3 The text stresses the number of years that the woman was ill (twelve) and her valiant, although futile, efforts to find a cure. It mentions nothing about the ritual impurity. Yet, it is difficult to read this text without the "unclean" overtones found in Leviticus (see especially Leviticus 15:25–33). If she is a member of the Capernaum community, she was likely well-known to those gathered around her, not least of which is Jairus. When Jesus declares her "clean" he may have been talking pointedly to Jairus, whose daughter is twelve years old!

way to help Jairus's daughter. She attempts to hide her desperation by secretively touching him. In a manner reminiscent of the paralytic healed earlier, Jesus recognizes the touch and the deeper yearning of her heart. Jesus' question, "Who touched me?" was for her benefit, not for his enlightenment. He knew who had touched him. Her confession allowed Jesus to explain how the healing came from the expression of her faith rather than some magical power in his cloak. Healing is not magical, even if it is miraculous.

Like the paralytic, she is healed by faith. Like Legion, she is restored to her community of faith. It may well be that Jesus asks, "Who touched me?" in order to call attention to her before Jairus and the others in the community. It is as though Jesus had said, "She is healed of her distress, welcome her in worship."

Jesus continues with Jairus. By this time, however, his daughter has died. Jairus is undoubtedly heartbroken. Further, he may have risked everything in his relationship toward the higher ups in the religious establishment. "Don't be afraid," Jesus says, "just believe."

A small crowd gathers outside the home mourning the child's death. When Jesus says the child is not dead, they mock him. Pushing them out of the house, Jesus takes Peter, James, John, and the parents and goes in to where the child was.

At her side Jesus says, "*Talitha koum,*" meaning, "Little girl, I say to you, get up." These may be the words her parents used to rouse her in the morning. They are not magic words any more than the "touch" of the woman was magic in her healing. These words spoken to the child imply a personal eyewitness observation of the event, likely Peter's. Then, like Peter's mother-in-law, she stands up and walks around as her parents give her something to eat.

What do we make of these two stories? Observe how the former serves as a wrapping around the latter, tying the two stories together to make a single point. Jairus and the woman represent Judaism. By tying these stories with the story of Legion, Mark is claiming both the Jewish world and the Gentile world stand in need of divine healing. Both are in the wilderness where suffering is the norm and where recovery is beyond their reach. And Jesus allows all to flourish.

Human efforts to help Legion failed. Similarly, human efforts are not helpful to Jairus. His daughter dies. Further, human efforts are not helpful to the woman. It may seem a little bit of a stretch to use these three stories to make the broader claim that the entire world stands in need of the good news Jesus is bringing. Yet, this is precisely what Mark is proposing. The wilderness is a universal reality. We all experience it.

Other New Testament passages make this claim using similar symbolism and hence lend support to this reading. For example, in the fourth Gospel, John states explicitly, "For God so loved the world that he gave his one and only Son, that whoever believes in him shall not perish but have eternal life" (John 3:16). In the context of this statement, John relates stories about three people: Nicodemus, a ruler of the Jews (John 3:1–15), a Samaritan woman (John 4:1–38), and a royal official from Capernaum whose son was sick (John 4:46–54). These people are similar to those used by Mark. In this instance, the purpose to have these three represent the whole world is explicit and clearly stated by John. It is implied in Mark.

The same symbolism happens again in the story of the early Church. Just before Jesus is taken up into Heaven, he informs his disciples, who have just become Apostles, that they will be his "witnesses in Jerusalem, and in all Judea and Samaria, and to the ends of the earth" (Acts 1:8). The message of salvation is for the whole world and again we have the noble Jew associated with Jerusalem, the less than noble Jew of Samaria, and the Gentile with the "uttermost part of the earth."

From a Jewish perspective, the world consists of Jews and Gentiles, and there are differences among the Jews: male and female; righteous and impure. From a Christian point of view, the salvation brought by Jesus is needed by everyone. This includes Jairus and Nicodemus every bit as much as the

Samaritan woman, the woman with the medical issue, and the Gentiles. It is for this reason that these three individuals are highlighted. That is to say, we know two of them by name.

Notice further that Jairus is discussed more significantly than his daughter. She is the one who is brought back to life and her name is not known. The miracle is for the daughter. The story is about Jairus.

The one person not named is the woman. In early Greek tradition she is given the name Bernice and in the Coptic tradition she is called Veronica. [4] The story is about her expression of faith. By her action, she acknowledged the authority of the one who heals.

As one examines the role of the disciples, one observes they simply form a backdrop for the stories about Legion, Jairus, and the woman. The disciples are primarily privileged witnesses to the healings and responsible for certain details of the stories. They have no speaking role except for the inconsequential observation that Jesus is surrounded by a crowd. The only other role is that which Peter, James, and John play in witnessing the resurrection of Jairus' daughter.

The contribution from the crowds, however, is a little more complicated. For our purposes in studying the drama, notice that Mark introduces us to several crowds. The woman who is healed is part of a crowd that is like the crowds in the first chapter. They are enthusiastic and expectant, gathering around Jesus as the miracle worker. The woman is one of them.

Mark adds a new crowd that has struggled to protect Legion whom they consider one of their own. They marvel at Jesus, and they also fear him and ask him to leave. We meet a third crowd at Jairus' home. This crowd ridicules Jesus and Jesus brushes them aside. The laughter of the crowd, which is described in some translations as "laughter to scorn," prevents them from

---

4 William Lane, *The Gospel According to Mark*, 194.

witnessing the little girl's healing. [5] It is a lack of faith on their part and it keeps them from the awe of the miracle witnessed by Peter, James, John, and the parents. No longer is the crowd a homogenous enthusiastic group awed by Jesus. Some crowds are awed but fearful, and others mock him.

Jesus responds differently to each of the three situations in this section. As a result, the reader is encouraged to move beyond merely being awed and amazed by Jesus. Jesus is asked to leave. He does. Jesus is mocked. The crowd becomes inconsequential. Such a change in how Jesus is portrayed interacting with the crowds challenges the reader. Beware, how you respond to Jesus may very well affect how he responds to you.

It is appropriate at this point to notice something about the possible function of the crowds, something that might have been quite familiar to the people of Rome. In some respects, the crowd functions in Mark's Gospel like the chorus in a Greek play. When there is doubt about how the audience is to react, the author of a Greek play lets the chorus inform the audience what reaction is appropriate.

If the same holds for Mark, we, as readers, will know exactly how to respond to Jesus. The story of Jesus should fill us with awe, and initially, this is what happens. However, there are times we may find ourselves fearful of Jesus. We may even ridicule him for what we understand to be foolish. As such the crowd continues to inform us how to react as the circumstances change.

The crowds once appeared very helpful. They were amazed by what Jesus did. As the story has progressed, they have become varied in their opinion of Jesus. How is he connected with *good news*? The crowd may still help us identify our own perceptions and may help us discover something about ourselves. For Mark,

---

5 The phrase "laughter to scorn" carries with it the lack of genuine sorrow on the part of the mourners. Their rapid change to laughter causes Jesus to quickly dismiss them as having a lack of integrity (William Lane, 197).

the crowds draw the reader into the story, inviting the reader to move beyond awe and amazement.

> "Isn't this the carpenter? Isn't This Mary's Son And
> The brother of James, Joseph, Judas and Simon?
> Aren't his sisters here with us?"
> —Mark 6:3

THE CARPENTER

When Jesus returns to his hometown, his neighbors see him as the little boy they remember growing up among them. They wonder how he could heal the sick and where he learned the Scriptures so well. He is a great teacher. They are skeptical.

> ***6*** *Jesus left there and went to his hometown, accompanied by his disciples.* [2] *When the Sabbath came, he began to teach in the synagogue, and many who heard him were amazed.*

One may safely assume the hometown reference here is to Nazareth as references to his family from Nazareth follow immediately. The people of his hometown will know him quite well. It is not a large community. Will they tell us who he is? This is important as there is much of the story in Nazareth that Mark does not provide. For instance, we do not have the teaching from the synagogue and so we cannot react to that teaching. Further, we have very little information about his hometown. What about the citizens of that town? They knew him.

In terms of Jesus' identity, Mark has been circumspect and perhaps even evasive. We have read stories of what Jesus does, some of his actions anyway. We have heard very little of his teaching. We do not understand the prejudicial and hateful response of the religious leaders, and we have learned that not all the religious leaders share the same opinion. We are surprised by the disciples and eventually we would like them to give us a clearer statement.

Up to this point, the best we can do is join one of the enthusiastic crowds: "Wow! This Jesus is someone special." Or, we may say, "Mark is telling an awesome story!" Or, alternatively, "Don't make me laugh, the dead (Jairus' daughter) do not come back to life." We know what question to expect in Nazareth. Will the people in Jesus' hometown tell us who he is? Will they recognize what the Lord has done in a manner similar to what Jesus envisioned when he sent Legion to his people and his hometown?

> *"Where did this man get these things?" they asked. "What's this wisdom that has been given him? What are these remarkable miracles he is performing? [3] Isn't this the carpenter? Isn't this Mary's son and the brother of James, Joseph, Judas and Simon? Aren't his sisters here with us?" And they took offense at him.*

They boast knowing who Jesus is! He is from their town, and he is known by his heritage and vocation. It is a correct identification. With it, Mark places Jesus historically and factually into an existential and universal setting. Like everyone, he has a geographic place where he lived, a family and their neighbors, and a means to support himself.

Unfortunately, this setting will not explain Jesus' ability to heal the sick, drive out evil spirits and raise the dead. Their identification of Jesus is nothing more than what the military might understand as name, rank, and serial number. Perhaps the Nazareth crowd knows the inadequacy of their own answers, perhaps not. In any case, the truthfulness of these answers is only partially helpful. It does not explain his charisma, his authority, or his destiny. More importantly, it seems to be unaware of how Jesus speaks with authority regarding the kingdom of God.

> [4] *Jesus said to them, "A prophet is not without honor except in his own town, among his relatives and in his own home."* [5] *He could not do any miracles there, except lay his hands on a few sick people and heal them.*[6] *He was amazed at their lack of faith.*

Jesus marvels at their lack of faith. They knew of the works he had done and dismiss him with a brief comment about his family. One wonders when they look upon him as Mary's boy if that is intended as an insult. The people of Nazareth certainly knew that Mary and Joseph were not yet married when Mary was pregnant with Jesus. Perhaps this is the reason Mark does not tell us much about Jesus' family.

Where there is faith there is hope. Jesus had complimented the woman who touched him for her faith and had specifically encouraged Jairus to keep faith. Now he finds people without faith. It makes no difference if they are from his hometown or even members of his own family. In fact, these people of Nazareth who watched Jesus grow up, and perhaps had to compete with him, show distain for him and for his work. In another Gospel, his brothers are represented as taunting him to reveal himself if he is who he says he is (John 7:3–5).

Mark does not dwell on the disbelief of the people from Nazareth—he merely lets us know the poverty of life without faith. He heals only a few people. In this way, Mark tells the reader that the full force of Jesus' story is lost without faith on the part of the person who would participate in it. Mark closes this portion of his story with a statement on how Jesus interprets what is taking place. Jesus is befuddled.

One of the most challenging conversations for any parent is that which is most important. My faith in Jesus is central in my life, and my greatest hope is that it is central for those I love. As a teacher, I enjoy sharing the knowledge and wisdom that comes from a lifetime of study. As a pastor, I enjoy sharing God's passion for his creation displayed through his own sacrifice.

I am now the elder statesman of the Jacobsen family. By the grace of God, I have learned to trust in God from the examples that have gone before me. Faith is essential to entering into a right relationship with the God who created us. My hope is that you have already seen the compassion Jesus has for every person. He has the same compassion for you in your situation. As we continue to go through the *good news*, keep in mind that God loves you.

PERSPECTIVE ON THE CARPENTER

The primary perspective in "The Carpenter" (Mark 5:1–6:6a) centers on the profiles of the three individuals. Mark has given them priority. More text is devoted to them, more detail, and even more personality than to any of the individuals previously except Levi, a disciple. Here we know the names of two of them. Mark uses them to make the claim of universal human hunger for a redeemer. Everyone—Gentile and Jew, male and female, young and old, religious leader and those who desire the benefits of physical health—all stand in need of someone other than themselves to provide that which they are unable to get on their own.

So, what about their need? The precipitating "need" for these people seems to arise out of ordinary life situations. Having a sick child could be anyone's experience. A physical illness and the proper remedy which escapes the examining eye of the attending doctor happens today as well as in the days of antiquity. A mental breakdown as a result of a trauma—at least this is supposed by several as the origin of Legion's illness—happens to nearly everyone even if the trauma is not as devastating. To be sure, we can overcome many of our obstacles with medicine and counseling, but not all. Sometimes we mask our problems to convince ourselves that the problem no longer exists. As long as we have what is often called the "human condition," we will have needs.

Mark is opening the door for his readers to recognize the needs they may have stemming from their human condition. Loss of a loved one, physical and mental impairment, separation and isolation from society, are all too common for the readers not to recognize them in their own personal lives. This would be especially true for the people of Rome under the cruel hand of Nero. The basic characteristic of this human condition, stated in terms of the prologue, is wilderness. Life is worth living, it just doesn't always flourish as intended.

Further, whatever healing Jesus provides for the stated need is a temporary solution for a specific problem, not a change in the person. The needs themselves are secondary to the primary point Mark is making. Each of these three will continue to face the same or similar needs in the future. Legion might be traumatized again; Jairus' daughter may face another terminal illness; Jairus himself may again feel helpless and desperate; the woman with the issue may develop another debilitating disease.

Whatever threatening challenges they may encounter, they will always remember how Jesus met their earlier needs with grace and compassion. The point of the stories is to affirm Jesus' ability to address the needs of all humankind. Let it also be noted that concern from Jesus for those outside the covenant with Abraham means that the *good news* is for all human beings. Everyone is in the scope of God's kingdom.

Let us not forget that all three have other needs as well. Jesus addresses these needs too. Legion needs to return home to his family and friends. His exile is over, and he is restored. The crowds know full well the woman has been absent from worship. By calling public attention to her healing, Jesus has reinstated her into the worshiping community. Jairus's trust in Jesus may have jeopardized his service in the synagogue, and when the daughter is brought to life again, Jairus would feel vindicated.

Consider also the following: First, there is no mention in these three narratives of any personal responsibility for whatever malady any of the three suffers. It is not as though Jesus said, or could have said, "Your sin is forgiven, go and sin no more." The only time Jesus has said this so far is in his comment about the paralytic (Mark 2:1–12). There is, however, an act of worship common to all three. They fall at Jesus' feet in deep humility.

There are two major references to faith: one with the woman and the other with Jairus. Faith was first mentioned in the story of the paralytic and his friends. When Jesus saw "their faith" (Mark 2:5), he spoke to the paralytic concerning both his forgiveness and the end of the paralysis.

In this act Jesus identifies faith as the explanation for the woman's healing and he encourages Jairus not to lose faith. Jesus encourages people to believe, to trust him and his word. Faith results eventually in soundness of mind, body, and soul. Jesus baptizes with the Spirit, an act much greater than washing with water.

If we are correct in assessing this act, Mark is expanding Jesus' role into the larger world. The *good news* about the kingdom of God will include people from all over the world. How that will happen we have yet to see. What we can tentatively infer is that the compassion Jesus has on the people who are sick is the same compassion he has on the whole world.

ACT THREE

“Who Do People Say I Am?” (6:6b–9:29)

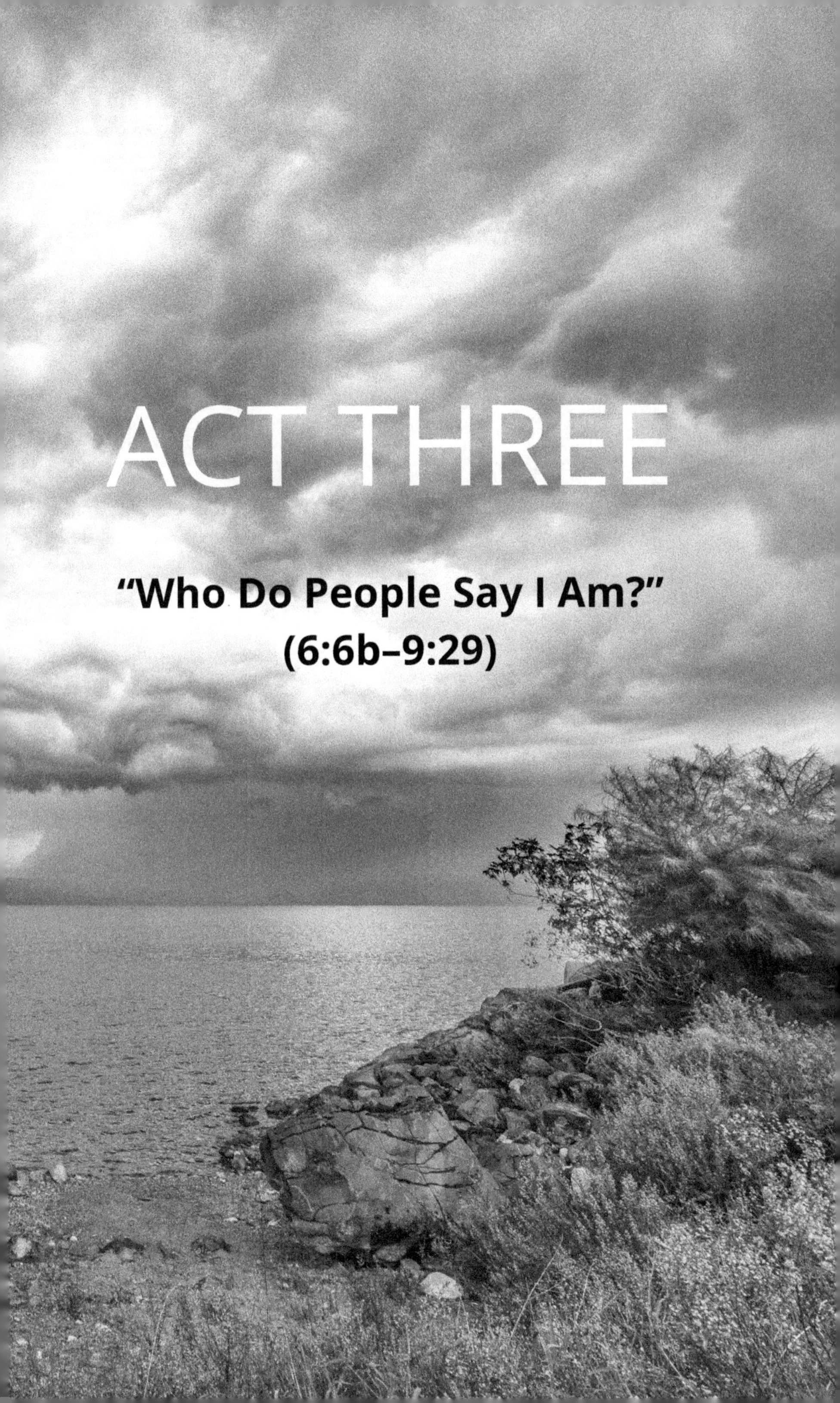

Setting: Disciples Heal / John Beheaded (6:6b–32)

Vocational aptitude requires knowledge, skill, proper training, and experience for the novice to learn the trade. When Jesus said, "Follow me, I will make you fishers of men," the disciples were on the front end of their training. [1] One wonders how much of that call they understood. The first four called were all fishermen and so they understood the fishing industry of the day. "Fishers of men" might have some similarity to their fishing but it is not quite the same. For one thing, working as a fisherman did not require a call.

When a call to ministry comes, it is expected that the person called will continue to develop a personal relationship with God—whom s/he wishes to represent. We see this expectation in the relationship Jesus has with the Father. He is the Son with whom the Father is well pleased. Similarly, the Apostle Paul recognizes how each one of us needs to relate to God. He advises Timothy, "Do your best to present yourself to God as one approved, a workman who need not be ashamed and correctly handles the word of truth" (2 Timothy 2:15).

The disciples have been observers so far. They have not fully established their personal relationships with Jesus. Yes, they each responded to the initial call to follow him. They have listened to him teach, they have observed him drive out demons, and they

---

1 Gilbert Bilezikian refers to this period in the life of the disciples as their "training period." Jesus is preparing them for the demands of discipleship and their "shocking failure" to grasp His teaching (Gilbert Bilezikian, page 83).

have witnessed his healing power. They have also been surprised that Jesus can still a storm, and probably a little frustrated that the people of Nazareth see him only as a boy from their village.

Now Jesus commissions them to preach, to heal the sick, and to cast out demons. The call to ministry is advancing beyond observation. This section shifts attention from what the disciples have witnessed to what they will be doing. They are becoming active fishers of men, temporarily at least. In a sense, they are entering into an apprenticeship for ministry.

> *Then Jesus went around teaching from village to village.* [7]
> *Calling the Twelve to him, he began to send them out two by two and gave them authority over impure spirits.*
>
> [8] *These were his instructions: "Take nothing for the journey except a staff—no bread, no bag, no money in your belts.* [9]
> *Wear sandals but not an extra shirt.* [10] *Whenever you enter a house, stay there until you leave that town.* [11] *And if any place will not welcome you or listen to you, leave that place and shake the dust off your feet as a testimony against them."*
>
> [12] *They went out and preached that people should repent.*
> [13] *They drove out many demons and anointed many sick people with oil and healed them.*

At what appears to be the same time the disciples are preaching repentance, Mark tells us a different story—one without repentance. It concerns King Herod and John the Baptist.

> [14] *King Herod heard about this, for Jesus' name had become well known. Some were saying, "John the Baptist has been raised from the dead, and that is why miraculous powers are at work in him."*
>
> [15] *Others said, "He is Elijah."*

And still others claimed, "He is a prophet, like one of the prophets of long ago."

16 But when Herod heard this, he said, "John, whom I beheaded, has been raised from the dead!"

*17 For Herod himself had given orders to have John
arrested, and he had him bound and put in prison. He did
this because of Herodias, his brother Philip's wife, whom
he had married. 18 For John had been saying to Herod,
"It is not lawful for you to have your brother's wife." 19
So Herodias nursed a grudge against John and wanted to
kill him. But she was not able to, 20 because Herod feared
John and protected him, knowing him to be a righteous
and holy man. When Herod heard John, he was greatly
puzzled; yet he liked to listen to him.*

*21 Finally the opportune time came. On his birthday
Herod gave a banquet for his high officials and military
commanders and the leading men of Galilee. 22 When the
daughter of Herodias came in and danced, she pleased
Herod and his dinner guests.*

*The king said to the girl, "Ask me for anything you want,
and I'll give it to you." 23 And he promised her with
an oath, "Whatever you ask I will give you, up to half
my kingdom."*

24 She went out and said to her mother, "What shall I ask for?"

"The head of John the Baptist," she answered.

25 At once the girl hurried in to the king with the request: "I want you to give me right now the head of John the Baptist on a platter."

[26] The king was greatly distressed, but because of his oaths and his dinner guests, he did not want to refuse her. [27] So he immediately sent an executioner with orders to bring John's head. The man went, beheaded John in the prison, [28] and brought back his head on a platter. He presented it to the girl, and she gave it to her mother. [29] On hearing of this, John's disciples came and took his body and laid it in a tomb.

After John the Baptist is killed and buried, the disciples of Jesus return from their preaching assignment. They are now called Apostles as they had been sent on a mission. Mark does not elaborate on the story of their adventure beyond the indication that they were in need of rest.

[30] The apostles gathered around Jesus and reported to him all they had done and taught. [31] Then, because so many people were coming and going that they did not even have a chance to eat, he said to them, "Come with me by yourselves to a quiet place and get some rest."

[32] So they went away by themselves in a boat to a solitary place.

THE DISCIPLES AND JOHN THE BAPTIST

Commissioning the Twelve

Practical experience in ministry for the disciples is rightly expected to reinforce the significance of the Spirit's power in the wilderness, driving away anything that would destroy the creation. Jesus tells them from the beginning that they will drive out demons and heal those who are sick. This power of the Spirit is from God and, somehow, it comes to them through Jesus.

Seen by itself, the story Mark shares of the disciples' activity is somewhat frustrating. Not one episode of their mission is reported. There is no story of any particular healing, no mention of a location where a sermon was preached, no record of a town refusing them entry, and no shaking off dust from their sandals. Nothing! Although they are presumed to have done all these things, all the reader knows is that they have accountability because they return to Jesus and report everything to him. He apparently accepts their report and offers them some rest.

Clearly, Mark's report on the disciples is not about their mission. Mark is focused on establishing the disciples as qualified to identify Jesus. They have come a long way since leaving their fishing boats. They have witnessed Jesus perform the same things they just accomplished. They have studied privately with Jesus explaining what these things mean. It is as though they have done the coursework in their discipleship program and are now ready for an internship.

In terms of the story, we may wonder if the disciples are yet prepared to tell us who this Jesus is or if they need still further instruction. We may also wonder why Jesus does not plainly tell them who he is. However, before we learn anything about their mission experience, Mark tells the twisted story of John the Baptist's cruel and unjust execution.

The story is about sheer evil in the world, an evil that can appear to silence the good permanently. For the church in Rome familiar with the excesses of Nero, there is little in the story of John the Baptist that surprises them about life in a cruel, authoritarian, political world. Mark seems to have an intention of explaining *good news* in the context of such cruelty.

The Execution of John the Baptist

Mark begins this story with Herod, a superstitious man and likely paranoid. He hears about the ministry of the disciples and fears Jesus is John the Baptist come back to life knowing all along he has killed John. There is, of course, a connection. John was announced as the forerunner to the Jesus, a voice in the wilderness regarding one baptizing with the Spirit.

For Herod, a person trying to silence his own guilty conscience, John the Baptist has been "raised from the dead." Herod's guilt resurrects many ghosts. It also foreshadows the resurrection of another sufferer.

Mark wants the reader to remember that when John the Baptist was put in prison the readers were to look for the One whose sandals John felt unworthy to untie (Mark 1:14). Now that John is dead, the "voice" in the wilderness is silent. The storyline shifts to the identification of Jesus: "the one more powerful than I."

Before picking up on the narrative, reflect for a moment on Herod and Herodias and the newly identified characteristics of the wilderness we see in them. Life in the wilderness is not merely life which does not thrive by virtue of the lack of natural resources such as water, or by the presence of disease, or from the loss of loved ones. Life in the wilderness is threatened by the hostility of enemies everywhere. Sometimes the enemy can be someone close to us, someone who seeks a personal advantage at our expense.

Further, many of the problems we face are of our own making. When Herod took his brother's wife for his own, the Baptist specifically confronts Herod with his transgression of the law. Herod did not like being called out and neither did Herodias. The accusation prompts Herodias to hate John and eventually to instigate his murder. Let us also note that sin which is not confessed can lead to further sin in order to hide or cover up the first. Does killing the messenger of God really change the sins of greed or lust.

Herod is complicit with Herodias. He overreacts before his guests out of pride. He traps himself with his own words which he should have either qualified beforehand or retracted. What a strange turn of events that has Herod justifying his behavior by keeping the pledge spoken in the presence of his guests, instead of honoring God by refusing to execute a man who spoke the truth and was known to be "a righteous and holy man." He turns a deaf ear to the truth using a self-serving desire for his reputation to justify a great evil. Both Herod and Herodias act out of selfish ambition and neither respects the law.

The young girl, Salome, seems innocent yet she abdicated her choice in favor of her mother's wishes. Even though corrupted by her mother, some responsibility is carried by her, too. The unfortunate soldier commanded to carry out the deed simply had done what he was told, and he did it with haste. The web of sin is intricately woven and strangles human life. It is powerful in its own right, though it lacks integrity. In time, it can appear to silence any and every voice crying in the wilderness.

We might observe that if Herod and Herodias had emulated the people of Jerusalem who came to John confessing their sins, they might have been forgiven and John the Baptist would have been spared. Unfortunately, not everyone who sins looks for forgiveness.

One might wonder how much pillow talk, like that of Herodias with Herod, was happening in Rome. Perhaps some of the persecutions were the result of jealousies and sexual immorality. This speaks to us today as well. Guard against the selfish desires, greed, and envy. For where there is envy and selfish ambition, there you find disorder and every evil practice (James 3:16). We, like those in Rome, have in the example of Herod a call to repent.

Thankfully, this is also a story about a greater good. When John the Baptist is gone from the scene the promise of one more powerful than he will come to baptize with the Spirit. Evil will not have the last word.

The One more powerful has come. He is Jesus, the carpenter, the son of Mary. Demons call him the Holy One of God; Jesus calls himself the Son of Man; the disciples in their fear ask who he is when he stills the wind and the waves.

A lot of time has passed since the storm at sea and the disciples should be better prepared to answer their own question. You may be sure they already know the inadequacy of identifying Jesus merely in terms of his family and his vocation. This is especially true after they have a successful experience carrying out their own mission. The disciples are beginning to experience God's power working through them—a fact recognized by Herod (through his fear) that it is the same source of power that energized John the Baptist. The disciples knew they could not claim the power to heal as their own power. They have received it from Jesus.

The juxtaposition of these stories ends in a rather surprising fashion. John, having completed his work, is beheaded and killed. The disciples, having fulfilled their commission, are both exhausted and followed by the crowds—so much so that they did not have time to eat. Jesus invites them to rest.

We come now to the center of the Gospel. In it, we find a brilliant literary strategy calling attention both to the question of Jesus' identity and to its answer. Initially, the strategy involves a collection of four stories. This collection has a brief conclusion before being followed by a second collection of four stories. Together the collections make a single point. They form the basis for Jesus to ask the disciples, "Who do you say I am?" The first four are listed below without any intervening commentary. Remember, the focus is on the disciples, who are still learning to be fishers of men.

First Set of Four Stories (6:33–7:37)

FEEDING FIVE THOUSAND

*33 But many who saw them leaving recognized them and
ran on foot from all the towns and got there ahead of them.
34 When Jesus landed and saw a large crowd, he had compassion on them, because they were like sheep without a
shepherd. So, he began teaching them many things.*

*35 By this time it was late in the day, so his disciples came
to him. "This is a remote place," they said, "and it's already
very late. 36 Send the people away so that they can go to the
surrounding countryside and villages and buy themselves
something to eat."*

37 But he answered, "You give them something to eat."

They said to him, "That would take more than half a year's wage! Are we to go and spend that much on bread and give it to them to eat?"

38 "How many loaves do you have?" he asked. "Go and see."

When they found out, they said, "Five—and two fish."

*39 Then Jesus directed them to have all the people sit down
in groups on the green grass. 40 So they sat down in groups
of hundreds and fifties. 41 Taking the five loaves and the*

two fish and looking up to heaven, he gave thanks and
broke the loaves. Then he gave them to his disciples to dis-
tribute to the people. He also divided the two fish among
them all. 42 *They all ate and were satisfied,* 43 *and the dis-*
ciples picked up twelve basketfuls of broken pieces of bread
and fish. 44 *The number of the men who had eaten was*
five thousand.

WALK ON WATER

45 *Immediately Jesus made his disciples get into the boat*
and go on ahead of him to Bethsaida, while he dismissed
the crowd. 46 *After leaving them, he went up on a moun-*
tainside to pray.

47 *Later that night, the boat was in the middle of the lake,*
and he was alone on land. 48 *He saw the disciples straining*
at the oars, because the wind was against them. Shortly
before dawn he went out to them, walking on the lake.
He was about to pass by them, 49 *but when they saw him*
walking on the lake, they thought he was a ghost. They
cried out, 50 *because they all saw him and were terrified.*

Immediately he spoke to them and said, "Take courage! It
is I. Don't be afraid." 51 *Then he climbed into the boat with*
them, and the wind died down. They were completely
amazed, 52 *for they had not understood about the loaves;*
their hearts were hardened.

53 *When they had crossed over, they landed at Gennesaret*
and anchored there. 54 *As soon as they got out of the boat,*
people recognized Jesus. 55 *They ran throughout that whole*
region and carried the sick on mats to wherever they heard

he was. [56] *And wherever he went—into villages, towns or countryside—they placed the sick in the marketplaces. They begged him to let them touch even the edge of his cloak, and all who touched it were healed.*

CONFRONTING PHARISEES

7 The Pharisees and some of the teachers of the law who had come from Jerusalem gathered around Jesus [2] *and saw some of his disciples eating food with hands that were defiled, that is, unwashed.* [3] *(The Pharisees and all the Jews do not eat unless they give their hands a ceremonial washing, holding to the tradition of the elders.* [4] *When they come from the marketplace they do not eat unless they wash. And they observe many other traditions, such as the washing of cups, pitchers and kettles.)*

[5] *So the Pharisees and teachers of the law asked Jesus, "Why don't your disciples live according to the tradition of the elders instead of eating their food with defiled hands?"*

[6] *He replied, "Isaiah was right when he prophesied about you hypocrites; as it is written:*

"'These people honor me with their lips, but their hearts are far from me. [7] *They worship me in vain; their teachings are merely human rules.'*

[8] *You have let go of the commands of God and are holding on to human traditions."*

[9] *And he continued, "You have a fine way of setting aside the commands of God in order to observe your own traditions!* [10] *For Moses said, 'Honor your father and mother,'*

and, 'Anyone who curses their father or mother is to be put
to death. 11 *But you say that if anyone declares that what*
might have been used to help their father or mother is
Corban (that is, devoted to God)— 12 *then you no longer*
let them do anything for their father or mother. 13 *Thus*
you nullify the word of God by your tradition that you
have handed down. And you do many things like that."

14 *Again Jesus called the crowd to him and said, "Listen*
to me, everyone, and understand this. 15 *Nothing outside*
a person can defile them by going into them. Rather, it is
what comes out of a person that defiles them." 16

17 *After he had left the crowd and entered the house,*
his disciples asked him about this parable. 18 *"Are you so*
dull?" he asked. "Don't you see that nothing that enters a
person from the outside can defile them? 19 *For it doesn't*
go into their heart but into their stomach, and then out of
the body." (In saying this, Jesus declared all foods clean.)

20 *He went on: "What comes out of a person is what defiles*
them. 21 *For it is from within, out of a person's heart, that*
evil thoughts come—sexual immorality, theft, murder, 22
adultery, greed, malice, deceit, lewdness, envy, slander,
arrogance and folly. 23 *All these evils come from inside and*
defile a person."

TWO MIRACLES

24 *Jesus left that place and went to the vicinity of Tyre. He*
entered a house and did not want anyone to know it; yet
he could not keep his presence secret. 25 *In fact, as soon as*
she heard about him, a woman whose little daughter was

possessed by an impure spirit came and fell at his feet. [26]
The woman was a Greek, born in Syrian Phoenicia. She begged Jesus to drive the demon out of her daughter.

[27] *"First let the children eat all they want," he told her, "for it is not right to take the children's bread and toss it to the dogs."*

[28] *"Lord," she replied, "even the dogs under the table eat the children's crumbs."*

[29] *Then he told her, "For such a reply, you may go; the demon has left your daughter."*

[30] *She went home and found her child lying on the bed, and the demon gone.*

[31] *Then Jesus left the vicinity of Tyre and went through Sidon, down to the Sea of Galilee and into the region of*
the Decapolis. [32] *There some people brought to him a man who was deaf and could hardly talk, and they begged Jesus to place his hand on him.*

[33] *After he took him aside, away from the crowd, Jesus put his fingers into the man's ears. Then he spit and touched*
the man's tongue. [34] *He looked up to heaven and with a deep sigh said to him, "Ephphatha!" (which means "Be*
opened!"). [35] *At this, the man's ears were opened, his tongue was loosened, and he began to speak plainly.*

[36] *Jesus commanded them not to tell anyone. But the more*
he did so, the more they kept talking about it. [37] *People were overwhelmed with amazement. "He has done everything well," they said. "He even makes the deaf hear and the mute speak."*

These four stories form part one of Mark's literary structure. Each story has independent value. Together, these first four deal with crowds, disciples, religious leaders, and individuals who are in need of healing. They seem to mimic the earlier sections in this manner, and they offer deeper insights into both the kingdom of God and the identity of Jesus. In contrast to stories from Act 1, the response to Jesus is more than just awe: "People were overwhelmed with amazement. 'He has done everything well.'"

We may make several valuable observations on these passages. Let us begin with the crowds. Their number has grown considerably. Everyone around the Sea of Galilee is on the lookout for Jesus and when they see him, they descend upon him confident of some healing benefit. The only solitary place for Jesus and his disciples to rest is in a boat. The crowds still watch for them and so when they come ashore the crowds have already gathered. Jesus continues his compassion for the crowds and begins to teach them again. Interestingly, we know nothing of what he taught. We do know the crowds are growing.

As the hour grows late, the disciples get concerned about the crowd not having food to eat. There may also be some unexpressed concerns as they no longer seem able to have any time alone with Jesus. They are unaware that Jesus is about to teach them an important lesson by asking the disciples to feed the crowd. They predictably complain they cannot because the cost to feed so large a crowd is prohibitive. Their resources are limited, as they have only five loaves and two fish. Yet, in Jesus' eyes, this will be enough for their lesson (let alone enough food for five thousand or more people).

Jesus feeds all five thousand who have been enjoying his teaching so much that they have not left for home even though the hour was late. By staying late, they get treated to a miraculous meal. Whether they know the inside story about the bread and the fish they consume, or not, is unknown to us. They are enamored with Jesus and they trust him. As long as Jesus is available, they will bring their sick to him and listen to his teaching. In the end, they will be overwhelmed with amazement reminding us of the enthusiasm of the crowds when Jesus began his ministry. Now, however, the size of the crowd is a quantum leap above what it used to be.

After the feeding of the five thousand and collecting the leftover pieces of bread and fish, Jesus sends the disciples ahead in a boat while he dismisses the crowd (Mark 6:45). At this point, it is important to remember something about the crowds. By including a statement dismissing the crowds, Mark is informing the reader that the crowd is not always available to help the reader know how to react. This highlights the importance of each reader engaging with Jesus to determine one's own relationship with him.

Jesus prepares for his next step by retreating to pray. It is the second time we hear of him secluding himself (see Mark 1:35). This brief notation is important even though Mark does not elaborate on it just yet. It will become clearer later.

From the shore Jesus can see the disciples straining at the oars. He walks on the water toward them. When they see Jesus walking on the water, they believe they are seeing a ghost and are profoundly fearful. After Jesus gets into the boat and the wind dies down, we would expect the disciples to remember the last time they were in a storm at sea. Regardless, Mark tells us they did not understand about the bread. Perhaps reflecting on their lack of understanding, Mark also tells us they are miles away from their original destination. They are in Gennesaret and not Bethsaida. Mark concludes their hearts were hardened. They were not the only ones with hardness of heart.

The Pharisees come to Jesus and ask why Jesus' disciples do not wash their hands before they eat. Jesus does not answer their question. Rather, he responds by calling the Pharisees hypocrites. He goes on to explain the hypocrisy and then teaches the crowds gathered around him on the true meaning of clean and unclean.

The disciples are perplexed and do not understand what he is saying. How long will it take before the bewildered disciples are able to realize what is taking place right before their very eyes? In teaching the difference between what comes from within a person and what a person eats, he declares all foods clean. Peter will not understand this until years later when the Lord calls him to Cornelius' house (see Acts 10).

Jesus further explains the moral side of behavior. From within a person come the motives that result in sinful behavior. Instead of evaluating specific acts which are thought to be moral or immoral, Jesus directs the attention of his disciples toward the motives from which the actions stem. He provides a list of twelve motives to increase our understanding (Mark 7:20–22).

The list of motives is partially a comment on Herod, Herodias, and their crowd. Among her motives, Herodias harbors sexual immorality, murder, and adultery. Herod practices arrogance; the young girl, Salome, folly; and the guests, envy and greed. To be sure, Mark wants the emphasis on motives to apply to his readers as well. Pay attention to what people do—*and* to the motivations for their behavior.

The teaching is in some sense simple. What enters the body is not what makes one clean or unclean. It is what comes out of a person that reveals the heart as clean or not.

The final narrative is about healing the daughter of a Syrophoenician woman and healing a man who is deaf and dumb. The latter is in Jewish territory and the former in Gentile territory. This juxtaposition mirrors the earlier stories of Jairus's daughter (Jewish) and the Gerasene demoniac (Gentile). Mark is emphasizing that *good news* is for all people.

In these stories, the woman believes Jesus can heal her troubled daughter. In the dialogue there is again a reference to bread and the woman is content with crumbs falling from the table. The deaf man's ears were opened, and his tongue freed to speak. Those observing his healing give a climactic assessment of Jesus as a healer: "He does everything well!"

Mark provides us a theme to hold these stories together by the many references to food. Jesus feeds the five thousand with five loaves of bread and picks up twelve basketfuls when the meal is over. The disciples, who do not comprehend the loaves, are amazed but incredulous. The Pharisees and the teachers of the law wonder about clean hands when eating and are scolded by Jesus for missing something much more important about food. Lastly, the Syrian Phoenician woman seems content with crumbs falling from the table.

The implication is that there is enough food from Jesus for everyone; food for the body and food for the soul, metaphorically, either nourishing crumbs from under the table or baskets full of bread after the meal is served. Is the *good news* that everyone has enough?

We turn now to the second collection of stories. Again, the four stories will be given without intervening commentary.

Second Set of Four Stories (8:1–26)

FEEDING FOUR THOUSAND

8 During those days another large crowd gathered. Since
they had nothing to eat, Jesus called his disciples to him
and said, 2 "I have compassion for these people; they have
already been with me three days and have nothing to eat.
3 If I send them home hungry, they will collapse on the
way, because some of them have come a long distance."

4 His disciples answered, "But where in this remote place
can anyone get enough bread to feed them?"

5 "How many loaves do you have?" Jesus asked.

"Seven," they replied.

6 He told the crowd to sit down on the ground. When he
had taken the seven loaves and given thanks, he broke them
and gave them to his disciples to distribute to the people,
and they did so. 7 They had a few small fish as well; he gave
thanks for them also and told the disciples to distribute
them. 8 The people ate and were satisfied. Afterward the
disciples picked up seven basketfuls of broken pieces that
were left over. 9 About four thousand were present. After
he had sent them away, 10 he got into the boat with his
disciples and went to the region of Dalmanutha.

REJECTING PHARISEES

[11] The Pharisees came and began to question Jesus. To test him, they asked him for a sign from heaven. [12] He sighed deeply and said, "Why does this generation ask for a sign? Truly I tell you, no sign will be given to it." [13] Then he left them, got back into the boat and crossed to the other side.

NO BREAD IN THE BOAT

[14] The disciples had forgotten to bring bread, except for one loaf they had with them in the boat. [15] "Be careful," Jesus warned them. "Watch out for the yeast of the Pharisees and that of Herod."

[16] They discussed this with one another and said, "It is because we have no bread."

[17] Aware of their discussion, Jesus asked them: "Why are you talking about having no bread? Do you still not see or understand? Are your hearts hardened? [18] Do you have eyes but fail to see, and ears but fail to hear? And don't you remember? [19] When I broke the five loaves for the five thousand, how many basketfuls of pieces did you pick up?"

"Twelve," they replied.

[20] "And when I broke the seven loaves for the four thousand, how many basketfuls of pieces did you pick up?"

They answered, "Seven."

[21] He said to them, "Do you still not understand?"

HEALING A BLIND MAN TWICE

> 22 *They came to Bethsaida, and some people brought a*
> *blind man and begged Jesus to touch him.* 23 *He took the*
> *blind man by the hand and led him outside the village.*
> *When he had spit on the man's eyes and put his hands on*
> *him, Jesus asked, "Do you see anything?"*
>
> 24 *He looked up and said, "I see people; they look like trees*
> *walking around."*
>
> 25 *Once more Jesus put his hands on the man's eyes. Then*
> *his eyes were opened, his sight was restored, and he saw*
> *everything clearly.* 26 *Jesus sent him home, saying, "Don't*
> *even go into the village."*

Switching only a few details, Mark uses four similar contexts for his second collection of stories. This time the confrontation with the Pharisees comes before the boat story. There is only one person being healed, not two. However, the blind man in this collection needs two efforts from Jesus for the healing to be complete.

The two collections of stories are intentionally repetitious, and apparently pertinent to the point Mark wishes the reader to see.

Notice the similarities. Both collections report the miraculous feeding of thousands of people: the feeding of five thousand, and then shortly afterward, of four thousand. Their connection is also obvious when Jesus ties them together with his question of how many basketfuls of bread were retrieved in each case (Mark 8:19–21).

Notice further, the crowd is dismissed after the feeding of the five thousand and, likewise, the crowd is sent away after the feeding of the four thousand. The role of the crowd in responding to Jesus is no longer needed. The best they can do is express amazement at the end of the first collection: "Jesus does everything well!" It will soon become the disciples turn to share what they have learned.

There is a crowd at the end of the second collection too. However, unlike the crowd that says Jesus does everything well, this crowd, which brings the blind man to Jesus, does not witness the blind man's healing. Jesus takes the blind man away from them and even after restoring sight to him, instructs the blind man to go home and stay away from the village. By implication, stay away from the crowd.

Why stay away? Is it because it took two efforts to heal the man? At first the man claimed people looked like trees walking and later he saw clearly. Why did Jesus heal the man in two steps? Why did Jesus need the testimony of the man regarding what he was able to see? Is the concluding testimony of the first collection, namely, he does everything well, different from the concluding testimony of the blind man's healing? Why stay away from the crowds?

Mark's literary style seems to raise questions rather than provide explanations. It may not yet be clear why he chooses this style. It may be that, like the blind man, there is a greater clarity yet to come.

Food, primarily bread, is an important theme in both collections. Bread is obvious in the stories of the two feedings. It is mentioned in the first boat story, and it dominates the concluding boat story where it leads into a puzzling conversation. They had no bread with them in the boat; they had one loaf.

What is Mark saying? No bread in the boat? Or one loaf? Does Mark contradict himself? Is there a loaf in the boat? Or is there no bread at all in the boat? You might end up looking in vain at the passage itself for a suitable answer. There is none, just a paradox.

Earlier in the text, I shared some about my enjoyment of studying Martin Luther—especially with "A Mighty Fortress." Luther also inspired many thoughts on the subject of paradox within the faith. *Simul justus et pecator* (at the same time, saint and sinner). [2] In modern society, paradox is rarely understood for what it is. As a pastor, I want to encourage people to spend time in solitude with God, reflecting on the kingdom of God in this manner. Believers are in constant need of repentance, and at the same time in full assurance of being fully forgiven children of God.

In connection with the Pharisees, Mark reminds us that not all bread is the same. There is a bread that lasts and there is a bread that spoils, namely, bread with yeast. With this reference to the yeast of the Pharisees and that of Herod, Mark recalls their pact to kill Jesus (Mark 3:6). He even reminds us of Herod's role in killing John the Baptist (Mark 6:14–29). Beware of the yeast.

The Pharisees ask for a sign. Did he not feed thousands? Isn't this sign enough? Jesus refuses to provide the Pharisees with the sign they claim to need. Why should he? They fail to cherish the bread already provided.

Jesus goes a little further, stating that this generation is looking for a sign. One might observe the many signs already given. Each seems to be missed. And one might reflect upon our own tendencies to look for more than what is plainly there to be seen. Remember, the crowds are not present here. *How do we respond?*

The disciples seem to miss the implication of the bread, too. They worry about not having bread in the boat. Jesus asks them, "Do you have eyes but fail to see? Ears but fail to hear? How many basketfuls did you collect after the feeding of the five thousand? After the feeding of the four thousand?"

---

2 In Martin Luther's *Lectures on Romans,* he explains St. Paul's claim: "Wretched man that I am!" (Romans 7:24). Luther notes Paul is the same person subject to the law of God and the law of flesh. He writes, "Now notice ... the saints, at the same time they are righteous are also sinners; righteous because they believe in Christ, whose righteousness covers them and is imputed to them, but sinners because they do not fulfill the Law ..." (Martin Luther, page 336).

They answer the questions about baskets full of bread correctly: five loaves feed thousands and twelve baskets full are left over; seven loaves feed thousands and seven baskets full are left over. Do they understand? Mark clearly implies they do not. When Jesus asks pointedly, "Do you understand?" They do not even answer.

Because the crowds can no longer help us, we wonder if the disciples can. We know they are Jesus' hands when it comes to serving the bread. Yet, they understand very little. We wonder if we knew the meaning of Jesus' question about how many basketfuls of pieces of bread had been collected on two separate occasions, would we have had the requisite insight? The disciples knew the obvious answer, didn't they, twelve and seven? Are the obvious answers the correct ones? Or is there an insight they lack? Could we do any better?

More than one person has looked for an answer in the numbers twelve and seven. [3] Mark does not provide one. If we fail to understand, perhaps we do not need to worry too much as the disciples did not get it either, even with their collective effort. Of what help are they?

Fortunately, there are hints at the right answer. There is no bread in the boat. However, the one who creates bread and who is himself the Bread of life, is in the boat. When Jesus is there with the disciples, why do they worry about no bread? They worry because they still do not understand. Cherish the Bread!

Marvel if you will, at Jesus' patience. These disciples have been with him for a long while and they are slow to learn. The crowds, like the disciples, have been around for a long while too. Gratefully, they are willing to give God the glory in their amazement. You may be like either one of them, and you may

---

3 Bargil Pixner notes the value of "twelve" as symbolic of completion from a Jewish perspective and "seven" representing perfection from a Gentile perspective. With both of these numbers represented, Mark is stating that Jesus represents the fullness of and to all creation.

be ready to draw your own conclusion. Or, would you rather be like the obtuse religious leaders, seeing one piece of evidence after another and still be looking for a sign from Heaven? Do you ask for signs? The signs have already been given, and Mark is laying them out in plain sight.

As the second collection of stories comes to a close, there is no concluding summary such as, "He does everything well," which we found in summarizing the first collection. Both sets of stories have provided insight into Jesus and the kingdom of God.

Regarding the kingdom, there is healing and nourishment that goes far beyond our needs. The winds are calm, there is bread enough for everyone, and all who look to God find healing, both Jew and Gentile. Despite these indicators, many fail to see the kingdom because they find themselves looking for something else.

Regarding Jesus, each story affirms his power and authority. His ability to provide, nurture, calm, heal, and restore is evident in each pericope. In addition, he is able to understand even those who try to deceive him—particularly the religious leaders. Seeing beyond their futile question for a sign, he challenges each of us to see him as he is. This leads us to the central question of Mark's Gospel narrative.

Jesus' Question: Who Do You Say I Am? (8:27–30)

"Who do you say I am?"
—Mark 8:29

27 *Jesus and his disciples went on to the villages around Caesarea Philippi. On the way he asked them, "Who do people say I am?"*

28 *They replied, "Some say John the Baptist; others say Elijah; and still others, one of the prophets."*

29 *"But what about you?" he asked. "Who do you say I am?"*

Peter answered, "You are the Messiah."

30 *Jesus warned them not to tell anyone about him.*

Following the dramatic literary technique of repetition the story has built up to a point of climax. Jesus asks of his disciples, "Who am I?" This is the central question of *good news*—and the central question for the entire Gospel of Mark.

The importance of Jesus' identity is affirmed in three ways:

First, it is Jesus who asks the question. By itself this makes the question of identity preeminently important. The reader will also notice Jesus does not give away any answers to it. It is not like the same episode reported by Matthew in which Jesus asks,

"Who do men say the Son of Man is?" (Matthew 16:13). In Mark's Gospel, Jesus offers no help in answering the question.

Second, up to this point Mark has provided only tainted identifications of Jesus. Demons who can't be trusted. Crowds who are amazed. Religious leaders who feel threatened. Testimonials from those who have been healed. And disciples who don't fully understand. This is your opportunity (and mine) as a reader to engage with this question.

Third, there is a significant turning point in terms of the story. In the first two chapters Mark has described Jesus in terms of his authority. He has not yet been properly identified. John the Baptist came the closest. As the voice in the wilderness, John prepared the way for him and identified him with the Spirit.

Jesus works miracles out of compassion for the needs of others. The beauty and hope in the Gospel come from Jesus' treatment of the sick and the troubled. He heals illnesses such as leprosy and even raises the dead. He drives out evil spirits. He appears to be invincible. No power on earth is superior and no demonic power can overcome him. He makes everyone who seeks his help healthy and well. Our inability to identify him is more than a little frustrating. However, we have come to believe that nothing can stand in the way of his authority.

Mark is now confronting the question of Jesus' identity directly. The disciples answer it both in terms of the opinions of others and in their own opinion. It brings satisfaction to the reader to have a clear and definitive identification of Jesus as this. Finally, we will learn who this Jesus is! But do we really?

The setting for this identification is significant and I do not wish to pass it by. Jesus has traveled to the villages around Caesarea Philippi. This region boasts of having perhaps the greatest harvesting seasons in the whole world, in some cases more than a dozen harvests of some crops in a single year. It has a constant rich source of water from the melting snow on Mount Hermon to the north. Water simply gushes out of the ground forming the head waters for the Jordan River. The climate is stable. It is a lush area. In stark contrast to the wilderness, if ever there were a place for life, this is it.

It is here in full view of the abundant harvest, in the midst of rich life-giving water, at the foot of Mount Hermon, that Jesus asks, "Who do you say I am?" The setting alone affirms that, with Jesus, life flourishes. It is not the wilderness which one encounters at the southern end of the Jordan where Jesus was baptized by John. At the north end it is life and life abundant. To quote another evangelist, "I have come," says Jesus, "that they may have life, and have it abundantly" (John 10:10). For Jesus and the disciples, there is no place richer with life than Caesarea Philippi.

Peter's answer, "You are the Christ!" must have come to Peter and to everyone around him as a relief. It is as though the disciples could finally say to each other, "We get it! We understand both the feeding of the five thousand and of the four thousand! You are the one who feeds the world! Everyone should have you in the boat! We understand! You are not John the Baptist as Herod had thought, not Elijah, and not one of the Prophets. We know better. You, Jesus, are the Holy One of God, the Savior, the Healer, the One Anointed by God, the Christ!"

If this is what they thought, then it would be most satisfying if Jesus had confirmed Peter's testimony. He does not. This suggests we may not have the right answer just yet. Jesus commands Peter to be silent indicating there is something about the confession that is not quite right. It may be something Peter does not understand or something that radically redefines what it means to be the Christ. It does not take long before Peter reveals how little he comprehends about his own confession. In the blink of an eye, the story changes, taking on a tone of what appears to be unavoidable, dark, and foreboding.

Son of Man Must Be Killed (8:31–9:1)

31 He then began to teach them that the Son of Man must
suffer many things and be rejected by the elders, the chief
priests and the teachers of the law, and that he must be killed
and after three days rise again. 32 He spoke plainly about
this, and Peter took him aside and began to rebuke him.

33 But when Jesus turned and looked at his disciples, he rebuked
Peter. "Get behind me, Satan!" he said. "You do not have in
mind the concerns of God, but merely human concerns."

34 Then he called the crowd to him along with his disciples
and said: "Whoever wants to be my disciple must deny
themselves and take up their cross and follow me. 35 For
whoever wants to save their life will lose it, but whoever
loses their life for me and for the gospel will save it. 36 What
good is it for someone to gain the whole world, yet forfeit
their soul? 37 Or what can anyone give in exchange for
their soul? 38 If anyone is ashamed of me and my words
in this adulterous and sinful generation, the Son of Man
will be ashamed of them when he comes in his Father's
glory with the holy angels."

***9** And he said to them, "Truly I tell you, some who are*
standing here will not taste death before they see that the
kingdom of God has come with power."

Jesus has certainly faced hostile forces. He was tempted by Satan in the wilderness and confronted with demons. Amazingly, the demons abided by his authority to abandon their hosts and to remain silent regarding his identity. Compared to demons, what can any other hostile force expect to accomplish?

Notably, what can the religious and civic leaders of society hope to gain by opposing Jesus? Mark has already indicated that many of these leaders were actively seeking opportunity to kill Jesus.

Jesus refers to himself in this section as the Son of Man. [4] Mark intentionally places this reference closely juxtaposed with Jesus being identified as the Christ. By doing so, Mark is making the connection of Jesus as fully God and fully human. More will be said about the importance of this phrase throughout the remainder of the Gospel. At this point, it is important for the reader to recognize that Jesus is identifying himself with the creation.

Jesus says he will be killed—and that he must suffer at the hands of those same civic and religious leaders. The announcement is jarring, it comes immediately after Peter identifies Jesus as the Christ. From the point of view of the disciples, the death of Jesus at the hands of the authorities cannot be true. If it is, it changes everything. Hence, this is the turning point in the Gospel narrative. We may call it the climax or crisis of the story. From this point on, we know how it will end, Jesus will be killed, even if we do not yet know how this is *good news*.

Notice Peter's reaction. And remember, Mark's perspective is informed perhaps more from Peter than any other. Together with the other disciples, they have watched Jesus with awe. They have become a part of the ministry as they were empowered to

4 In *A Theology of Mark's Gospel*, Garland argues there is no well-defined concept of the "Son of Man" that parallels the title "Son of God." He suggests this is a phrase intended to identify Jesus with his humanity while enabling him to maintain the messianic secret; namely, that he is the Son of God (David Garland, pages 251–258).

drive out demons. They seemed to have moved closer to understanding who Jesus must be in order to explain his power and authority. Surely, there is nothing capable of standing in Jesus' way. Jesus will have the victory over every evil force controlling the wilderness. Or so it appears. Then, suddenly, we learn that he must suffer and die.

Further, this is a moment of personal crisis for the disciples who have identified themselves with Jesus. Jesus called them to be fishers of men. They left everything behind to follow him. Why? Especially if Jesus is going to die in the end. The thought of following him in vain, only for him to die, is an existential question of their purpose—and it is similar to the question of Christians in Rome to whom Mark is writing.

So, Peter pulls Jesus aside. Imagine the conversation. Peter, the follower, attempts to inform Jesus that his prophecy cannot possibly be true. Is this not reminiscent of the serpent telling Eve, "You will not certainly die" (Genesis 3:4)? Jesus responds harshly, as he might to the serpent: "Get behind me, Satan!" (Mark 8:33).

For us as the readers, this change in focus is likewise significant. We have identified with the disciples. The crisis reverses expectations for everyone, for Jesus, for the disciples, for Rome, for the religious leaders and for us. Jesus is to be identified in terms of his death and not his life. It is an identification which had previously been kept hidden. Is this how we too will be identified?

There is more to the kingdom of God in this passage than is evident on first read. In his rebuke of Peter, Jesus includes that Peter (and perhaps the disciples—or even we the readers) is not focused on the things of God. Rather, we are concerned only with human things. With this simple statement, Jesus is transforming our very understanding of life and death.

Remember the parable of the sower. This is the only parable for which Mark included Jesus sharing his explanation. "Unless the seed falls into the ground and dies ...." The kingdom of God is like this. We must first enter into the rich soil.

He continues to explain that, in order to save one's life, you must first lose it. For those focused on worldly things, this is utter nonsense. Yet, Jesus also ends this section with a word of comfort: that some standing in their midst would see the power of the coming of the kingdom of God.

To prepare for the crisis, Mark reminded us of the respective roles of the disciples and of John the Baptist. John's role as forerunner had come to an end. The role of the disciples as fishers of men is beginning to mature. Jesus sent the twelve to preach and cast out evil spirits. They apparently achieved those tasks. All twelve were experienced fishers of men.

Yet, before Mark reported on the success of the disciples, he interjected a brief narrative regarding the death of John the Baptist. John's task was finished. Jesus, whom he announced, is here. And all attention is directed toward Jesus from this point forward.

The disciples, via Peter, celebrate that Jesus is the Christ. Yet, in one swift move Mark puts Peter, the disciples and his readers back into a quandary—an even greater crisis.

In the absence of help from the crowd we thought the disciples might help. Briefly, we thought Peter had given us the right answer. Instead, we found a Satanic ambush. How could Peter be so wrong in the understanding of his answer that Jesus would rebuke him so strongly? Nowhere else does Jesus address one of his disciples with words like these, "Get behind me Satan!" It must have crushed Peter who so clearly thought he had it right.

Keep in mind the context for Mark's Gospel. The church in Rome had certainly experienced its fair share of suffering, persecution, and death. Would they have recognized Peter's pulling Jesus aside as an attack from Satan? I suspect they might have—especially given the importance of maintaining the integrity of their faith, despite that integrity leading to greater persecution and certain physical death.

Jesus has been keeping a most important piece of information from his disciples, namely, he would suffer and die at the hands of the religious and civic leaders. This news comes with devastating power. The enthusiasm and all the wonderful expectations of Peter and the other disciples come abruptly to an end. Following Jesus takes a new and unexpected turn. There is a choice to be made, not just a benefit to be received. If Jesus is going to die, why follow him?

How do we understand this sudden shift in Mark's Gospel? There has not been the slightest hint from Jesus of his suffering up until now and no mention of being killed let alone rising from the dead. At this point in time, we probably do not comprehend it any better than Peter. We do have a suggestion, however, provided by the literary strategy.

Remember the man who needed to be healed twice before he could see clearly? Peter is like that man. He is at the point where people look like trees, or better, where he knows Jesus is the Christ, and he does not yet see Jesus clearly. He does not understand the Christ will suffer.

The healing of the blind man is told as a parable intended, in context, only for the disciples and the blind man. Hence, Jesus takes the blind man by the hand away from the village.

By extension, the blind man is a parable for us too. Like him, what we think we understand at one point is subject to a deeper understanding at some other point. Many of us have heard the story of Jesus several times and found our understanding growing as we heard it again. We thought we knew it at one point but then a later examination lets us know how little we understood.

It takes considerable time before Peter and the other disciples can comprehend what Jesus is teaching about his death. It reminds us how difficult it can be to learn the truth. At times, we all seem to process things slowly, especially in the realm of the spirit.

Thankfully, just as Jesus does not give up on Peter or on his disciples, he does not give up on us as readers either. He may become a little exasperated with us, as he did with them. He doesn't quit on us. Such is the nature of divine compassion. We thought Peter had gotten it right, and like him, we often think we have it right, too.

Mark has employed a magnificent strategy to get his point across to us. Not only does he provide two collections of similar stories, he even has a living parable. Then Mark presents the central question knowing whatever answer we give; it is likely to be in need of modification. In some measure Mark is calling us to humility. In greater measure, he is calling us to realize the depth of our own participation in the wilderness where life on every level does not flourish as it should. We are created to flourish.

A few other items are worth mentioning. For those who have a strong familiarity with the history of the Hebrews, the two stories of multiplied bread have obvious precedence in the story of the Hebrews wandering in the wilderness (see Exodus 16 and Leviticus 11). It is God who provides the manna, a flake which is a type of bread, for daily nourishment.

In the stories of the multiplied bread with more than enough left over, there is sufficient parallel to link Jesus with the God who provides food in the wilderness. The story of Jesus healing the daughter of Jairus may be reminiscent of Elijah raising the son of the widow of Zarephath (I Kings 17:17f). Jesus walking on water may remind others of Moses parting the Red Sea.

For those familiar with these stories, the impact Jesus might have on the disciples and the crowds is astounding.

Earlier, in my comments near the end of the prologue, I shared that the heart of my message in drafting this text is this: God loves you. With this section—focused on the "Jesus Question," I want to revisit that simple message. It is important to know that God loves you. It is equally important to know who that God is.

God is not the image depicted by the religious leaders. That includes the images of the modern church, whether viewed as icons, stained glass, marble statues, or simple and unadorned hard wooden pews. The God who loves you came himself to die. The denouement that follows sharpens our understanding of why this is the *good news*.

From the perspective of an old Norwegian, I want to encourage each of you to consider the Jesus Question: *Who do you say I am?*

"This Is My Son, Whom I Love" (9:2–13)

2 After six days Jesus took Peter, James and John with him
and led them up a high mountain, where they were all
alone. There he was transfigured before them. 3 His clothes
became dazzling white, whiter than anyone in the world
could bleach them. 4 And there appeared before them
Elijah and Moses, who were talking with Jesus.

5 Peter said to Jesus, "Rabbi, it is good for us to be here. Let
us put up three shelters—one for you, one for Moses and
one for Elijah." 6 (He did not know what to say, they were
so frightened.)

7 Then a cloud appeared and covered them, and a voice
came from the cloud: "This is my Son, whom I love.
Listen to him!"

8 Suddenly, when they looked around, they no longer saw
anyone with them except Jesus.

9 As they were coming down the mountain, Jesus gave
them orders not to tell anyone what they had seen until
the Son of Man had risen from the dead. 10 They kept the
matter to themselves, discussing what "rising from the
dead" meant.

[11] And they asked him, "Why do the teachers of the law say that Elijah must come first?"

[12] Jesus replied, "To be sure, Elijah does come first, and restores all things. Why then is it written that the Son of Man must suffer much and be rejected? [13] But I tell you, Elijah has come, and they have done to him everything they wished, just as it is written about him."

It takes a week before Peter's confession, "You are the Christ," receives a confirmation. Peter, along with James and John, is invited to witness the second time that God affirms Jesus' identity. The first was at his baptism. John the Baptist both witnessed and gave testimony at that time. This time, it is for this inner group of disciples. Once again, a voice from Heaven affirms that Jesus is the Son of God.

Peter's identification of Jesus as the Christ was accurate. However, it is important not to be confused between his statement and its interpretation. Peter's statement was correct. His interpretation was not. His understanding implied Jesus would not suffer and die. Jesus strongly rebuked his interpretation, although the statement had not yet been either affirmed or denied.

Here, again, Jesus is referred to as the Son of Man. However, in this instance, that reference comes immediately following God's affirmation of Jesus as "This is my Son." The dual nature of Jesus as fully divine and fully human is being made stronger. The incarnation, by which God becomes part of creation, is unique. It creates a paradox that religious leaders neither accept nor understand. Yet, Jesus performs things only God can do before their very eyes.

There is a second paradox to notice within this section. Jesus, alongside Elijah and Moses, is glorified in bright white raiment—and concludes by repeating the prophecy that the Son of Man must suffer, be rejected, and die. And Jesus also hints at the hope of *good news* by instructing Peter, James, and

John not to discuss what they have seen until after he is risen from the dead.

Jesus goes to the top of a high mountain with three of his disciples. The truth of Peter's confession is validated in grand fashion for the three disciples. Peter, James, and John are granted a truly rare opportunity as Jesus is transfigured before them. The experience proves to be more than a little unsettling when Elijah and Moses appear with Jesus. How the disciples could identify them is not stated. And then, to top it all, there is a voice from above that proclaims Jesus as "my Son." No wonder Peter, James, and John were afraid.

Their fear is a reminder of the fear felt by Mary (Luke 1:29) and some shepherds (Luke 2:9) when angels appeared to them. "Fear not!" said the angels. But to Peter, James, and John there are no angels calming them and they are terrified. [5] How long does it take before the pounding heart in one's chest quiets down? At times like this people say many things that make no sense. Peter is no different.

"Let us build three shelters," he says. Peter is speaking out of his anxiety—wanting to do something. Jesus invited him there to witness what God is doing. As a pastor, I have all too often witnessed people wanting to do something in place of simply being present during a significant moment. This is a significant moment. [6]

The shelters are reminiscent of the tabernacle, the Tent of Meeting, in the wilderness. It assured them of God's presence at

---

5 See *The Idea of the Holy* for further discussion regarding the many references to fear experienced by individuals when confronted by divine or heavenly powers. The phrase used by Otto is *mysterium et fascinans* (Rudolph Otto).

6 This is an important moment. Personally, it is important for me. Paul Thompson, one of my associates in ministry, practiced well the presence of the Lord. This practice extended beyond his devotion to Jesus to every area of his life. For example, when asked by family what gifts he would like for his birthday, Paul would simply respond, "I just want to spend time with you." That is what God requests from us. And wouldn't it be wonderful if more people would come to spend time with him?

the same time it protected the people from a direct encounter with the Holy God (Exodus 40:34–38).

When a cloud settled on the Tent of Meeting, the people did not move from one location to another. They remained fixed where they were until the cloud lifted. No one, not even Moses, could enter the Tent of Meeting while the glory of the Lord was there. Notice, in verse 7, that the cloud settled over them. One significant difference from Moses's experience in the wilderness is that Peter, James, and John are present within the cloud. They are in the very presence of God.

A second interpretation of the significance of this moment may be connected with the story of Jesus' baptism. It is likely that at least John was familiar with the account of Jesus' baptism, including the voice from Heaven calling out. John refers to the baptism in his own Gospel account. It is also unlikely that any of Peter, James, or John were present at the baptism. Together, they have truly had a rare and likely unique experience.

It is no wonder Peter did not know what to say! The passage is especially interesting in light of the certainty Peter exhibited just six days earlier. Then, he rebuked Jesus saying Jesus would not die. Now, less than a week later, in a state of fear, he is speechless and anxiously mumbles something about building tents.

Everything seems to have become disconnected for Peter. He is awkwardly amazed and seemingly still until they begin down the mountain. At that point, Jesus begins to explain what they have just witnessed.

Undoubtedly, the disciples know something about the significance of Elijah and Moses. Moses is the one who delivers the Hebrews from captivity in Egypt, he is the Father of the nation and the recipient of the Law by which the people would govern themselves before God. Elijah is a Prophet during the reign of several kings demanding that the rulers of the kingdom honor the Lord, keep the Law, and remove the idols from their nation.

For us as readers, the cloud and the voice clearly recall the moment of Jesus' baptism. Mark makes sure of that. At the baptism, John the Baptist was the privileged observer, now there are three disciples who are likewise privileged. Yet, for Peter, the words "Listen to him!" must have been burning. It is as though the voice had said, "Peter, instead of you telling Jesus what lies ahead for him, let him tell you his destiny. If you do not understand it, then ask for wisdom and be silent until you get it." Jesus tells them to tell no one what they have seen until a later time.

The three of them appear to have heeded Jesus' advice as they discuss two different issues they had difficulty understanding. First, they discussed what did Jesus mean by rising from the dead. This subject is left hanging. Mark is not yet telling the reader what it means.

Then the disciples ask Jesus, "Why do the Prophets say Elijah must come first?" In answer to this question, Mark returns to the manner in which he began—telling the narrative of the disciples sent out to preach and to heal wrapped around the story of John the Baptist's execution. Here, Jesus speaks plainly that John the Baptist is the Elijah who has come. In doing so, he adds that the people to whom Elijah had come did what they wanted to with him. They killed him. Then, in contrast to the successes the disciples experienced earlier, Mark reports the disciples' failure to heal a sick boy.

As we go forward, pay attention to how Mark is using Semitic literary styles. There are intentional repeats, as we have seen with the two sets of four stories. This is another repeat. However, in this case, there are significant changes. Before the Jesus Question, the disciples have no understanding and are yet able to perform healing by the authority with which Jesus sends them forward. After (correctly) answering the question, it is as though the disciples have not only failed to understand the significance of who Jesus is, they have also become disconnected from his authority.

Disciples Unable to Heal (9:14–29)

14 When they came to the other disciples, they saw a large
crowd around them and the teachers of the law arguing
with them. 15 As soon as all the people saw Jesus, they were
overwhelmed with wonder and ran to greet him.

16 "What are you arguing with them about?" he asked.

17 A man in the crowd answered, "Teacher, I brought you
my son, who is possessed by a spirit that has robbed him
of speech. 18 Whenever it seizes him, it throws him to the
ground. He foams at the mouth, gnashes his teeth and
becomes rigid. I asked your disciples to drive out the spirit,
but they could not."

19 "You unbelieving generation," Jesus replied, "how long
shall I stay with you? How long shall I put up with you?
Bring the boy to me."

20 So they brought him. When the spirit saw Jesus, it
immediately threw the boy into a convulsion. He fell to
the ground and rolled around, foaming at the mouth.

21 Jesus asked the boy's father, "How long has he been like this?"

"From childhood," he answered. 22 "It has often thrown
him into fire or water to kill him. But if you can do any-
thing, take pity on us and help us."

23 "'If you can'?" said Jesus. "Everything is possible for one who believes."

24 Immediately the boy's father exclaimed, "I do believe; help me overcome my unbelief!"

25 When Jesus saw that a crowd was running to the scene, he rebuked the impure spirit. "You deaf and mute spirit," he said, "I command you, come out of him and never enter him again."

26 The spirit shrieked, convulsed him violently and came out. The boy looked so much like a corpse that many said,
"He's dead." 27 But Jesus took him by the hand and lifted him to his feet, and he stood up.

28 After Jesus had gone indoors, his disciples asked him privately, "Why couldn't we drive it out?"

29 He replied, "This kind can come out only by prayer."

The disciples want to drive out the evil spirit but are unsuccessful. Their failure was frustrating. After all, they were called to be fishers of men and they had previously healed many people and even cast out evil spirits (Mark 6:6b–13). We can only imagine how elated they were as they made their earlier report to Jesus (Mark 6:30) and how frustrated they are this time.

Mark concludes with their ineffectiveness and their frustration. We can hear their disappointment as they ask Jesus, "Why couldn't we drive it out?"

This failure leads the disciples into confrontation with the teachers of the law who pick an argument with them, presumably dealing with the powers of the world of the dark spirits. The precise content of the argument is not known, but we may assume the disciples, who have been shielded from criticism up until now, are feeling some of the negativity Jesus has been experiencing all along. It adds to their frustration.

The father of the boy is also frustrated and confesses as much when Jesus asks them to bring the boy. "If you can do anything, take pity on us and help us." Just the same, the father holds out in hope for his son. Jesus answers, "Everything is possible for those who believe." To that the father responds, "I believe, help my unbelief."

As far as faith is concerned, the confession, "I believe, help my unbelief," is honored by Jesus. Even the timid can make their requests known. The boy is restored.

One of the greatest paradoxes of the Christian faith is found in this very simple and honest prayer. "Lord, I believe, help my unbelief." At the heart of this prayer is God's grace that allows us to have faith in his sovereignty. There is also a recognition of who we are without God.

Ole Hallesby understands this aspect about prayer: "Behold I stand at the door and knock" (Revelation 3:20). [7] God is always there, waiting. We still need to open the door—even if we don't fully comprehend who God is or how he will answer our prayer. My prayer is that all who have benefited from my ministry will similarly open the door and ask for God to secure confidence in faith.

We are not given any reaction from the crowds and so we are not counseled by them on how we might respond to this scene. Instead, there seems to be an effort to heal the boy before the crowds arrive and render them unable to respond. When the crowds finally do approach, Jesus commands the spirit to come out of the boy.

Later, as Jesus and the disciples discuss the experience, Jesus reminds them on the importance of both faith and prayer. We are led to believe that some experiences will be beyond us even

---

7 In *Prayer*. To pray is to let Jesus come into our hearts (Ole Hallesby, page 13).

as this one is beyond the disciples. They are, after all, still functioning as apprentices.

The reference to prayer is important. Remember, Mark told us Jesus prayed as this larger narrative was beginning (Mark 7:46). Jesus' words to his disciples at this juncture is a reminder to them that they are not the source of any healing. It is God who heals, and the glory belongs to God. They must realize that thinking they are the ones who heal, even after being commissioned to heal, grabs glory for themselves. No wonder they ask, "Why couldn't *we* do it?" Truth is, they never could! It was always and only God.

There are some translations of this passage that add fasting to praying. The word may be absent from the earlier manuscripts, yet the thought is worth observing. Fasting has its own significance in terms of support for clear thinking in prayer.

Mark has made his point. The repetition of stories in the two collections, the parable in the double healing of a blind man, the confession of faith by Peter when he lacks an accurate understanding of the Christ, and this weak confidence from the father of a boy possessed by an evil spirit, add up to little more than a mustard seed of faith. His faith is enough! Faith in God exercised through prayer opens the door to the work of God.

More importantly, Mark has made a brilliant observation regarding the question, "Who do you say I am?" Jesus asks it regarding himself. Peter answers it, "You are the Christ." This seems to be so true that there was (and is) no way to deny it. However, when Jesus explains his destiny is to suffer and die at the hands of the religious leaders, Peter protests. Jesus' reprimand is as strong as one can ever imagine. "Get behind me, Satan." Jesus explains, Peter's mind was on human concerns and not the things of God. For the reader, I want to remind you that the temptations continue long after Jesus overcomes them in the wilderness.

Notice Jesus is posing the identity question for the disciples. They need to ask, "Who am I?" about themselves. At this point, their minds are set on earthly things. If their minds are open, Jesus can help redirect their minds to the things of God.

This is the climax of Mark's Gospel. In this sequence, he ties together many themes: the failure of the disciples to understand and to heal; the ongoing intent of demons to destroy; the importance of honoring faith, however small; Jesus' compassion for others; the limited role of the crowds; the importance of prayer before God, for whom nothing is impossible; and the counsel for the disciples regarding their failure. All of this comes together in the ambiguity of the question: *Who am I?*

PERSPECTIVE ON "WHO DO PEOPLE SAY I AM?" SON OF MAN? SON OF GOD?

The disclosure of Jesus' identity is the primary focus for Act 3. "You are the Christ," says one of the disciples, not knowing what that meant. "This is my Son," exclaims the voice in the cloud. The opening words of the prologue, "The beginning of the Gospel of Jesus Christ the Son of God," have finally been responsibly, if not mysteriously, affirmed. The affirmation comes as a special revelation to three of the disciples after they had identified Jesus as the Christ but failed to understand his destiny.

It is significant to notice that the temptations for Jesus (and for the disciples) have continued. By Peter pulling Jesus aside to comfort him, and telling him that he will certainly not die, he is tempting both Jesus and himself. Peter expects that Jesus will be the hero. The hero does not die. [8] Yet, Jesus rebukes Peter. In this same way, we will see that the temptations continue to the very end of the Gospel.

---

8 The hero does die. Jesus' death is the underlying theme of Mark. It is also a prominent theme in Greek tragedy. For this reason, Gilbert Bilezikian draws on Aristotle's *Poetics* to construct a useful outline for Mark's Gospel. Read Mark as a tragedy and the outline of Mark will be much clearer than other outlines. It was a personal challenge to me, from which I benefited greatly.

Mark understands the significance of the transfiguration as he presents the voice as a theophany identifying Jesus as the Son of God. However, before the scene is concluded he references Jesus as the Son of Man. These two identifications express the mystery of the incarnation. As Son of God, Jesus is divine; and as Son of Man, he is fully and truly human.

This mystery is emphasized by the Apostle Paul in his letter to the Romans as the fundamental teaching of the Christian faith. "Sin entered the world through the one man" (Romans 5:12), Adam, who is a type of the one to come. The first Adam is flawed while the last Adam is without sin (1 Corinthians 15:45-49). The first became a living being; the second is a life-giving spirit. Jesus, who is the second Adam, is the giver of righteousness and life that comes. As the Apostle says, "the gift of life reigns through one man, Jesus Christ" (Romans 5:17).

Paul continues, "There is no condemnation for those who are in Christ Jesus, because through Christ Jesus the law of the Spirit of life set me free from the law of sin and death. For what the law was powerless to do in that it was weakened by sinful nature, God did by sending his own Son in the likeness of sinful man to be a sin offering" (Romans 8:1–3a).

Paul links the two identifications of Jesus as Son of Man and Son of God in his letter prior to his visit with the church at Rome. It would be hard to imagine that Mark was not familiar with this letter. If he is aware of it, it would help account for the mystery Mark simply reports. There is a voice calling Jesus, "My Son," and Jesus is the Son of Man who will rise from the dead.

The disciples' best efforts do not yet include the mysteries of the incarnation and the sin-offering. The most they can do is proclaim, "You are the Christ," a judgment they themselves do not understand. It should be no surprise that Peter makes this observation. He and the other disciples have had more opportunity to know Jesus than anyone save, of course, Mary, the mother of Jesus. They know he is in a religious league by himself. For whatever reason, Mark does not tell us about Mary.

Hence, in Mark, our best insight into the identity of Jesus is through the experience of the disciples.

The disciples' role, to become fishers of men, requires them to listen to everything Jesus says and to observe all that he does. In this section, they have moved beyond observers, entering into a kind of internship. In the beginning of Act 3, they successfully perform several healings. It ends, however, with the disciples unable to heal a sick boy.

Jesus takes three disciples to a high mountain to witness the transfiguration. There they are enveloped in a cloud, they hear a voice from the cloud speaking to them, and when they look around, they see Moses and Elijah standing with Jesus whose clothes had become dazzling white.

The cloud is significant. It parallels the cloud at the baptism, and it also recalls the experience of the Hebrews being led through the wilderness: a cloud by day and a pillar of fire by night. The Lord who was with them in their trials was also the one leading them to the promised land. Now a new leader, one like unto Moses, would lead a new community through a different kind of wilderness to a new promised land. This is the kingdom of God, one that reflects the Father's glory. By being enveloped by the cloud, Peter, James, and John are revealed as part of that community. This is a magnificent promise!

The disciples learn slowly. They need remedial lessons. Even though they assist Jesus in the feeding of the five thousand and of the four thousand, they do not understand. They see a blind man healed twice but do not recognize the parable. They discuss why they could not heal the boy and then they hear a father say, "I believe, help my unbelief."

The disciples have struggled all along the way. In curiosity, they wondered who is this Jesus when he calmed the sea; they are bewildered when Jesus asks the significance of the two feeding miracles; they hear Jesus upbraid Peter; three of them tremble in fear when Jesus is transfigured; and the others are unable to heal someone who is sick.

It is clear the disciples have more to learn. So far, their attention has been focused on Jesus and on those surrounding him. They have not reflected on themselves except for a mild complaint, "Why couldn't we drive out the demon?" This is a critical question if they are to continue with Jesus.

I want to remind my colleagues in ministry (and, perhaps even more, myself), that it is God who acts through us. The disciples are certainly challenged to reflect on their inability to heal. We, too, should reflect on situations when we are ineffective in sharing the grace of God. For myself, it is a constant reminder of the call to repent.

In the concluding words of Jesus, the disciples are advised what to do about healing people and about themselves. Pray. There is a secret hiding in plain sight about the kingdom of God. It is found in relationship with God. Prayer is our opportunity to be in fellowship with God—and in a right, humble position. For it is by God's authority that we are able to do all things. The fullness of that power is not yet evident in Mark's Gospel.

ACT FOUR

Why the Son of Man Must Be Killed (9:30–13:37)

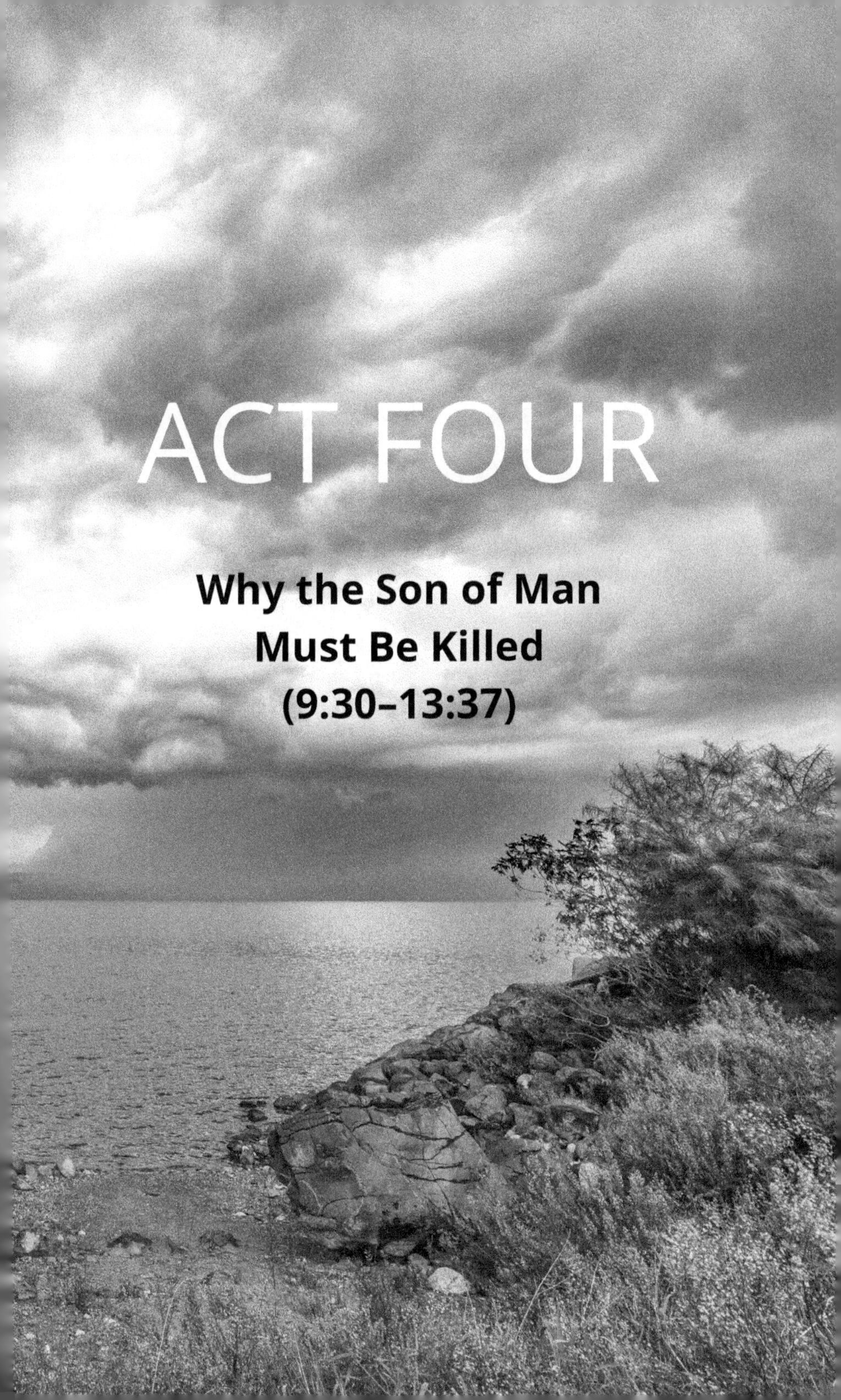

Teaching the Disciples (9:30–9:50)

The Son of Man did not come to be served, but to serve,
and to give his life as a ransom for many.
—Mark 10:43

The disciples have been privileged to receive profound spiritual instruction. All the parables have been explained to them. They have exercised dynamic spiritual authority: healing the sick and casting out demons. They have come to some understanding of Jesus as evidenced by Peter's proclamation at Caesarea Philippi: "You are the Christ."

Still, they do not comprehend Jesus' assertion that he will die. Similarly, they do not understand what Jesus means by "raised from the dead."

Jesus clearly knows what is coming and why. He repeats the account he shared at Caesarea Philippi about his death and then privately offers new teaching for the disciples. They need to know much more about themselves and their relationship with God than they realize. The next stage in their development involves the lesson on being a servant. This begins at Capernaum.

30 They left that place and passed through Galilee. Jesus did not want anyone to know where they were, 31 because he was teaching his disciples. He said to them, "The Son of Man is going to be delivered into the hands of men. They will kill him, and after three days he will rise." 32 But they

did not understand what he meant and were afraid to ask
him about it.

33 *They came to Capernaum. When he was in the house,*
he asked them, "What were you arguing about on the
road?" 34 *But they kept quiet because on the way they had*
argued about who was the greatest.

35 *Sitting down, Jesus called the Twelve and said, "Anyone*
who wants to be first must be the very last, and the servant
of all."

36 *He took a little child whom he placed among them.*
Taking the child in his arms, he said to them, 37 *"Whoever*
welcomes one of these little children in my name welcomes
me; and whoever welcomes me does not welcome me but
the one who sent me."

38 *"Teacher," said John, "we saw someone driving out*
demons in your name and we told him to stop, because he
was not one of us."

39 *"Do not stop him," Jesus said. "For no one who does a*
miracle in my name can in the next moment say anything
bad about me, 40 *for whoever is not against us is for us.* 41
Truly I tell you, anyone who gives you a cup of water in
my name because you belong to the Messiah will certainly
not lose their reward.

42 *"If anyone causes one of these little ones—those who*
believe in me—to stumble, it would be better for them if
a large millstone were hung around their neck and they
were thrown into the sea. 43 *If your hand causes you to*
stumble, cut it off. It is better for you to enter life maimed

than with two hands to go into hell, where the fire never goes out. [44] 45 And if your foot causes you to stumble, cut it off. It is better for you to enter life crippled than to have two feet and be thrown into hell. [46] 47 And if your eye causes you to stumble, pluck it out. It is better for you to enter the kingdom of God with one eye than to have two eyes and be thrown into hell, 48 where

"'the worms that eat them do not die, and the fire is not quenched.'

49 Everyone will be salted with fire.

50 "Salt is good, but if it loses its saltiness, how can you make it salty again? Have salt among yourselves and be at peace with each other."

PRIVATE LESSON ON BEING A CHRISTIAN SERVANT

"What were you talking about?" Jesus asks. When they do not answer, Jesus begins the next lesson with a discourse on who truly is the greatest. They will learn that Jesus knows them better than they know themselves. Not one of them spoke of greatness in terms of serving others and Jesus knew it. Remember, Act 1 left the crowds, including the disciples, in awe of the compassion and power of Jesus demonstrated by his miraculous acts on behalf of others, including Peter's mother-in-law.

Mark explains, "Jesus, sitting down, called the Twelve to him." The fact that Jesus sat down is significant. In the culture of that day, when the teacher sits down, the students are to pay close attention as the teaching that follows is important. Matthew presents a similar situation when Jesus begins the "Sermon on the Mount." Jesus sits down to teach. It is also done privately as there is no intention to bring public disgrace to any of them.

The fact that he calls the twelve implies they all need this lesson on greatness. In the minds of the twelve, the greater the person the more he rules over others or, perhaps, the more he is able to accomplish. Peter, James, and John might have thought highly of themselves because they were on the Mount of Transfiguration with Jesus. One may surmise these three could have told the other disciples who were unable to drive out a demon from the boy that they could have done it if they had been there. If this is so, then Jesus says to the three and to the others, the first must be last and the servant of all.

To illustrate his point, Jesus places a child before them. By itself this seems a simple illustration. The disciples, who spoke primarily Aramaic, knew that the Aramaic word for child was the same as the word for servant. [1] They would recognize the play on words. Roman society at large might not understand it. Here, the teaching is private and for the disciples alone. If they wish to repeat it for the benefit of the Roman Church, they may do so at another time. Mark provides opportunity for that to happen with this narrative.

If the disciples are to become accomplished fishers of men, they must become servants of others. With the child before the disciples, Jesus teaches them to welcome little children. New parents are likely to know exactly what Jesus means.

Children place demands on their parents especially in their younger years. Newborn children have very simple needs: food, cleanliness, and shelter. As they grow, they will also need vision, dreams, guidance, hope, love, comfort, and patience. Parents provide love, supervision, and guidance. The child does not demand service from the parents. Rather, it is in loving the

---

1 In *The Gospel According to Mark* (William Lane, page 340). Greatness is not tied to glory; rather, greatness is tied to serving others.

child, and knowing the needs of the child, that good parents are commanded to serve the child.

Parents have an awesome responsibility encouraging their children. "Train up a child in the way he should go," writes the wise teacher, "so that when he is old he will not turn from it" (Proverbs 22:6). Parents know what it means to sacrifice themselves for the sake of their children. They know that everything the child wants is not necessarily good for the child. They also know that children can resist their instruction. Unfortunately, parents are also inclined to live out their own fantasies through their children.

Jesus astounds the disciples by putting the lesson into perspective: he, Jesus, is the child who needs to be welcomed. Before their very eyes, the disciples can see Jesus with the child placed in their midst. Yet, do they see Jesus in the child? The disciples who learn to follow Jesus will become leaders in Jesus' name. In his name, they will need to see Jesus in the ones whom they are serving. If this is what Jesus is teaching, it revolutionizes interpersonal relationships and, in so doing, redefines leadership.

Many reading this text are likely familiar with at least the label of "servant leadership." I want to add just a brief comment. The leadership that Jesus is describing is not based in a desire for self-gratification. It is all too easy for religious leaders to get caught up in this concept in a way that boasts about being a great servant in order to gain notoriety as a leader.

Thomas Aquinas points this out regarding pride and humility.[2] He noted that, the very moment at which he achieved true humility, he becomes guilty of pride. In this manner, we ought to remind ourselves that true servant leadership comes from a constant heart of repentance and submission to the will of

---

2 In Thomas Aquinas's *Summa Theologica,* Question 162: "Pride is the source of all other sins. It is the vice which causes one to make more of oneself than he is. It is the deadliest for pride can enter the mind of those who do good."

God. Or, borrowing from the Aramaic, true servant leadership requires the heart of the child.

This time, the response to Jesus' message comes not from Peter but from John who together with Peter had witnessed the transfiguration. Avoiding a direct reference to welcoming children, John speaks of himself as serving Jesus by stopping someone from doing miracles in Jesus' name because this person was not one of the twelve.

There is irony in stopping someone from working a miracle when John knows his fellow disciples were unable to heal a young boy just moments ago. He heard Jesus say then that some miracles required prayer as God is the one who makes the miracle happen. So, for a second time, Jesus teaches his disciples whoever does something in Jesus' name is not a threat to them even if what they do is merely provide a cup of cold water. They will receive their reward.

The language Jesus uses to teach why this lesson is important is from Hebrew symbolism, yet clear enough for a Roman audience. Cutting off a hand or foot and gouging out the eye is not the point. To welcome a child is to welcome Jesus; to bring a child to Jesus is to bring the child to God. The Apostle James comments on this very point, "Religion that God the Father accepts as pure and faultless is this: to look after orphans and widows in their distress and to keep oneself from being polluted by the world" (James 1:27).

The private teaching closes with three comments on salt. The first, "Everyone will be salted with fire," is often thought to be connected with Hebrew worship in which grain offerings were salted before being offered in the fire (Leviticus 2:11–15). This perspective may be correct, although the Hebrew people themselves do not appear to be included in the salting. A better application may be found in the experience of Roman Christians suffering persecution under Nero. Whereas the Hebrew sacrifice of grain was to be salted before being put into the fire, many of the Christians in Rome lost their lives literally "salted" with fire. There is a sense in which Jesus is instructing the disciples to expect persecution simply because they are the salt. This remains true for us today.

Second, "if salt loses it saltiness, they cannot make it salty again." The Church in Rome faced persecution daily. For them to remain true to Jesus they would need a strong faith. If they capitulate under pressure, the salt that was theirs, namely their integrity, would be compromised and perhaps lost. Mark, alone among the Gospel writers, provides this reference in a pastoral manner to encourage faith for the believers in Rome.

Third, Jesus concludes, "Have salt in yourselves and be at peace with each other." Instead of the quarreling among his disciples over who is the greatest, Jesus teaches them to serve each other and then there will be peace. This contrasts with the yeast of the Pharisees (Mark 8:15) and is in agreement with the teaching of both the Apostle Peter and the Apostle Paul. Paul admonishes the Church at Colossae, "Let your conversation be always full of grace and seasoned with salt so that you may know how to answer everyone" (Colossians 4:6). Peter writes, "Live in harmony with one another ... Do not repay evil with evil ... but with blessing, because to this you were called" (I Peter 3:8–9). Both Apostles were mentors to Mark.

In a marvelous summation on the mystery of servant leadership, Jesus explains that acts on behalf of others are, at a deeper level, a service to himself (Mark 6:7–12). Then he adds, it is furthermore a service to the One who sent him. The dignity of leadership is derived from the context (before God) in which one serves, how one perceives the "child" (Jesus) being served, and, further, how the leader perceives himself (servant of the Lord). "If you want to be first, you must be the very last, the servant of all." Fishers of men are servants of those to whom they are sent.

We may be assured that the advice for the disciples applies to us as well. We, too, must work our way through the desires to rule and to be served until we realize we are called to a life of service for others. Life is not measured by the number of toys we call our own or the number of people over whom we preside. This is a childish understanding. Life is measured by care given to children, especially when they are in danger. Salt preserves and enables us gracefully to survive the challenges we inevitably encounter. Those who are truly great people are the salt of the earth.

The private lesson on servanthood is over. Jesus and the disciples leave the house and travel to Perea on the eastern side of the Jordan near Judea. They are on their way to Jerusalem. Jesus continues teaching them even though it is mediated through what he teaches others. The second lesson concerns hardness of heart. It begins with a question about divorce.

Individual Ethics (10:1–52)

HARDNESS OF HEART (10:1–16)

__10__ Jesus then left that place and went into the region of Judea and across the Jordan. Again, crowds of people came to him, and as was his custom, he taught them.

2 Some Pharisees came and tested him by asking, "Is it lawful for a man to divorce his wife?"

3 "What did Moses command you?" he replied.

4 They said, "Moses permitted a man to write a certificate of divorce and send her away."

5 "It was because your hearts were hard that Moses wrote you this law," Jesus replied. 6 "But at the beginning of creation God 'made them male and female.' 7 'For this reason a man will leave his father and mother and be united to his wife, 8 and the two will become one flesh.' So, they are no longer two, but one flesh. 9 Therefore what God has joined together, let no one separate."

10 When they were in the house again, the disciples asked Jesus about this. 11 He answered, "Anyone who divorces his wife and marries another woman commits adultery against her. 12 And if she divorces her husband and marries another man, she commits adultery."

13 People were bringing little children to Jesus for him to place his hands on them, but the disciples rebuked them. 14 When Jesus saw this, he was indignant. He said to them, "Let the little children come to me, and do not hinder them, for the kingdom of God belongs to such as these. 15 Truly I tell you, anyone who will not receive the kingdom of God like a little child will never enter it." 16 And he took the children in his arms, placed his hands on them and blessed them.

Before diving into the analysis of how Mark intends these stories to fit into the narrative of *good news*, it might prove valuable to remind ourselves of a key distinction Jesus has made at multiple points throughout the Gospel. The kingdom of God is different from human experience in the (fallen) creation. It is unlike even the visions of the religious leaders. In order to gain any insight into what the kingdom of God is like, therefore, it is necessary to change our thinking, feeling, and experience at every level. We need to be mindful, first, of the things of God.

God intended for male and female to be united as one flesh. For God, there is marriage. There is nothing else. Jesus explains that people's hardness of heart sometimes makes it seem impossible for a couple to remain together. Hardness of heart destroys relationships, even in the sacred union of marriage. Today, we recognize the many ways in which such stubborn, self-righteous attitudes become abusive. It is for this reason Moses wrote a law allowing divorce. It is out of compassion for the other spouse that God allows what is otherwise an abomination.

Mark recognizes that we are living in the wilderness. Jesus has come to introduce the kingdom of God, and in so doing, to transform the barren wilderness so that it brings life and flourishes. Regarding marriage, life in the wilderness requires laws regulating both the marriage and its dissolution. Within the kingdom, no such law about divorce is needed.

Everyone is infected with hardness of heart. A few people, like the Pharaoh of Moses's day, have a pronounced case of it (Exodus 7:13, *et passim*). Pharaoh needed to change, and he stubbornly refused. It is a character defect, one that Moses knew infected everybody. In time Moses would refer to those he leads out of Egypt as stiff-necked people.

Jesus explains that, in order to govern life with some degree of order and civility, Moses had to take into account the depth to which "hardness of heart" effects people in their interaction with each other. Each of us also has a hardness of heart which manifests itself in our own stubborn ways of doing things. Most of the time people can accept us with our faults and we move on, or we find a way to deny or cover up our faults. Honesty about our basic human relationships reveals a hardness of heart familiar to everyone. It shows up in every family unit whether in a marital union or in the treatment of a child.

In teaching this to his disciples and the gathered crowd, Jesus explains divorce and remarriage in terms of adultery. God has joined them together and they spurn what God has done. Hardness of heart characterizes the people living in the wilderness.

Next, Mark tells us about people who were bringing little children to Jesus. The disciples rebuke the parents and in doing so, they reveal their own hardness of heart. They violate the relationship Jesus has with children and seem to ignore the private teaching they had just heard. As such, they have a lot to learn about leadership and especially about themselves. In this narrative, they fail the first recorded opportunity for them to act in a righteousness manner toward children and to be the salt of the earth (Mark 10:13). Clearly, they have not yet learned and matured to what Jesus is teaching.

Notice what is called "hardness of heart" here is a teaching about sin. It is not about principles on how to raise a child nor about the sanctity of marriage. Irreconcilable marital difficulties illustrate the hardness of heart preventing couples from fulfilling God's call on their lives. Some get divorced, others do not. The former are often judged harshly. We should not be too quick to fault them. Nor should we be too quick to praise those who remain married as though they avoided any hardness of heart.

Have we not recognized the disciples' hardness of heart that they have failed to see in themselves? They are no different from couples getting divorced. They were just told that to receive a child was the same as receiving Jesus. Then, inexplicably, they turned the children away. This is tantamount to turning Jesus away. No wonder Jesus was indignant! Jesus emphasizes his lesson by welcoming the children with his own hands and blessing them.

Overcoming hardness of heart is not an easy matter. It certainly includes getting proper instruction (Mark 9:36, 37) and following good examples (Mark 10:16). These are not enough. Like the disciples listening to Jesus talk about accepting children and not recognizing their own behavior in rejecting them, we too have hardness of heart. Confession and forgiveness may assist us in overcoming some faults. Yet we continue to stumble on wobbly legs in our walk through the wilderness.

In the next narrative Mark explains how hardness of heart infects religious communities. It is possible for those who do what is right before the law to be guilty of their own hardness of heart. The disciples are amazed and ask a telling question.

PURPOSE OF THE LAW (10:17–31)

17 As Jesus started on his way, a man ran up to him and fell on his knees before him. "Good teacher," he asked, "what must I do to inherit eternal life?"

18 "Why do you call me good?" Jesus answered. "No one

is good—except God alone. [19] You know the commandments: 'You shall not murder, you shall not commit adultery, you shall not steal, you shall not give false testimony, you shall not defraud, honor your father and mother.'"

[20] "Teacher," he declared, "all these I have kept since I was a boy."

[21] Jesus looked at him and loved him. "One thing you lack," he said. "Go, sell everything you have and give to the poor, and you will have treasure in heaven. Then come, follow me."

[22] At this the man's face fell. He went away sad, because he had great wealth.

[23] Jesus looked around and said to his disciples, "How hard it is for the rich to enter the kingdom of God!"

[24] The disciples were amazed at his words. But Jesus said again, "Children, how hard it is to enter the kingdom of God! [25] It is easier for a camel to go through the eye of a needle than for someone who is rich to enter the kingdom of God."

[26] The disciples were even more amazed, and said to each other, "Who then can be saved?"

[27] Jesus looked at them and said, "With man this is impossible, but not with God; all things are possible with God."

[28] Then Peter spoke up, "We have left everything to follow you!"

[29] "Truly I tell you," Jesus replied, "no one who has left home or brothers or sisters or mother or father or children or

fields for me and the gospel [30] will fail to receive a hundred times as much in this present age: homes, brothers, sisters, mothers, children and fields—along with persecutions—and in the age to come eternal life. [31] But many who are first will be last, and the last first."

My son, who holds a doctorate in clinical psychology, might begin a response to this section differently. He might acknowledge that the rich man appears to be afflicted with Narcissistic Personality Disorder. Jesus recognizes this immediately when he somewhat ostentatiously begins, "Good Teacher." Narcissus would only compliment someone whom he expects would return the compliment. Jesus doesn't fall for the flattery. That being said, Jesus also responds to this young man from the context he presents.

Not very many people can claim to have kept the whole law—and none have actually achieved that claim. If someone does keep the law, or comes close to keeping it, most of us would commend that person. In this story, a wealthy man claims to have kept the law since he was a child. The disciples seem impressed, and Mark says Jesus loved him. In the narrative, we see Jesus' compassion in the way he addresses the man's hardness of heart, pointing the way toward trusting in God. In the end the rich man does not realize how his hardness of heart is blinding him to true righteousness.

Mark deals here with a fundamental Christian teaching. Mark knows hardness of heart is a life-destroying cancer. Everyone needs to be aware of it for the so called "innocent" are no less guilty than everyone else. In a marvelously simple sentence, the Apostle Paul writes, "All have sinned and fall short of the glory of God" (Romans 3:23). This comment is especially significant because Paul understands that his zeal for God caused him to persecute the Lord's anointed (Acts 9:1–22). For this reason, he calls himself the foremost of sinners (I Timothy 1:15).

For Mark, hardness of heart characterizes the rich man at the core of his being. However righteous he appears before the law, he becomes extremely selfish through his hardness of heart. The man is searching for a salvation and peace he craves, and he keeps thinking he can achieve it on his own. The Scripture teaches he cannot succeed because no one can attain to the perfection of righteousness which would make salvation unnecessary. Make no mistake; the demands of righteousness before God are exceptionally high. Jesus' instruction for him to sell what he has is designed to enlighten the man. Instead, it seems to bring him to a sense of hopelessness.

Several points are worth making about the narrative. First, as noted above, Jesus deals with the rich man with compassion. He will show love to him by speaking the truth and leading him to discover what is the true meaning of salvation. It is an excellent illustration of being a servant as he is demonstrating leadership.

When the rich man calls Jesus the good teacher, Jesus knows the man thinks he can become "good" by keeping the law. Jesus challenges him gently, and immediately, in this regard, reminding him only God is good. Unfortunately, the man does not understand how the affirmation that only God is good relates to himself. He will need to return to this affirmation after he discovers more about himself.

This is yet another identification of Jesus that misses the mark. It is right and true to identify Jesus as "good." However, Jesus challenges the rich young man to know what he is saying. The man fails to recognize the authority by which Jesus ministers. Likewise, he fails to understand how he might be able to enter into a good relationship with God.

Second, Jesus tells him to sell what he has and give it to the poor. We do not know whether the man has offered alms for the poor or not. Mark is silent on this point. If the man has not cared for the poor, he violates an ethical command to love his neighbor as himself. The man says he keeps the law and Jesus seems to affirm the man in this regard. Jesus does not accuse him of ignoring the poor, nor does he admonish him to care for them. Rather, Jesus directs the rich man to sell "all" he has and give it to the poor.

Clearly, when the rich man heard this he was dismayed. Likely, if he were to take Jesus' advice, what he saw in his mind was abject poverty. He would have lost control of his own future. This was unacceptable to him.

Notice, if Jesus intended to impoverish the man, then Jesus is moving beyond the commandments and moving way beyond the obligations of caring for the poor, even beyond what he himself accepts (see Mark 14:1–11). Jesus asks whether the man was so tied to his wealth that nothing, not even the love of God, which he claimed to seek, could separate him from it. By itself, selling all he has is not in the commandments and not an ethical mandate.

So, if Jesus is not addressing an ethical failure on the part of the rich man, what is he addressing? Mark reports the rich man so loved his wealth that it was preventing him from loving God and trusting in God's mercy. "How hard it is for the rich to enter the kingdom of God!" Jesus explains. The rich feel they can purchase a pardon rather than trust in God's goodness toward them. Remember, only God is good.

The disciples appear to recognize the point of the lesson when they ask, "Who then can be saved?" Jesus answers their question, "With man this is impossible, but not with God; all things are possible with God." Whether the disciples truly understand Jesus' answer Mark does not say. However, Mark will address their open-ended question when the narrative on salvation continues.

What do we make of hardness of heart regarding the rich man? For the rich man it is a blindness on two levels. First, the man does not comprehend that there is nothing we can bring to God but a humble and contrite heart (Psalm 51:17). Our efforts to impress God, whether with our money or with our acts of religious righteousness, are futile. They presume that goodness is within our reach and this assumption masks our selfishness and pride. In the narrative, the rich man does not see his inherent selfishness or the misguided pride.

Jesus' admonition is to help the man recognize he must approach God with nothing in his hand to bring. Give it all away! The rich man is selfish. If he were not selfish, he might have spoken on behalf of others and asked, "What can we do (emphasis on we) to inherit eternal life?" Or maybe, "What can I do to help my neighbor?" His concern is for himself only, "What can I do for myself to inherit eternal life?"

To put the matter in a stark fashion, suppose the man were able to gain eternal life by his own actions. What good would that do for anyone else? Can he share his accomplishment? Or, is he left to gloat over others where they failed, and he succeeded? Seeking righteousness in one's own works is inherently selfish. This righteous law keeper is guilty of not loving his neighbor as himself.

Second, on a higher level, the man is guilty of violating the first commandment. He has replaced God as the One to love with all our heart, soul, and strength. In place of God, he puts himself and his own wealth. Ignoring the commands to love God and to love one's neighbor results in the restlessness of his spirit.

Since the beginning, God has instilled in human beings a hunger to be at peace with God and with oneself. "You have made us for yourself, and our heart is restless until it rests in you." [3] Sin works against that peace. In his providence, God wrote the law on human hearts and on tablets of stone to assist us in the wilderness of human existence.

Laws enable people with varying degrees of hardness of heart to live together. Having no law to govern human affairs is chaos (see Judges 21:26). The point of the law before God

---

3 St. Augustine, *The Confessions of St. Augustine*, trans. John K. Ryan, 1.

is not to make people righteous. Paul writes, "No one will be declared righteous in his [God's] sight by observing the law; rather, through the law we become conscious of sin" (Romans 3:20). This is Mark's point in telling the story of the rich ruler! There is no righteousness before God by following the law. The result for the rich man was uneasiness and despair.

However, what is impossible for human beings is not impossible for God. Mark tells us God provides salvation. Paul announces there is "a righteousness from God, apart from the law" (Romans 3:21). The point of the law is to reveal sin and drive us toward God's mercy and goodness. "For the law was given through Moses; grace and truth came through Jesus Christ" (John 1:17). "For by grace you have been saved, through faith," writes the Apostle Paul, "and this is not from yourselves, it is the gift of God—not by works, so that no one can boast" (Ephesians 2:8, 9).

Martin Luther captured this truth in a disputation in Heidelberg when he argued that the Ten Commandments are not an aid toward righteousness. They are a hindrance. [4] The law judges and condemns.

Did the rich man understand this teaching? Not at all! He experienced it in his desire for it. He did not comprehend it. The rich man went away sorrowful rather than seeking God's grace. Mark makes this point about the rich man clearly.

Did the disciples understand? Remember this is a teaching session for them. Mark informs us Peter misses it completely as he protests that he made every sacrifice to follow Jesus and should not be without his reward. Talk about a blind spot! Talk about hardness of heart! In time, Peter will confess he was "called out of darkness into God's marvelous light" (I Peter 2:9).

Living with an awareness of all that is taking place brings with it the awareness that we did not see everything at first. We

---

4 "Heidelberg Disputation" in *Selected Writings of Martin Luther, 1520–1523,* ed. Theodore G. Tappert, 65.

sometimes need someone else to explain what we see and experience. That is the value of a proper education. However, even with good education, we are often blind to what we see because of our hardness of heart. As a result, Mark (in fact, the Holy Spirit) encourages us to be sensitive to the hardness of heart in ourselves and not be too quick to praise ourselves or criticize others. The Apostle John writes, "If we claim to be without sin, we deceive ourselves and the truth is not in us" (I John 1:8).

Jesus graciously assures him no sacrifice goes unnoticed or unrewarded. When we do see what God is doing, we are often called to humility and a softening of our heart, especially toward others. I think of countless examples of people I have seen caring for others during their time of need. That is true compassion—and it sometimes seems an easier sacrifice for those who are not in love with the wealth and riches they have accumulated. This is part of what John means by walking in the light, "If we walk in the light, as he [God] is in the light, we have fellowship with one another, and the blood of Jesus, his Son, purifies us from all sin" (I John 1:7).

We are not told how hardness of heart can be overcome, not yet anyway. Instead, Mark punctuates his story with a second reminder that Jesus will die. This time the lesson on servanthood will come to a spectacular conclusion.

The Son of Man Came to Serve (10:32–52)

REMINDER: SON OF MAN WILL DIE

> [32] *They were on their way up to Jerusalem, with Jesus leading the way, and the disciples were astonished, while those who followed were afraid. Again, he took the Twelve aside and told them what was going to happen to him.* [33] *"We are going up to Jerusalem," he said, "and the Son of Man will be delivered over to the chief priests and the teachers of the law. They will condemn him to death and will hand him over to the Gentiles,* [34] *who will mock him and spit on him, flog him and kill him. Three days later he will rise."*

Jesus' words are clear, and his resolve is unshakeable. He is on his way to Jerusalem and the disciples are with him. There is no hesitation in his step. He knows he is headed for betrayal and condemnation to death. His chosen destiny, which entails suffering at the hands of others, will be his glory whether at the hands of his disciples, the Jews, the Gentiles, or anyone else. He is going to die.

Jesus desires that his disciples have a better understanding of what is about to happen. That is not yet forthcoming. If they had understood the simpler lessons on servant leadership or on hardness of heart, they might have been ready for a more advanced lesson. They have not yet learned about their own hardness of heart as is evident in the response of two of them when Jesus again repeats he will die. James and John, who had stood alongside Peter on the mountain with Jesus, Moses, and Elijah, reveal their utter ignorance of what is being taught by Jesus.

EVEN THE SON OF MAN CAME TO SERVE

35 *Then James and John, the sons of Zebedee, came to him. "Teacher," they said, "we want you to do for us whatever we ask."*

36 *"What do you want me to do for you?" he asked.*

37 *They replied, "Let one of us sit at your right and the other at your left in your glory."*

38 *"You don't know what you are asking," Jesus said. "Can you drink the cup I drink or be baptized with the baptism I am baptized with?"*

39 *"We can," they answered.*

Jesus said to them, "You will drink the cup I drink and be
baptized with the baptism I am baptized with, 40 *but to*
sit at my right or left is not for me to grant. These places
belong to those for whom they have been prepared."

41 *When the ten heard about this, they became indignant*
with James and John. 42 *Jesus called them together and*
said, "You know that those who are regarded as rulers
of the Gentiles lord it over them, and their high officials
exercise authority over them. 43 *Not so with you. Instead,*
whoever wants to become great among you must be your

servant, 44 *and whoever wants to be first must be slave of all.* 45 *For even the Son of Man did not come to be served, but to serve, and to give his life as a ransom for many."*

The disciples have now been told three times about the Passion. Initially, rather than hearing what Jesus is saying, they (through Peter) deny it. The second time they (through John) ignore the Passion and continue with their own sense of superiority. They remain tied to the question about who is the greatest among the twelve. What a disappointment!

The third time Jesus instructs his disciples that he will die, James and John respond in a way that demonstrates they have not understood the lessons either on servanthood or on hardness of heart at all. They ask Jesus for seats of honor.

While I was serving as senior pastor of Northwest Covenant Church in Mount Prospect, Illinois, we had a group of people who wanted to drive home the point of Christian service. The group gathered for a day of service and had t-shirts and hats printed with "It's not about me." The humble spirit guiding their activities led to other service ministries for the local community and beyond. Would that we could have this spirit every day!

As one reads this story, one wonders if Jesus wasted his breath with the discussion about being the greatest. Truly, they did not hear him. For them, the privilege of discipleship is about themselves, not about others and certainly not about their teacher. Serving is the farthest thing from their minds. How often will Jesus need to repeat his lessons? Do they not see their hardness of heart?

Do they not see the struggle of their teacher? Three times Jesus has shared about his impending death. At no point did the disciples respond with empathy. Rather, they continued to focus solely on their own struggles.

Jesus gathers his disciples yet another time and explains even more clearly that they must be different from the rulers of the Gentiles. He implies that they will be different because he says they will eventually drink the cup he drinks. For now, Jesus keeps the focus on his own destiny. The Son of Man came to serve, not to be served. He came to give his life as a ransom for many. He is the model for the disciples to become fishers of men. Because the disciples do not realize their own hard-heartedness, they continue to misunderstand the lessons.

An explanation is in order. Jesus is the perfectly free Lord of all, and he has become the perfectly dutiful servant of all. [5] Unless you are free, you cannot truly serve. Typically, we serve with at least some awareness of how it benefits ourselves. We use service to build a good reputation, gain knowledge or skill in an area of interest, and even earn a paycheck. In each of these cases, we are bound by that which we gain. Jesus does not benefit through his service—he is already Lord of all creation. His service comes as a fully free choice. The disciples, like us, are bound by their self-interests; yet, their freedom will come as they understand more about Jesus and the kingdom of God.

Jesus uses the title "Son of Man" for himself. We encountered it first in the prologue. It is a title of one whose dominion will be everlasting (Daniel 7:14) and whose power and glory come from the Ancient of Days. His task will be to destroy the evil in the world with the power given him through his suffering. Jesus, in taking this title and in speaking about his death, confuses his disciples who think of the title in terms of unlimited power in an earthly dominion.

The time is getting late. A crisis is approaching, and the disciples do not appear ready to comprehend what is taking place before their very eyes.

THE BLIND AND THE VISUALLY IMPAIRED

46 Then they came to Jericho. As Jesus and his disciples, together with a large crowd, were leaving the city, a blind

5 "The Freedom of a Christian" in *Selected Writings of Martin Luther,* 1520–1523, ed. Theodore G. Tappert, 20.

man, Bartimaeus (which means "son of Timaeus"), was sitting by the roadside begging. [47] *When he heard that it was Jesus of Nazareth, he began to shout, "Jesus, Son of David, have mercy on me!"*

[48] *Many rebuked him and told him to be quiet, but he shouted all the more, "Son of David, have mercy on me!"*

[49] *Jesus stopped and said, "Call him."*

So, they called to the blind man, "Cheer up! On your feet! He's calling you." [50] *Throwing his cloak aside, he jumped to his feet and came to Jesus.*

[51] *"What do you want me to do for you?" Jesus asked him.*

The blind man said, "Rabbi, I want to see."

[52] *"Go," said Jesus, "your faith has healed you." Immediately he received his sight and followed Jesus along the road.*

As Mark brings this part of the teaching session to a close, he relates the story of a blind man whose request for mercy results in gaining sight. The blind man is a counter illustration to the rich ruler who does not ask for mercy and walks away downcast. Mark also uses this story to correct any false assumptions from the "double" healing of the blind man of Bethsaida (Mark 8:22–26).

Further, Mark uses this healing narrative effectively to reflect on the disciples who have eyes yet do not see. They have the teaching of Jesus but do not serve. They are visually impaired. Unlike the blind man who knows he is blind, the disciples do not recognize their blind spots. However, the healing of the blind man portends a healing for the disciples. It is a good omen. Jesus is patient with them (and with us). With this narrative, the two lessons come to a close: one on being the greatest and the other on hardness of heart.

At this point, Mark turns our attention to the events of the Passion.

Beginning with Palm Sunday, Jesus is orchestrating the final days until his death. Mark records the events of this week on a daily basis as a way to emphasize the Gospel of Jesus Christ the Son of God is nearing its conclusion. Mark emphasizes the crucifixion by highlighting the events of the days leading up to it. Note that this is the first time that Mark has allowed us to identify a particular time of year when any of these events were taking place. It is time for Passover.

Jesus assures the disciples that the day of resurrection will come. In the spirit of the Psalm, the day of resurrection will be a new day unlike any other. It will be "the day the Lord has made" (Psalm 118:24). It will be a reminder that what is impossible for man is possible for God. With the resurrection the kingdom of God has come. However, we are not finished with what Mark has to say about sin and salvation. Sin is not merely a personal matter. Rather, sin entangles us in relationships, leading to negative effects for every aspect of society. Salvation, therefore, must transform social structures every bit as much as each individual heart.

Walter Rauschenbusch introduced several concepts related to what became known as the Social Gospel Movement of the early twentieth century. [6] His contention was that social issues drove Jesus to the cross. Therefore, Christians ought to be focused on implementing social change regarding politics, racial relations, economic opportunities, and even religious structures. From this perspective, each area of social life is as much in need of salvation as the individual person—in fact, salvation for the individual is often viewed as hampered by the social conditions.

There are two key misunderstandings of Social Gospel theology that are important to address. First, many conservative

---

6 Walter Rauschenbusch, *A Theology for the Social Gospel.*

Protestant believers struggle with the theology of the Social Gospel Movement insomuch as it seemingly contradicts economic principles of the capitalist free market. This attitude is no different from that of the rich young man.

Second, some believe that any emphasis on social change results in minimizing individual responsibility for sin. Such an attitude dismisses social injustices, placing a higher burden on the individual to address all aspects of sinful behavior. This attitude is no different from that of the Pharisees who believe keeping the law is sufficient.

Paradox. We've discussed it often (and not enough). The effects of sin are felt throughout all aspects of the creation—including social structures. It is the individual and corporate responsibility of the Church to respond—and to respond in a way that advances the Gospel. It is less important to address the injustice; it is essential to share the *good news*.

As the final week begins, Jesus shifts attention away from personal hardness of heart and addresses social issues which are more troublesome. Social structures have no conscience. They are guided by things accepted in the society: the gathering of wealth, attainment of power, or some honor or prestige. Righteousness is not among these goals.

Human beings are made in the image of God, they have a conscience that can disturb them when acting immorally. [7] Society is not created in the image of God. Its goal is to preserve itself and protect self-defined values. There is no conscience in the society guiding it except for the possibility that a leader has a conscience and is willing and able to exercise it. If those

---

7 In *Moral Man and Immoral Society*, "The central thesis was, and is, that the liberal movement, both religious and secular, seem to be unconscious of the basic difference between the morality of individuals and the morality of collectives, whether races, classes, or nations. This difference ought not to make for a moral cynicism, that is, the belief that the collective must simply follow its own interests. But if the difference is real, as I think it is, it refutes many still prevalent moralistic approaches to the political order" (Reinhold Niebuhr, page ix).

governing the society are moved by conscience, they might have some influence over the direction that their society takes.

PERSPECTIVE ON RIGHTEOUSNESS BY THE LAW: REVIEWING THE STEPS TOWARD THE PASSION

With the disciples, we have taken steps toward Jesus' Passion, steps that put us on the threshold of Jerusalem and the final week of Jesus' life. Jesus will suffer, die, and then, he tells us, rise again. As we move on to the final week, we will take additional steps. Before then, let us review where Mark has brought us.

Mark began with Jesus announcing the coming kingdom, calling for repentance and faith, and then gathering his disciples, the witnesses who will become fishers of men. The first miracle they witness is the healing of a demon-possessed man in Capernaum. They watch in awe with the crowds who are amazed (Mark 1:27). They observe the crowds looking for every opportunity to be near Jesus (Mark 1:37 and 45). The crowds express wonder even when they are not in the center of the story. If they are present when the focus is on religious leaders or on the disciples (Mark 2:12), they are always in awe. Initially we read Jesus has compassion on them.

Wherever Jesus goes, the crowds seem to follow. They gather in Gentile territory (Mark 5:20) and in Jewish territory (Mark 5:21) expressing their amazement, listening to Jesus' teaching and looking for what he will do next.

We notice their role begins to change with the story of Legion as the crowd asked Jesus to leave. It continues to change with the story of Jairus as the crowd mocks Jesus when he says the daughter is not dead.

The overwhelming response to Jesus is amazement. After the feeding of the five thousand, when Jesus dismisses them, they affirm, "[Jesus] has done everything well" (Mark 7:37). There is little more for them to do positively other than worship the Lord with loud praises. Their ability to inform the reader on how to react has reached its limit. Consequently, Jesus sends them away after feeding the five thousand.

When next we see them, the crowds have a new role. On Palm Sunday as they welcome Jesus into the city of Jerusalem, they unintentionally intimidate the religious leaders thus protecting Jesus against an arrest.

The religious leaders in the Gospel are the guardians of the faith. At first, they exercise their responsibility by correctly reminding us that ultimately God alone forgives sin. They also know anyone usurping the prerogatives of God commits a blasphemy. Jesus confounds them when he pronounces forgiveness of sin. They are unable to decide which is easier: forgiving sin or telling a lame person to walk. Their legitimate concern grows to nitpicking until they conclude Jesus deserves to be condemned.

Jesus adjusts his approach toward the religious leaders. This is more interesting than their response to him. At first, Jesus gives them opportunity to react with faith, but soon after is angered at their insensitivity to human need (Mark 3:5). Later, Jesus chastises them for elevating tradition above the word of God (Mark 7:9). After Jesus multiplies enough food to feed four thousand people, the Pharisees ask for a sign from Heaven. Jesus rightfully refuses to engage them (Mark 8:12). He writes them off and warns his disciples about them (Mark 8:15). Still, Jesus is not done with them. He meets with them one more time during his final week.

Mark does not develop the character of the demons. There is no "character" to develop with the spirits that merely destroy. They know who Jesus is and they are willing to acknowledge Jesus publicly. Jesus silences them. Their role comes to an end when Jesus begins his teaching concerning his own death (Mark 9:14–32). They do not figure overtly in the story again.

What have we learned from the narratives? We have learned that having faith is important even if the faith is small (Mark 9:24). To confess there is some unbelief at the same time as believing is not unusual. Mark tells the story of a father whose boy is possessed by a "dumb" spirit in order to teach this point. Mark also uses Peter to make the same point though Peter was not aware just how "dumb" his interpretation of the Christ was. When we believe, we should not be discouraged if our belief is accompanied by some unbelief.

We learn the importance of prayer (Mark 9:29). The disciples who had previously been successful in driving out demons and in healing people suddenly fail. The implication from Jesus' comment that only prayer (and fasting) can bring about some healing is a reminder that every healing is from the Lord. Healing is not from the one praying. Prayer involves praising God and humbly making our requests known. The power to heal is not ours. God is not our servant according to our own wishes.

The first time Jesus repeats his teaching concerning his death, we learn the importance of servant leadership and we are comforted when Jesus promises to demonstrate that leadership. It is one of the profound mysteries of life. Those who seek their own life lose it, while those who work on behalf of others find a fulfilling life.

We learn that righteousness does not come by following the law (Mark 10:32–34). We learn there is in human nature a hardness of heart in everyone. It is sometimes easy to see it in others as, for example, when watching someone pass by another in need and does nothing to help. It is harder to see it in someone as righteous as the young rich ruler. It is somewhat comical to see it in the disciples who hear a teaching on treating children as though they were treating Jesus and then turn around and rebuke parents for bringing their children to Jesus. These narratives all illustrate the truth that by human effort salvation is not possible.

We are encouraged not to despair over human weakness and over hardness of heart for with God all things are possible. God is patient and long-suffering with us just as he is with Peter, James, and John. Jesus is the "Son of Man," the Savior of the world, of all creation, and his dominion has no end. He does not come to condemn, but to redeem. Jesus explains, "For even the Son of Man did not come to be served, but to serve, and to give his life as a ransom for many" (10:45).

The disciples have a special role to play. Called to be fishers of men at the very beginning of the story (Mark 1:16–18), they are present with Jesus as he heals people and they receive privileged instruction. As their knowledge increases, Jesus invests them with authority to do the works he does (Mark 6:7); they are not always successful (Mark 9:28). They observe many details about Jesus but are unable to put it all together. On one occasion, Jesus marvels at them, "Do you still not understand?" (Mark 8:21). On another occasion, Jesus takes one of them to task (Mark 8:33) even though that one person identified Jesus as the Christ. Their inability to pick up on Jesus' predictions about suffering, death and rising again are noteworthy (Mark 9:31f). The disciples are portrayed as stuck in their own desire for power and honor, a hardness of heart that will need to change (Mark 9:33f and 10:35f). Their story is fascinating and an encouragement to anyone having similar difficulty believing the way to a "flourishing life" is through the death of the One greater than John the Baptist.

Jesus is patient with the disciples. He establishes a good rapport with them before telling of his impending death. Jesus has nurtured them carefully, often repeating his lessons for clarity and emphasis. In particular, he is determined for them to accept his statements about his dying. Mark makes this purpose clear by various strategies, notably, by repetition. Like someone who would place stepping stones leading up to the front door of the house, Mark places three announcements leading to the dreaded conclusion, Jesus is dead, crucified. The way of suffering, the *via dolorosa*, is Jesus' path to his ultimate destiny.

Why must he die? There is a partial answer to this question in what we have read so far. In the wilderness, we find physical and mental illness and death. We also find sufficient hostility for some people to plan carefully how they can kill others. The demons entering the pigs and drowning them illustrate what people in this world do to each other. Religious and political people alike can be just as deadly in their treatment of others as are the demons.

One of the reasons Jesus must die is that he has entered the world in which this evil hostility reigns. It is the kingdom where the Herods of this world decapitate righteous individuals and where the Neros crucify Christian believers. It is not in the nature of this world to promote love and peace, however much these words are used. Its true motives are selfish even under the best of circumstances and they include evil thoughts, fornication, theft, murder, adultery, coveting, wickedness, deceit, licentiousness, envy, slander, pride, and foolishness. Jesus has no chance in this world. Or does he?

As the final week of Jesus' life begins, we know the disciples still do not see clearly who Jesus is or why he must die. Blind Bartimaeus appears to see it as he prays, "Jesus, Son of David, have mercy on me" (Mark 10:47). As Saint Anselm pointed out years ago in "Cur Deus Homo,"[8] what we need is something we cannot provide for ourselves. The disciples' lack of self-awareness prevents them from deeper insight into the Son of Man and his impending death.

---

8 "The work is in two sections (books). In the second, Anselm shows 'by plain reasoning and fact that human nature was ordained for this purpose, viz., that every man should enjoy a happy immortality, both in body and in soul; and that it was necessary that this design for which man was made should be fulfilled; but that it could not be fulfilled unless God became man, and unless all things were to take place which we hold in regard to Christ." From "Cur Deus Homo" in *St. Anselm: Basic Writings,* trans. S. N. Deane, 177–178.

Triumphal Entry (11:1–11)

THE BEGINNING OF PASSION WEEK

Every expectation is that Jesus will enter Jerusalem triumphantly. Imagine Jesus riding into the city, leading his troops to vanquish his enemies. He sits majestically on a warhorse, facing the gates from the eastern slope of the Mount of Olives. Beside him and on either side are soldiers ready for battle. Welcoming them, the people of the city gaze upon the horizon with the early morning sun glistening off the armored battalion.

This is the expectation from a worldly perspective. God's expectation is different. The kingdom of God meets his expectation.

In truth, Jesus is surrounded only by his disciples and a handful of followers—fishermen, not soldiers. It is a small crowd; he is riding a colt, not a warhorse; he comes in peace weeping over the city that did not recognize the peace prepared for it.

It is true that he comes over the Mount of Olives from the east. It is also true that Jesus enters the city of Jerusalem to the triumphant cheers of the crowd shouting, "Hosanna!" (Psalm 118:25) and "Blessed is he who comes in the name of the Lord" (Psalm 118:26). Jesus, however, is about to transform all expectations for the Messiah.

The cheers are quotations from the Scriptures for the Jewish celebration of the Passover. The celebration begins on the fourteenth day of Nisan in the Jewish calendar, which is less than a week away. "Hosanna" is a cry for salvation, a cry for liberation, a cry of hope and a cry of celebration. It means "Save!" Though this time it might mean more—perhaps a desperate cry from a whole community emphatically meaning "Save us now!" The miracle worker from Galilee comes raising the hopes of the people, hopes that may well have included a political aspect for freedom from Roman occupation. In some respect, Jesus is the warrior, just not the kind that depends upon an army.

For many years at Wheaton I taught a course entitled "Christ and Culture" which was developed based on the work of H. Richard Niebuhr. This course has been seminal to my ministry in teaching, administration, and the pastorate. Among the lessons in this course is a discussion on three types of power referenced throughout Scripture: creative, coercive, and submissive.

Creative power refers to a power reserved primarily for God, insomuch as only God is able to create ex nihilo, "out of nothing." There is a sense in which we, as human beings, can create new things out of what already is. After all, we are created in the image of God.

Coercive power may be understood best as "brute force." We often expect that God will just make it happen. Perhaps that was the expectation of many for how the Messiah would overthrow the oppressors. Throughout the Old Testament, this power is expressed as the "right hand of God." This power necessarily is enforced upon someone else—there is no freedom of the one who is coerced.

Submissive power is different—and stronger. This is characteristic of the kingdom of God. Submission refers to how we are to approach God. Jesus demonstrates this power by submitting to God's will. It involves an active, freely chosen obedience. This power has an absorptive quality. The Apostle Paul references this quality with his description of the armor of God, "In addition to all of this, take up the shield of faith, with which you can [absorb] all the flaming arrows of the evil one" (Ephesians 6:16).

When faced with challenging situations, we often look to how we can either (creatively) change or escape the situation or (coercively) overcome the situation. My encouragement to every one of us, is to (submissively) look first to God's will in the situation; then, trust and obey.

Consider how other verses from Psalm 118 might have been seen in support of their hopes. Their cry looks to the Lord God who has "become my salvation" (Psalm 118:5, 14 and 21). The psalmist enjoins the faithful: "With boughs in hand, join in the festal procession" (Psalm 118:27). These boughs are seen as the palm branches mentioned by John (John 12:13). Some in the entourage may have thought perhaps this is the day the Lord sets his people free from the Roman occupation.

It is near the time to remember the Passover, the day the angel of death passed over the homes in Egypt which had blood from a recently sacrificed lamb put on the doorposts and the lintel. The significance of the Passover lends ominous weight to Jesus' impending death and his blood on the cross.

However, note that the precise chronology of the events in Passion week is open to some debate based on the variations in the four Gospels. [9] In spite of the variations, the Christian Church begins the story of Jesus' Passion with Palm Sunday.

For Mark, the Triumphal Entry on Palm Sunday is followed by the cursing of a fig tree and a "cleansing" of the temple on Monday (Mark 11:12–19). On Tuesday morning, (Mark 11:20f) the disciples notice the fig tree is dead. After a brief interaction with his disciples, Jesus enters into discussions with the chief priests, and the scribes and the elders.

Mark uses these discussions to expand on the reasons why he who comes uniquely in the name of the Lord will die. Salvation

---

9 See William Lane's *The Gospel according to Mark* for a rich discussion on the variations of the chronology of Passion week.

involves more than a personal response to the question of who can be saved, much more. Social structures are also at stake. It is indeed only with God that all things are possible, and his sacrificial death is a part of his plan for salvation.

DAY ONE: PALM SUNDAY: THE TRIUMPHAL ARRIVAL IN JERUSALEM

***11** As they approached Jerusalem and came to Bethphage*
and Bethanyat the Mount of Olives, Jesus sent two of his
disciples, [2] saying to them, "Go to the village ahead of you,
and just as you enter it, you will find a colt tied there,
which no one has ever ridden. Untie it and bring it here.[3]
If anyone asks you, 'Why are you doing this?' say, 'The
Lord needs it and will send it back here shortly.'"

[4] They went and found a colt outside in the street, tied at
a doorway. As they untied it, [5] some people standing there
asked, "What are you doing, untying that colt?" [6] They
answered as Jesus had told them to, and the people let
them go. [7] When they brought the colt to Jesus and threw
their cloaks over it, he sat on it. [8] Many people spread their
cloaks on the road, while others spread branches they had
cut in the fields. [9] Those who went ahead and those who
followed shouted,

"Hosanna!"

"Blessed is he who comes in the name of the Lord!"

[10] "Blessed is the coming kingdom of our father David!"

"Hosanna in the highest heaven!"

[11] Jesus entered Jerusalem and went into the temple courts. He looked around at everything, but since it was already late, he went out to Bethany with the Twelve.

Palm Sunday is a spectacular day. Notice how sparingly Mark records the events of that day. The enthusiasm of the crowd is matched only by their expectation that the prophetic voice of the psalmist (Psalm 118) is, in all likelihood, being fulfilled before their very eyes. Mark does not tell us how the crowds came to expect Jesus to be entering Jerusalem on this very day. He does make it eminently clear that the crowds connect his entry into Jerusalem with the prophecy.

The familiarity of Psalm 118 and the popularity of Jesus result in a great procession down the Mount of Olives, across the Kidron Valley and right up to the temple in Jerusalem. The city opens for the king who enters it riding on a colt, fulfilling the vision of the Prophet Zechariah.

Rejoice greatly, O Daughter of Zion!
Shout Daughter of Jerusalem!
See, your king comes to you, righteous
and having salvation,
gentle and riding on a donkey, on a
colt, the foal of a donkey.
—Zechariah 9:9

Mark makes no mention of this prophecy. Instead he is content to report only the psalmist suggesting the kingdom of David is about to be restored. When the hour grows late, Mark tells us Jesus looks around, implying Jesus knows what he will do next. The stage is set. We are in Jerusalem at the start of Passover week.

Social Ethics (11:12–12:44)

Religious Corruption (11:12–33)

DAY TWO: MONDAY: THE SYMBOL OF THE FIG TREE

Monday begins with a curious reference to a fig tree that seems a little out of place following the powerful story from the temple.

[12] The next day as they were leaving Bethany, Jesus was hungry.[13] Seeing in the distance a fig tree in leaf, he went to find out if it had any fruit. When he reached it, he found nothing but leaves, because it was not the season for figs. [14] Then he said to the tree, "May no one ever eat fruit from you again." And his disciples heard him say it.

[15] On reaching Jerusalem, Jesus entered the temple courts and began driving out those who were buying and selling there. He overturned the tables of the money changers and the benches of those selling doves,[16] and would not allow anyone to carry merchandise through the temple courts. [17] And as he taught them, he said, "Is it not written: 'My house will be called a house of prayer for all nations'? But you have made it 'a den of robbers.'"

[18] The chief priests and the teachers of the law heard this and began looking for a way to kill him, for they feared him, because the whole crowd was amazed at his teaching.

[19] When evening came, Jesus and his disciples went out of the city.

THE HOUSE OF PRAYER FOR ALL NATIONS

One of the most challenging aspects of faithful living is the simple concept of trust. All too often we try to take certain things into our own hands—especially financially. Even within the Church, we have a habit of focusing concern on the money to pay for things. It is true that some funds are necessary. Yet, we tend to look for ways to profit from those things, too. By doing so, we miss the point of trusting God.

Jesus comes into the temple. He knows its purpose. When Solomon dedicated the temple to the Lord, he consecrated the house of the Lord as a place of refuge and solace for Israel and, also, a house of prayer for people of all nations (II Chronicles 6:12–42; Isaiah 56:7; and Jeremiah 7:11). It is not to be a marketplace for business ventures. The house of God stands for grace, not sales; mercy, not extortion; generosity, not barter and profit (see also: I Timothy 3:1–5).

Some may defend the selling of animals for sacrifice by the temple priests. They were in financial competition with those who sold animals for this purpose just across the valley on the Mount of Olives. However, that defense does not justify their action. Jesus is making at least two points. The first is that the temple is reserved for worshipping God. The second is more subtle: the section of the temple mount being used for the purpose of selling animals is an area dedicated for the purpose of Gentiles gathering for prayer. By inserting a place to conduct business, the priests have displaced people God has called.

Therefore, Monday is a day of housecleaning and judgment

so that people approaching the house of God with humility may find peace with God. Jesus calls for spiritual purity and religious integrity by removing obstacles that might be a detraction. His action is a warning to those who are selling merchandise to change their ways. The religious authorities who are to serve the people are commissioned to encourage prayer and devotion. More importantly, Jesus is restoring the temple as a place dedicated to worship and placing trust in God.

DAY THREE: TUESDAY: A LESSON ON PRAYER FROM THE FIG TREE

With the removal of the moneychangers and the animals from the temple area, the temple can once again be reserved for its singular purpose. It is a place for prayer where petitioners can seek the mercy and grace of a loving God.

Holy week should be a time for prayer and for many it is. On this particular day, it is an opportunity for Jesus to expose the religious authorities who fail to seek repentance themselves. By their example, they fail to lead the people in repentance. It is a day to confront spiritual poverty in high places.

> 20 *In the morning, as they went along, they saw the fig tree*
> *withered from the roots.* 21 *Peter remembered and said to*
> *Jesus, "Rabbi, look! The fig tree you cursed has withered!"*
>
> 22 *"Have faith in God," Jesus answered.* 23 *"Truly I tell you,*
> *if anyone says to this mountain, 'Go, throw yourself into*
> *the sea,' and does not doubt in their heart but believes that*
> *what they say will happen, it will be done for them.* 24
> *Therefore I tell you, whatever you ask for in prayer, believe*
> *that you have received it, and it will be yours.* 25 *And when*
> *you stand praying, if you hold anything against anyone,*

forgive them, so that your Father in heaven may forgive you your sins."[26]

As Jesus and his disciples walk into the city on Tuesday, Peter observes, "Rabbi, look! The fig tree you cursed has withered," implying the damning of the tree was not a random act of Jesus. It is more likely a parable in action. What does it mean?

The symbolism is extensive. The fig tree represents the grace of God in providing the law that was delivered by Moses. In years past, God spoke to Moses from a burning bush saying, "I have indeed seen the misery of my people in Egypt. I have heard them crying out because of their slave drivers, and I am concerned about their suffering. I have come down to rescue them ... and to bring them ... into a land flowing with milk and honey ... So now, go. I am sending you to bring my people the Israelites out of Egypt" (Exodus 3:7, 8, 10).

Moses faced obstacle after obstacle as he went to Pharaoh with the demand to set the Israelites free. Not least of the obstacles was Pharaoh, whose heart was hardened. Moses had support, too. For it was God, whose heart was softened when he heard his people cry, who commanded Moses to confront Pharaoh.

In the end, it was a reversal of Pharaoh's decree that set the Israelites free. Pharaoh had ordered that every boy born to a Hebrew woman be thrown into the Nile (Exodus 1:22). God decreed that he would strike down every firstborn—both men and animals—unless blood from a year-old sheep or goat was put on the sides and tops of the doorframes of the houses in which a special meal was eaten. The tragedy would pass over the house covered with the blood of the lamb. The Passover was to become an annual festival celebrating freedom and the start of a new life.

The justice of God made the exodus possible. Pharaoh was not able to place any obstacle in Moses' way, not armies, not natural borders, not a desert in the Sinai. The integrity of God honors the promises made to the patriarchs Abraham, Isaac, and Jacob. The love of God for his people sets them free. Moses will receive commandments to govern the life of the Hebrews as they become a new nation. These commandments would be the sweet laws of freedom and not the bitter reality of slavery. Among the commands there would even be instructions on sacrifices for sins.

In the land of promise, milk and honey would represent the lives of the shepherd and the farmer. The farmer would harvest orchards and grape vines while the shepherd tended sheep and goats. In this light, "honey" in the promise of the land is a promise of sweet fruit such as the fig and the honeycomb. In religious terms it promises the comfort of God for the people who obey his commands. The law of the Lord is sweeter than the honeycomb (Psalm 19).

The condemning of the fig tree suggests that the "sweet" law is about to be replaced. The land of milk and honey is being surpassed by something greater and better. The once revered fig tree is not the tree planted by streams of living water bearing fruit in season, although it foreshadows one that will. The fig does not have the necessary nutritional value of a sacrifice once and for all time, although it provides temporary benefit (Hebrews 10:1–10). The business of the temple will be replaced (Hebrews 8:13–9:10) and a new tree planted. It will come from a seed that will enter the earth and die. In time the law will be seen by Jesus' Apostles in an altogether new light. Instead of an aid to righteousness, it will be seen as the law of sin and death (Romans 3:19–26; 8:1–4).

Day three is a call to faith and prayer. It presupposes there is a captivity greater than that experienced in Egypt. Because God heard and answered prayer then, and because nothing is impossible for God, true believers should reach out again to God.

Many will assume the new "Egypt" is the Roman Empire. Prayer to God will rid the nation of Roman occupation and influence. However, the damning of the fig tree suggests Rome is not the real enemy. Something other than Rome, something much more powerful than Rome is the enemy. Something human beings cannot overcome. God can. Prayer is the best way to defeat it.

If the disciples were observant, they would remember how Jesus prayed often (Mark 1:35; 6:41; 8:6). Most recently, they observed him praying for the healing of a boy with an evil spirit (Mark 9:20). There is unlimited power and authority in God. The power is not magical. It is not found simply in the prayer. Rather, it is found in the one to whom we pray. Prayer is a portal, a door for the penitent to open. It opens the opportunity for the suppliant, the one praying, to join in the work of bringing in the kingdom of God.

Jesus connects prayer with the need of forgiveness. He does so by first stating that the disciples should bring their concerns to God in prayer. As they pray, they ought to have confidence that God is already responding favorably to their prayer. Then he adds that they who are praying need to forgive anyone who has wronged them so that God may be able to forgive them. Prayer does not serve envy or greed; rather, it serves the needs of the penitent sinner.

OPPOSITION FROM RELIGIOUS LEADERS

The Pharisees and the teachers of the law have not been able to accept Jesus at face value. They suspect Jesus will be doing something detrimental to their interests. They have been attempting to kill him and would prefer a justification for their actions witnessed by the people. They claim they want to know what authority lies behind Jesus' teaching and his miraculous wonders. Unfortunately, they are not after a truthful answer at all. Rather, they are trying to trap Jesus so they can arrest him and turn the people against him. Their bias, their hardness of heart, keeps them from hearing the truth so that when they question Jesus, their questions lack integrity. They are no more successful than the withered fig tree in the parable. They do not bear fruit. In time, the disciples who remember the fig tree was cursed will make this connection.

THE RELIGIOUS LEADERS QUESTION JESUS' AUTHORITY

> [27] *They arrived again in Jerusalem, and while Jesus was walking in the temple courts, the chief priests, the teachers of the law and the elders came to him.* [28] *"By what authority are you doing these things?" they asked. "And who gave you authority to do this?"*
>
> [29] *Jesus replied, "I will ask you one question. Answer me, and I will tell you by what authority I am doing these things.* [30] *John's baptism—was it from heaven, or of human origin? Tell me!"*
>
> [31] *They discussed it among themselves and said, "If we say, 'From heaven,' he will ask, 'Then why didn't you believe him?'* [32] *But if we say, 'Of human origin' ..." (They feared the people, for everyone held that John really was a prophet.)*
>
> [33] *So they answered Jesus, "We don't know."*
>
> *Jesus said, "Neither will I tell you by what authority I am doing these things."*

It has been a long while since Mark spoke of John the Baptist. The primary reason for not speaking of him was his work was finished. If John is no longer available to call people to repentance, then the one John said was more powerful would be preaching instead. The religious leaders had opportunity to listen to John: repent. Had they done so, perhaps they would have been calling for repentance. Instead, they rejected John, and now reject Jesus, in order to maintain their power and prestige. Jesus, who knows of their duplicity, uses their rejection of John to expose them. He calls out the chief priests, the teachers of the law and the elders on their lack of integrity.

As readers of this Gospel, we know that the rulers had taken counsel together with the Herodians on how they might kill Jesus. For this reason, they could not very well betray their allegiance to the Herodians. Remember, it was Herod himself who had ordered the execution of John the Baptist. Jesus also knew they were afraid to answer the question for fear of the crowd. With one question, Jesus neutralizes their attack on him with their own duplicity: "What was John's authority in calling for repentance?"

The religious leaders do not answer Jesus. Neither does Jesus answer their question. Lest they miss the point, Jesus confronts them with a parable. In the parable, he quotes from the very same Psalm that prompts the people to sing "Hosanna." He says, "The stone the builders rejected has become the capstone" (Psalm 118:22, 23).

This begins a series of four questions, reminiscent of the *Mah Nishtanah.* [10] Mark cleverly ties in Jesus' interactions with three separate religious groups (Pharisees, Sadducees, and Scribes) acting as children during the Seder.

The four questions asked by children during the Seder focus on the primary question: How is this night different? For our purposes, the questions themselves are less important than the subject matter they introduce. The children are asking questions that deal with slavery and freedom. The answers to each question are a reminder of both the slavery endured by the Hebrews in Egypt and the freedom God brought about through Moses.

---

10 *Mah Nishtanah* are the first two Hebrew words in the phrase "Why is tonight different from all other nights?" and all of the four questions typically asked by the youngest child attending a Passover Seder.

Judaism is an historical religion. Events in its history have opened the door to a theological understanding of themselves in relationship to a sovereign being. Their freedom from captivity in Egypt is one of the most important of those events. It will need to be told from one generation to the next.

The Seder at Passover is one way to tell the story and to impress the message of God's leading upon the next generation. In the telling of the story, there is a clear understanding that four types of children are listening: wise, wicked, simple, and quiet.

- The wise child eagerly asks about the significance of Passover and is rewarded with a full explanation.
- The wicked child scoffs at the story—having failed to experience the hardship of slavery, this child seems to have no sense of the value (or cost) of freedom.
- The simple child asks a simple question. Like the wise child, the simple child is rewarded with an answer, although a simple one, that s/he can understand.
- The quiet child asks nothing and is there to observe and hear the story being told.

Four Questions (12:1–44)

JESUS RESPONDS TO THE RELIGIOUS LEADERS WITH A PARABLE

***12** Jesus then began to speak to them in parables: "A man*
planted a vineyard. He put a wall around it, dug a pit for
the winepress and built a watchtower. Then he rented the
vineyard to some farmers and moved to another place. 2
At harvest time he sent a servant to the tenants to collect
from them some of the fruit of the vineyard. 3 *But they*
seized him, beat him and sent him away empty-handed.
4 *Then he sent another servant to them; they struck this*
man on the head and treated him shamefully. 5 *He sent*
still another, and that one they killed. He sent many
others; some of them they beat, others they killed.

6 *"He had one left to send, a son, whom he loved. He sent*
him last of all, saying, 'They will respect my son.'

7 *"But the tenants said to one another, 'This is the heir.*
Come, let's kill him, and the inheritance will be ours.' 8
So they took him and killed him, and threw him out of
the vineyard.

9 *"What then will the owner of the vineyard do? He will*
come and kill those tenants and give the vineyard to
others. 10 *Haven't you read this passage of Scripture:*

"'The stone the builders rejected has become the cornerstone;[11] the Lord has done this, and it is marvelous in our eyes'?"

[12] Then the chief priests, the teachers of the law and the elders looked for a way to arrest him because they knew he had spoken the parable against them. But they were afraid of the crowd; so, they left him and went away.

The religious leaders understood themselves as the builders and the protectors of the temple. Jesus insists they were only the custodians. He chastises them for failing to care for the vineyard of the Lord. The most recent Prophet, John the Baptist, had been killed with tacit approval from these religious leaders. Jesus, who is the remaining prophetic voice, is next. Jesus knows it; yet, without any fear, he confronts the antagonists.

One frustrating aspect, especially concerning the chief priests, teachers of the law, and elders, is that they are the ones responsible for the spiritual health of the community. Yet, they are not even able to keep themselves spiritually pure and healthy. Worse, they seem to be willfully blind to their own selfish ambition. This causes them to react to Jesus with defensive anger, seeking to kill him because he dared to call out their pride. Personally, I consider this a constant check in my own ministry.

Slavery exists in many forms.

There is an historic slavery. For the Jews, this is the experience in Egypt. During Holy Week, this slavery is foremost in the minds of those coming to celebrate the Passover.

There is also a slavery for the people living in Jerusalem under Roman rule. Some of the crowds celebrating the Triumphal Entry may very well have been looking to Jesus to overthrow Roman oppression.

There is a slavery that Jews have to their own traditions—much like we all do. Being part of any group, there are rules, expectations, and traditions by which we must abide. The religious traditions often miss the original intent as they are reduced to the tradition without the teaching. Think of how Christmas has become about the gifts rather than the birth of Christ. In much the same fashion, Passover has become less of an historic event during which God freed his people. Rather, it is something that is done because it is tradition.

Jesus has come to bring the *good news* of freedom from yet another slavery. Mark has not yet fully explained it—although he continues to call for repentance. Perhaps that is another reason Mark reminds us of John the Baptist at this point in the Gospel. This new freedom has something to do with the coming of the kingdom of God.

SETTING TRAPS FOR JESUS

Jesus' message was transparent. The chief priests and other religious leaders knew he was talking about them in the parable. They despised him and increased their resolve to kill him.

To capture Jesus and to kill him will be a challenge. Jesus temporarily has the protection of the supportive crowd intimidating the rulers. In time, the religious leaders will succeed in killing him, but first they need to capture him. What kind of traps will the authorities build to capture Jesus?

Notice that Mark cleverly uses situations that remind us of slavery and freedom in a manner like the questions of the Seder. The first trap recalls the hard slavery of Egypt and the heavy taxation of Rome.

TRAP NUMBER ONE: TAXES

> [13] *Later they sent some of the Pharisees and Herodians to Jesus to catch him in his words.* [14] *They came to him and said, "Teacher, we know that you are a man of integrity. You aren't swayed by others, because you pay no attention*

to who they are; but you teach the way of God in accordance with the truth. Is it right to pay the imperial tax to Caesar or not? [15] *Should we pay or shouldn't we?"*

But Jesus knew their hypocrisy. "Why are you trying to trap me?" he asked. "Bring me a denarius and let me look at it." [16] *They brought the coin, and he asked them, "Whose image is this? And whose inscription?"*

"Caesar's," they replied.

[17] *Then Jesus said to them, "Give back to Caesar what is Caesar's and to God what is God's."*

And they were amazed at him.

The alliance of Pharisees with Herodians continues. They are confident that the question they frame is sure to drive a wedge between Jesus and the protective crowd. They know taxation is seldom applauded by people when the tax benefits a foreign occupying power. Further, they have their own tax. The Pharisees will have their say about the tithe due to God. The Herodians, with whom they are engaged, have sided with the Romans and they will have their say also. So, which is it, God or Caesar?

The rulers are driven by hostility. It is not integrity that motivates them to interrogate Jesus. Hoping to trap Jesus, they intend to turn the crowd against him. They pick taxes as their first entrapment.

Jesus' answer is both political and religious. Politically, the coin belongs to Caesar, and hence the citizens of Jerusalem must pay their taxes to the Romans. Religiously, however, all human beings, including Caesar, are created in the image of God. Hence, both Caesar and his tax belong to God.

They are amazed! Their trap so cleverly devised had an answer. A good one! (see Romans 13:1–7). Note the trap backfired because those who were trapped were the religious and political leaders, the Pharisees and Herodians. In this sense, they remain slaves to their own ambition.

TRAP NUMBER TWO: MARRIAGES

The Sadducees, another group claiming religious leadership, also build a trap.

> [18] *Then the Sadducees, who say there is no resurrection, came to him with a question.* [19] *"Teacher," they said, "Moses wrote for us that if a man's brother dies and leaves a wife but no children, the man must marry the widow and raise up offspring for his brother.* [20] *Now there were seven brothers. The first one married and died without leaving any children.* [21] *The second one married the widow, but he also died, leaving no child. It was the same with the third.* [22] *In fact, none of the seven left any children. Last of all, the woman died too.* [23] *At the resurrection whose wife will she be, since the seven were married to her?"*
>
> [24] *Jesus replied, "Are you not in error because you do not know the Scriptures or the power of God?* [25] *When the dead rise, they will neither marry nor be given in marriage; they will be like the angels in heaven.* [26] *Now about the dead rising—have you not read in the Book of Moses, in the account of the burning bush, how God said to him, 'I am the God of Abraham, the God of Isaac, and the God of Jacob'?* [27] *He is not the God of the dead, but of the living. You are badly mistaken!"*

The duplicity continues. Even though the Sadducees do not believe in a resurrection, they ask a question about it. Jesus' answer shows them, ironically, to be in a position of undeserved authority. They do not know the faith they are representing.

There are at least two key issues in this interaction. At face value, the Sadducees attempt to trap Jesus by asking a question about something they expressly do not hold to be true. Their ignorance is a premise of the question they ask. Jesus exposes how little they know about God and life that is eternal. Because of their unbelief, they are clueless about even what has been revealed to them.

There is a second, more subtle theme in Jesus' response. The resurrection is not some future event as we understand time. It is. As God is. For it is this same God who said, "I am who I am." Those who are part of the resurrection are already known (to God), and he is their God, and they are alive. This is indeed *good news* for those who believe. The subtlety of this theme also foreshadows what is to come for Jesus. The resurrection already begins with him.

The Sadducees remain slaves to their lack of faith as evidenced by their unbelief. Like the Pharisees, their question trapped themselves.

TRAP NUMBER THREE: JEWISH LAW

There is one more effort to build a trap. It comes from a scribe and has a slightly different tone to the interaction.

> 28 *One of the teachers of the law came and heard them debating. Noticing that Jesus had given them a good answer, he asked him, "Of all the commandments, which is the most important?"*
>
> 29 *"The most important one," answered Jesus, "is this: 'Hear, O Israel: The Lord our God, the Lord is one* 30 *Love the Lord your God with all your heart and with all your soul and with all your mind and with all your strength.'* 31

The second is this: 'Love your neighbor as yourself.' There is no commandment greater than these."

[32] *"Well said, teacher," the man replied. "You are right in saying that God is one and there is no other but him.* [33] *To love him with all your heart, with all your understanding and with all your strength, and to love your neighbor as yourself is more important than all burnt offerings and sacrifices."*

[34] *When Jesus saw that he had answered wisely, he said to him, "You are not far from the kingdom of God." And from then on no one dared ask him any more questions.*

One often gets the impression that no one in the Jewish establishment had sympathetic feelings of any kind for Jesus. That is not true. Several were devoted to Jesus, and at least three significant religious leaders are mentioned by name: Nicodemus (John's Gospel), Joseph of Arimathea, and Jairus, who are included in Mark. Now there is one other leader who appears open to Jesus' words, a teacher of the law. After what he observed about Jesus' answers to the previously attempted traps, he is not out to trap Jesus.

Several things are interesting in this interchange. To begin, the answer to love God and the neighbor is reminiscent of Jesus' interchange with the rich ruler. Further, the commands underscore the importance of love, not so much as an emotion, more as of character, disposition, and behavior. Further yet, love can be commanded and cultivated. When love becomes a part of character, it flows into all of life. It is what allows Augustine to summarize Christian law as, "Love God and then do as you wish." [11]

---

11 In *The Enchiridion on Faith, Hope, and Love,* Augustine argues that all wisdom comes from God and that true wisdom for man is piety. God is to be worshipped with faith, hope, and love. Be sure you know the true God (the Apostle's Creed), approach God

Those who truly love God will love what God loves and do those things that bring glory to God. They will recognize truth when they hear it and they will speak truth. The teacher of the law acknowledges Jesus' answer as truthful. Jesus commends him, as someone not far from the kingdom of God.

It is noteworthy that no one else asks Jesus a question. His comment to the scribe seems to call for at least one more question: what would it take to be in the kingdom of God?

A QUESTION ON SCRIPTURE: IF DAVID CALLS HIM "LORD," HOW CAN HE BE DAVID'S SON?

The interrogation is over. It is time for Jesus to ask his own question as he challenges the religious establishment. A large crowd listens with delight.

> 35 *While Jesus was teaching in the temple courts, he asked, "Why do the teachers of the law say that the Messiah is the son of David?* 36 *David himself, speaking by the Holy Spirit, declared:*
>
> *"'The Lord said to my Lord: 'Sit at my right hand until I put your enemies under your feet.'"*
>
> 37 *David himself calls him 'Lord.' How then can he be his son?"*
>
> *The large crowd listened to him with delight.*
>
> 38 *As he taught, Jesus said, "Watch out for the teachers of the law. They like to walk around in flowing robes and be greeted with respect in the marketplaces,* 39 *and have the*

---

properly (the Lord's Prayer), and know the proper objects of love (love God and love your neighbor). Love without faith and hope is not true love. True love stems from the love of God that sent Jesus into the world to die for the sins of the world (St. Augustine, page 46).

> *most important seats in the synagogues and the places of honor at banquets. [40] They devour widows' houses and for a show make lengthy prayers. These men will be punished most severely."*

It is one thing to answer the questions of people wishing to trap you and escape the traps. It is another to identify the unjustified self-serving pride and greed of those who lay the traps. Jesus does this by asking a question of Scriptural interpretation that leaves the teachers of the law speechless.

Many of the religious leaders think and act like they are more important than anyone else. They are proud in their own eyes and glory-seeking. Jesus warns those listening not to be fooled by their behavior or by their appearance. It is likely that some of the leaders asking questions of Jesus were wearing long flowing robes. The appearance on the outside is inconsistent with the reality on the inside. Such people cheat widows and orphans (Matthew 7:15 and James 1:27). There are enough of these hypocrites to justify a caution for the crowds and the disciples concerning them.

Mark brilliantly uses Judaic tradition to teach everyone what is different about Jesus. As questions are used in the Seder to teach children the significance of the Passover, Jesus has used the questions from childlike religious leaders to teach about the significance of the Passover that is right before them. God is once again acting in the midst of human history to bring freedom for the slaves.

After the children ask their questions, the host, presumably the father of the children, will ask a question of biblical interpretation which none of the children are able to answer. This last question stresses the humility of human beings in the light of the sovereignty of God. It is a teaching question.

In this case, Jesus turns his attention away from the petulant religious leaders. Looking toward the crowd he asks, how can one who is addressed as "Lord" be the "son of him who speaks?"

Notice, too, that the crowds are again amazed—only now they are also listening intently.

The crowd paying attention to Jesus, as well as the Christians in Rome, would understand Jesus' reference to the Messiah as the promised Son of David. They would be familiar with the prophecy that the Messiah would sit on the throne of David forever.

In the following story, Jesus highlights the hypocrisy of the religious leaders by contrast to a lowly widow. She comes to the temple with her humble offering of only two small copper coins. Jesus knows the heart. He is not fooled by pomp and circumstance or "flowing robes." He knows who is genuine. Jesus observes as the woman gives what little she has. He uses her gift to illustrate for his disciples something else about the kingdom of God. It is a powerful object lesson for the disciples—and for us.

A POOR WOMAN'S EXTRAVAGANT GIFT

> 41 *Jesus sat down opposite the place where the offerings were put and watched the crowd putting their money into the temple treasury. Many rich people threw in large amounts.* 42 *But a poor widow came and put in two very small copper coins, worth only a few cents.*
>
> 43 *Calling his disciples to him, Jesus said, "Truly I tell you; this poor widow has put more into the treasury than all the others.* 44 *They all gave out of their wealth; but she, out of her poverty, put in everything—all she had to live on."*

The story is often referred to as "The Widow's Mite." In so far as Mark reminds us that Jesus called his disciples to witness the offering, Mark wants you, the reader, to learn from it, too.

Notice Jesus is seated as he calls the disciples to him. This should remind us that what he is about to say is important.

Mark contrasts this poor widow with the religious leaders of the previous story. One gets the impression, which is soon to be made explicit, that the religious leaders are not caring for the widows and orphans (see James 1:27).

The religious leaders hardly realize that their livelihood comes in part from the sacrificial giving of people like this widow. Very soon, they will use money that comes from faithful people (like the widow), thirty pieces of silver, to preserve their status in the society by putting a bounty on Jesus' head. It is better to be like the poor widow than any of the false teachers of the law!

There is one more important comparison involving the widow. In the beginning of this Act, Mark recounted the story of a man who asked Jesus what he must do to inherit eternal life. The man had kept the law. Jesus responded by telling him to do one more thing: sell everything you have and follow me. That man went away sad because he had great wealth. Mark has closed the frame on the four questions with a story of a poverty-stricken widow. Who is in possession of that which is most valuable: the man or the widow?

The interrogation section with the hypocritical religious leaders is over. It is clear that political and religious systems offering structures for society are beneficial for stability in communal living. Unfortunately, it is also clear that people responsible for the administration of these structures are often ill-equipped to bring justice and stability to that same society. A new society, a new kingdom, a new social structure of a different order is necessary. This new society will be led by the Son of David whom David calls "Lord." And it is unlike any of the social structures we know.

God's Redemption of the Created Order

(13:1–37)

Before the day itself ends, Jesus offers his disciples one more insight explaining why salvation is not possible for human beings.

13 As Jesus was leaving the temple, one of his disciples said to him, "Look, Teacher! What massive stones! What magnificent buildings!"

2 "Do you see all these great buildings?" replied Jesus. "Not one stone here will be left on another; every one will be thrown down."

3 As Jesus was sitting on the Mount of Olives opposite the
temple, Peter, James, John and Andrew asked him pri-
vately, 4 "Tell us, when will these things happen? And what
will be the sign that they are all about to be fulfilled?"

5 Jesus said to them: "Watch out that no one deceives you.
6 Many will come in my name, claiming, 'I am he,' and
will deceive many. 7 When you hear of wars and rumors
of wars, do not be alarmed. Such things must happen, but
the end is still to come. 8 Nation will rise against nation,
and kingdom against kingdom. There will be earthquakes
in various places, and famines. These are the beginning of
birth pains.

9 *"You must be on your guard. You will be handed over*
to the local councils and flogged in the synagogues. On
account of me you will stand before governors and kings as
witnesses to them. 10 *And the gospel must first be preached*
to all nations. 11 *Whenever you are arrested and brought*
to trial, do not worry beforehand about what to say. Just
say whatever is given you at the time, for it is not you
speaking, but the Holy Spirit.

12 *"Brother will betray brother to death, and a father his*
child. Children will rebel against their parents and have
them put to death. 13 *Everyone will hate you because of*
me, but the one who stands firm to the end will be saved.

14 *"When you see 'the abomination that causes desola-*
tion' standing where it does not belong—let the reader
understand—then let those who are in Judea flee to the
mountains. 15 *Let no one on the housetop go down or enter*
the house to take anything out. 16 *Let no one in the field go*
back to get their cloak. 17 *How dreadful it will be in those*
days for pregnant women and nursing mothers! 18 *Pray*
that this will not take place in winter, 19 *because those*
will be days of distress unequaled from the beginning,
when God created the world, until now—and never to be
equaled again.

20 *"If the Lord had not cut short those days, no one would*
survive. But for the sake of the elect, whom he has chosen,
he has shortened them. 21 *At that time if anyone says to*
you, 'Look, here is the Messiah!' or, 'Look, there he is!'
do not believe it. 22 *For false messiahs and false prophets*
will appear and perform signs and wonders to deceive, if

possible, even the elect. 23 *So be on your guard; I have told*
you everything ahead of time.

24 *"But in those days, following that distress,*

"'the sun will be darkened, and the moon will not give its
light; 25 *the stars will fall from the sky, and the heavenly*
bodies will be shaken.'

26 *"At that time people will see the Son of Man coming in*
clouds with great power and glory. 27 *And he will send his*
angels and gather his elect from the four winds, from the
ends of the earth to the ends of the heavens.

28 *"Now learn this lesson from the fig tree: As soon as its*
twigs get tender and its leaves come out, you know that
summer is near. 29 *Even so, when you see these things hap-*
pening, you know that it is near, right at the door. 30 *Truly*
I tell you; this generation will certainly not pass away
until all these things have happened. 31 *Heaven and earth*
will pass away, but my words will never pass away.

32 *"But about that day or hour no one knows, not even the*
angels in heaven, nor the Son, but only the Father. 33 *Be*
on guard! Be alert! You do not know when that time will
come. 34 *It's like a man going away: He leaves his house*
and puts his servants in charge, each with their assigned
task, and tells the one at the door to keep watch.

35 *"Therefore keep watch because you do not know when*
the owner of the house will come back—whether in the
evening, or at midnight, or when the rooster crows, or
at dawn. 36 *If he comes suddenly, do not let him find you*
sleeping. 37 *What I say to you, I say to everyone: 'Watch!'"*

What has been assumed throughout this essay, namely, that the readers are intentionally engaged by Mark, is no longer in question. Quite pointedly, Mark has Jesus turn from the disciples and clearly say to the readers, "Watch!" But what are we to watch in this last teaching section?

The day ends with a private seminar for the disciples with whom we are now numbered. The early portion of the seminar suggests that Jerusalem is about to be destroyed, "not one stone here will be left on another." The signs predicting the destruction of Jerusalem include reports of false Christ's, wars and rumors of wars, earthquakes, and famines.

These will be difficult personal times. The disciples should expect flogging from the religious community, betrayals of one family member by another, and something called "the abomination that causes desolation."

Make no mistake about this teaching. Just like salvation is not possible based on individual effort such as that of the rich man, so also it does not come about through political and religious governmental channels. Religion and politics belong to the world of darkness.

A new kingdom and a new religious structure will be needed. Peter stresses this new kingdom in his epistle (see especially I Peter 2:9) and Mark acknowledges it in the duplicity of the religious leaders of Jesus' day.

Then, as if trial and suffering on earth were not enough, Jesus speaks of signs in the heavens. The sun, the moon, and the stars are all involved! The teaching of Jesus becomes apocalyptic. For some, this passage is prophetic regarding the last times. However, for reasons stated by Jesus earlier, this is perhaps better understood as a comment on salvation.

With individual human beings, earning salvation is not possible. Similarly, the coordinated effort of human beings in social structures will never be sufficient to provide a secure society. We live in a desolate wilderness.

The amazing aspect of this teaching is that salvation

ultimately depends on a "new creation" which only the Creator of the universe can provide. Literally, with God all things are possible. All creation needs to be included in redemption—there will be a new Heaven and a new earth.

The reign of peace is where lions and lambs cohabit the same space, where children play over the adder's nest without fear, where all tears are dried up and where continuous praise is offered in harmonious song. This is the work of God. Jesus, the seed of that new work, has been implanted into human experience and will certainly die. His death will create new life, a resurrection that is found only in and through him.

There is a theological point that is both important enough to include and challenging enough to separate from the rest of the text. Simply stated, in his death Jesus defeated death itself. The Apostle Paul makes this argument in his first letter to the Church at Corinth (I Corinthians 15):

- The last enemy to be destroyed is death (verse 26).
- The sting of death is sin, and the power of sin is the law. Thanks be to God! He gives us the victory through our Lord Jesus Christ (verses 56–57).

Throughout his ministry, Jesus has been transforming tradition. In his baptism, he transformed the notion of repentance for one's own sin to affirm God's love for all creation in a manner that invites all to be in right relationship with God. Throughout the text, Mark has demonstrated how the kingdom of God is different from our understanding—demons, wind, storms all obey Jesus; the Sabbath is made for man (and not man for the Sabbath). In that same manner, the Christ has come as the Servant to die.

In his death, Jesus is again transforming our understanding. Notice, his ministry was affirmed at both his baptism and the transfiguration. In each case, God identified Jesus and expressed his pleasure with him. In his death, Jesus is inviting all creation to participate in eternal life.

One final point: it is sin, which was not created, that introduced death into the world. Sin requires death as a natural consequence for those who have separated themselves from God. The paradox is that by his death, Jesus who knew no sin, is introducing new life to a sinful world. This is *good news*.

What is the wonder of all this? When God redeems the creation, the amazing lesson is not a single person will be forgotten. There will be grace and truth available for everyone. Again to use Peter's orientation, "Though you have not seen him [Jesus Christ], you love him; and even though you do not see him now, you believe in him and are filled with an inexpressible and glorious joy, for you are receiving the goal of your faith, the salvation of your souls" (I Peter 1:8–9).

Eventually, the Son of Man comes in the clouds, says Jesus, and his faithful are gathered to him. Count on it! Count on a favorable outcome even though you do not know the day or hour when it will happen. Be prepared! Heaven and earth will pass away. The words of Jesus will not. Learn the lesson of the fig tree! Watch for the owner to return.

All of you, watch!

PERSPECTIVE ON "WHY THE SON OF MAN MUST BE KILLED"

What is different about Jesus? Mark has moved us through the first three acts from a point of wonder and amazement toward a true identification of Jesus as the Christ. The question Jesus asks, "Who am I?" is central to the entire Gospel. Also central to the Gospel is his mission that he has come to die. In Act 4, Mark begins to explain the importance of Jesus being the Christ—and it is quite different from any expectation.

As the curtain opens on Act 4 Jesus is once again privately teaching his disciples. He said to them, "The Son of Man is going to be delivered into the hands of men. They will kill him, and after three days he will rise" (Mark 9:31). Although they still do not comprehend that his purpose is to die, Jesus continues to teach them: his death is central to the *good news*.

On this occasion, he uses an argument among the twelve to transform their understanding of God and his kingdom. While they argued over who is the greatest, Jesus teaches them that the first must be last, and servant of all. He brings a child in front of them, taking advantage of the Aramaic language in which *servant* and *child* come from the same root word. And he completes the transformation by identifying himself with the child. Welcome the child, welcome me—and, ultimately, welcome God.

Mark provides subtle yet significant insights into the relationship among Jesus and his disciples. In each situation, Jesus addresses more than just the face value view of what is happening. He consistently uses simple illustrations to reveal God's intentions.

In this manner, Mark tells of the disciples being worried that someone else is doing good in Jesus' name by driving out demons. They think they are doing right by telling the man to stop. They don't understand. Jesus responds by affirming anyone doing good in his name is doing good. And God is glorified.

Jesus returns to the illustration of a child three times in this section, interspersed with teaching about the effects of sin and the compassion of God. On each occasion, he elevates the child and rebukes the adult. The values of the world in which we live are so familiar to us that we are blind to their failures. These values are "created" by human beings. They are both insufficient and inadequate. The kingdom of God is not as we expect—it is as God designed.

Sin has entered God's creation. It has infected every individual human heart. It has entangled every social structure—especially those that are political and religious. It has even affected nature itself. Everything is tainted by sin. The entire universe is a wilderness. Separated from God's love by sin, it is a place where no life can flourish.

In Act 4, Mark walks the reader through the perils of sin. He begins with identifying how pervasive the problem of sin truly is: it hardens every heart. This point is illustrated through several interactions Jesus has with his disciples, religious leaders, and crowds. He begins and ends this series with contrasting stories of individuals.

The rich young man is likely everything to which we aspire: wealthy, presumably handsome, kind, law-obeying, educated, pious, and well-spoken. In his interaction with Jesus, he genuinely appears zealous in his desire to enter the kingdom of God. Jesus responds compassionately yet challenges the young man to sell what he has, give it to the poor, and follow him. The man goes away distraught because he was very wealthy.

The kingdom of God is closed to the worldly interests represented by the rich young man. If our striving is to be like him, our love is focused in the wrong direction.

For a third time, Jesus returns to teaching the disciples about his death. The disciples fight among themselves for recognition and places of honor. They avoid what Jesus is saying; namely, that he has come to die. Jesus responds to them by once again transforming their understanding. They must first learn to serve. And this time, Jesus goes further, by stating that even he has come to serve, and to give his life as a ransom for many.

The disciples have watched Jesus. They know he has come to serve. He has performed many miracles, healed the sick, and cast out demons. They've heard him, now three times, teaching them about his purpose: to die. Yet, there is little evidence that they understand what Jesus is saying—even now, as Mark begins the Passion narrative.

It is important for the reader to understand that Jesus knew his purpose. In this spirit, Mark records Jesus' decisive steps beginning with Palm Sunday. Jesus, the One who comes in the name of the Lord, enters Jerusalem, surveys the situation and then prepares his strategy for the week that follows. This is all his doing, his decision. It is deliberate.

Entering Jerusalem, Jesus shifts the focus away from teaching the disciples and toward fulfilling his purpose. One often wonders who might have been among the crowd shouting, "Hosanna!" during the Triumphal Entry. The practice of making a pilgrimage to Jerusalem at Passover was common, as it is today (see Luke 2:41–46). Therefore, many of the people in the crowd may have traveled great distances to be there.

If Mark teaches anything, it is the enthusiasm the people of Galilee have for their teacher. The crowds believe he does everything well. It is likely that the crowds included people familiar with Jesus' ministry. Perhaps some were present when he fed the five thousand or the four thousand. It is conceivable that even some of those he healed—like the paralytic, Jairus or his daughter, the deaf and dumb man, the woman who touched his robe, or the blind man—were there to welcome Jesus. These would be people who had reason to be expectant.

As with the disciples, Jesus continues to transform the understanding of the crowds, who represent our point of view as the readers, regarding how things are. We expect that the rich young man is the exemplar for who we should be—Jesus identified that he was missing something. Similarly, we expect the Messiah to be a hero warrior that will overthrow oppression. He does, although not as we expect. This gives us insight into the character of God: he fulfills his promises, although in ways that are beyond our understanding.

Social structures existed that were largely unchallenged, especially the religious structures. Jesus does two things to unexpectedly address the sin that withers these structures: he condemns a fig tree, and he overturns the money tables outside the temple.

With this "fig tree" gone, he calls people to trust in God, have faith and pray. Instead of insisting on one's personal rights and complaining about someone else's shortcoming, instead of defending yourself, learn to forgive because forgiveness is what you truly need if you wish to deal with your own hardness of heart.

Hence, Jesus encourages the disciples to move beyond consideration of themselves as individuals. He calls them to reflect on God's concerns for the structures and laws of society. In the debates with the Pharisees, Sadducees, and the teachers of the law, Jesus affirms the love of God and of one's neighbors. The kingdom of God does not emerge from the tenants of human society, even those that are religious. Rather, there is a need for social structures to be cleansed, much like the purification of the heart, in order to enter the kingdom of God.

The best we can do now is approximate the ideal. Even if it were possible for an individual to be moral, society would still be immoral. [12] The individual has a conscience, whereas society, which has no conscience, merely endeavors to preserve itself. The old way of doing things needs to pass away. A new kingdom is needed to replace the old. Interestingly, the new kingdom is more akin to the "original," archetypal kingdom as intended from before the creation (see comments on 1:1). As Jesus puts it to the religious leaders, King David calls his son, his Lord. How can this be?

Mark makes the point clear with a simple and devastating comparison. Those who walk around in magisterial religious robes sporting ostentatious behavior devour the wealth of widows. God knows, for he sees the heart. True devotion flourishes in the heart of a humble and poor widow who gives all she has, two copper pennies, to the temple treasury. Hardness of heart languishes in the wilderness of self-centeredness.

By highlighting the widow, Jesus is also drawing comparison back to the rich young man, who went away distraught because he had great wealth. The widow, who does not even interact directly with Jesus, is nonetheless joyful in giving all she had. Our social expectations have it all backwards. His wealth will

---

12 See *Moral Man and Immoral Society* (Reinhold Niebuhr).

fade away to nothing, leaving him desolate in the wilderness. Her faithful giving brings life to the congregation. She will be rewarded for her faith. Life flourishes in her wilderness.

A lesson such as this is often a fitting close to a discussion. Mark has more in mind. The disciples open the next subject in their preparation to become fishers of men with a comment on the beauty of the temple. Jesus informs them the stones will be torn down. Once down, the old system will no longer be practiced. In its place will be *good news* that will be proclaimed to all nations regardless of opposition, even fierce opposition. Just as the fig tree has withered and the stones tumbled, Heaven and earth will pass away.

Sin troubles the earth with the distress of earthquakes and famines. All creation groans while awaiting consummation (Romans 8:18–22). No wonder Jesus said salvation was impossible for man! For some, this seems like "It's the end of the world as we know it." Indeed, it is. And "I feel fine" [13] because this is the culmination of God's redemptive plan of salvation. It is a salvation that is open, given freely to all, where penniless widows are often closer to membership than the highest religious or political figures. It is for the whole of creation.

Searching for personal salvation in this light seems myopic and hopelessly selfish. Each of us, I suspect, has moments in which we consider the vastness of the universe and our limited presence in it. Perhaps, we also consider the brevity of life in the context of all history. In these moments, as individuals, we are seemingly insignificant. Peter remembers that the Prophet who spoke of a voice crying in the wilderness. He quotes Isaiah, "All men are like grass and all their glory is like the flowers of the field; the grass withers and the flowers fall, but the word of the Lord stands forever" (I Peter 1:24 with reference to Isaiah 40:6–8).

Now, we go back to the central question: *Who am I?* This

---

13 "It's the End of the World as We Know It" (R.E.M.).

question is beginning to be understood in its duality. It is still the question Jesus asks. Yet, it is also the question we ask of ourselves.

As individuals, we strive to be like the young rich man. In our institutions, we strive for clarity of expectations and fairness in allocations. Sin has affected every aspect of this world. It holds us captive, individually and corporately. We belong to the wilderness.

Jesus began his ministry quite literally in the wilderness as he subjected himself to temptation by the devil. His incarnation, temptation, and ministry have all been focused on his singular purpose: to die and to give his life as a ransom for many.

Jesus' purpose in dying gives us yet another precious new insight into the character of God. Prior to the incarnation, we knew God to be creator, sovereign, powerful, compassionate, and holy. We also knew of God's passionate, righteous anger. He demonstrated his judgment many times: the fall, the flood, Sodom and Gomorrah, Pharaoh, and even against Moses and his entire generation. God's holy nature has no room for compromise.

Mark brilliantly illustrates how God is transforming our sinful nature in order to bring us back to himself. He parallels the four types of children identified during the Seder service. [14] The Seder commemorates the Passover—a time when God's judgment results in the slaughter of Egypt's firstborn and the freedom of the Hebrews. The simile sets up the final act of the Gospel, when Jesus will transform our understanding at the Last Supper (which is a Seder meal)—a time when God's mercy

14 The four types of children identified during the Seder include the wise child, wicked child, innocent child, and child unable to inquire. To each child, the parent has an obligation to respond. For the wise child, the parent acknowledges the work of God toward freedom for his creation. For the wicked child, the parent is firm with a response that God has done this work for those he frees, and not for the wicked. For the other two children, the parent has an obligation to declare the work that God has done on their behalf.

results in the slaughter of God's firstborn and the freedom for all who place their trust in him.

Jesus has come to die. He has revealed God to us in a new way.[15] There is strength in humility. There is wealth in poverty. There is joy in suffering. And there is life in the wilderness. With God, all things are possible: for God, incarnate in the weakness of human flesh and subjected to death on a cross is stronger than all the forces of evil.

God is stronger in submission to death than all the coercive forces of evil. This theme has been a constant message in both my teaching and preaching. Heavily influenced by Luther, I recognize the absurdity this concept presents for those who do not believe. For believers, however, it is the very crux of our faith.

Neil Murray, a colleague from North Park College, once illustrated this concept beautifully through a sculpture known as the *Christus Victor*. The statue stands about 3 feet tall, depicting Jesus on the cross. There is no cross supporting his body. Instead, he is elevated on a pedestal (perhaps as a reference to Moses lifting the serpent in the wilderness).

Those who study the sculpture will note that Jesus' head is not hanging to one side, nor does he appear defeated. Rather, he holds his head lifted up and back, with his hands outstretched like a runner crossing the finish line. Indeed, he has finished the race victorious!

What a wonder, what an incredible wonder! In a work providing redemption and salvation for all creation and for all the nations of all time, there is a spirit of hope for individuals available at any time and anywhere.

---

15 See *How New Is the New Testament?* for a discussion on the transformational shift from preparing for a Messiah to an eschatological reality (Donald A. Hagner).

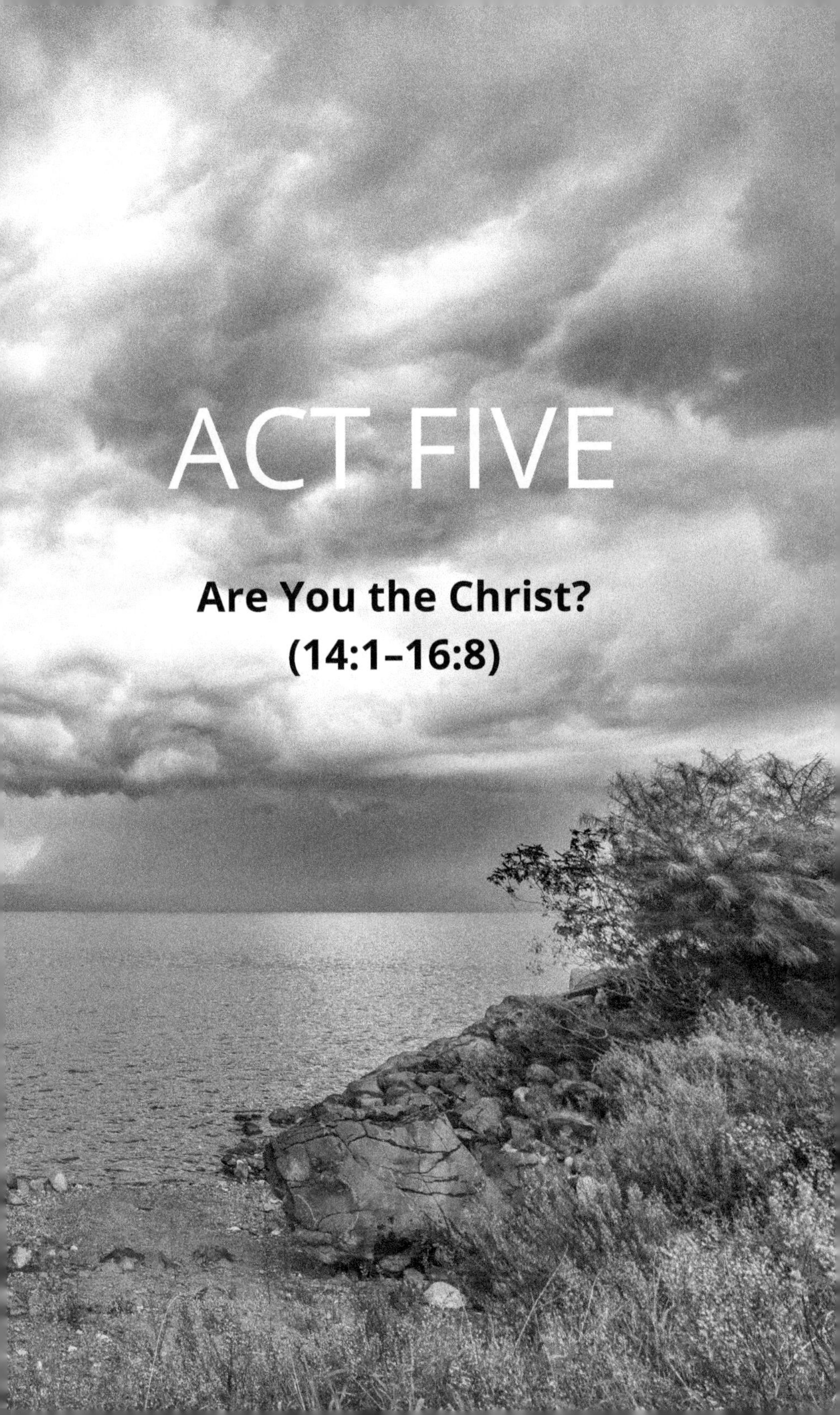

ACT FIVE

Are You the Christ?
(14:1–16:8)

Setting: Anointed for Burial (14:1–9)

"Abba, Father," he said, "everything is possible for you.
Take this cup from me. Yet not what
I will, but what you will."
—Mark 14:36

Throughout Mark, and throughout this text, we have highlighted the way Jesus transforms human understanding to introduce the kingdom of God. He has transformed how we consider wealth, service, greatness, healing, the Sabbath, and virtually everything we know about God through the Mosaic law. The most significant transformations are yet to come: transforming Passover and transforming life itself. All these efforts are part of God's plan of discipleship—making fishers of men.

Jesus lived to die. In this final act, Mark records the immediate events surrounding Jesus' death, beginning with an anointment for burial and ending with the pronouncement of his resurrection. Between these events, Mark provides insight into the dichotomy between this world and the kingdom of Heaven through stories of betrayal, abandonment, and human judgment surrounding the sharing of the Passover meal at the Last Supper. Ultimately, Jesus fulfills his purpose, and we find *good news* in his crucifixion.

ANOINTING FOR BURIAL BEFOREHAND

Mark resumes the Passion narrative to open the final act. It is a few days after Palm Sunday, two days before the Passover. In Jewish homes, the time before Passover is used to clean the house and make ready for the feast of freedom. Every scrap of leavened bread is to be removed. The year-round dishes and utensils are replaced by those reserved for this feast. Indeed, the whole house is readied.

> ***14*** *Now the Passover and the Festival of Unleavened Bread were only two days away, and the chief priests and the teachers of the law were scheming to arrest Jesus secretly and kill him. 2 "But not during the festival," they said, "or the people may riot."*
>
> *3 While he was in Bethany, reclining at the table in the home of Simon the Leper, a woman came with an alabaster jar of very expensive perfume, made of pure nard. She broke the jar and poured the perfume on his head.*
>
> *4 Some of those present were saying indignantly to one another, "Why this waste of perfume? 5 It could have been sold for more than a year's wages and the money given to the poor." And they rebuked her harshly.*
>
> *6 "Leave her alone," said Jesus. "Why are you bothering her? She has done a beautiful thing to me. 7 The poor you will always have with you, and you can help them any time you want. But you will not always have me. 8 She did what she could. She poured perfume on my body beforehand to prepare for my burial. 9 Truly I tell you, wherever the gospel is preached throughout the world, what she has done will also be told, in memory of her."*

The first scene is set in a home east of Jerusalem just over the Mount of Olives in the village of Bethany. Jesus is a guest of one Simon the Leper. We do not know who he is. One can only wonder if he is the leper who was healed when Jesus began his ministry (Mark 1:40–45).

As Jesus was reclining, a woman comes and anoints his head with perfume. The anointing is *for my burial*, says Jesus. We will note at the end of Mark's Gospel that there is an attempt at another anointing. At that time, several women come to the tomb to anoint the body of Jesus. He has already been anointed! The two anointing stories serve as a dramatic literary framework for the concluding announcement of *good news*.

If the woman who anoints Jesus is the same person mentioned in John's Gospel (John 12:1–8), it is Mary the sister of Martha and Lazarus. Mark does not give her name. He does tell us, however, that she did a beautiful thing and that whenever the story of Jesus' Passion is told she will be remembered.

Mark sets her devotion to Jesus in contrast to Judas and several other guests, in particular, the guests who would have preferred she sell the perfume and provide for the poor. They are indignant in their failure to recognize all that was happening.

What a great lesson on human behavior! One person does something nice, even extravagant, for someone else, and there are several others waiting to criticize because they would have done something "better" with the perfume. Jesus does not let them get away with the ignorance of their criticism. They can give to the poor anytime they want. Let the gifts they designate come from their own pockets.

The setting is now complete. The religious leaders continue to scheme against Jesus. The disciples have witnessed his being anointed. Jesus has again announced his death, stating that he will not always be with his disciples. He is now fully prepared to complete his purpose: Jesus is ready to die.

Plotting the Betrayal of Jesus (14:10–11)

> *[10] Then Judas Iscariot, one of the Twelve, went to the chief priests to betray Jesus to them. [11] They were delighted to hear this and promised to give him money. So, he watched for an opportunity to hand him over.*

Earlier we mentioned how the time before the Passover is a time of preparation and house-cleaning. It is important for us to remember how Jesus warned his disciples about the spiritual yeast of the Pharisees (Mark 8:15). Jesus is preparing his house, too. The removal of Judas from the presence of the twelve is the cleansing of Jesus' house.

Judas has been watching for an opportunity to betray Jesus. Mark does not tell us why Judas betrays Jesus or why he wants to be paid for it. His watchfulness is quite different from the command Jesus gave to "watch." Judas wants an opportunity to act in a particularly subversive manner. Jesus wants his disciples to observe what is happening in order to understand his parable about the owner of the house coming back to take charge of his property.

It is tempting to ask what prompts Judas. One may wonder if Judas was behind the criticism of the woman with the perfume. If she had sold the perfume for a large sum of money, the proceeds might have been given to Jesus for dispersal. Judas was the treasurer for the group and had at times helped himself to the available money (John 12:6).

Did Judas carry a debt? Was selling the perfume a temptation for him to pay off a debt? If selling the expensive perfume failed, would he need money from an alternative source—the high priest and the teachers of the law? We do not know.

Alternatively, we could surmise Judas was trying to force Jesus into a course of action different from the one Judas expected. We are not told.

What we do know is this: Judas, who had witnessed everything of Jesus' ministry, conspired with those who have been trying to kill Jesus. I suspect that there are many throughout history who have had opportunity to witness God's awesome presence who have similarly acted out of selfish ambition—selling out God for a few coins. My prayer is that each of us pays attention to what we do. Watch!

The kingdom of God is much more valuable. The wealth of the rich young man wasn't enough to gain entry, yet the pennies from a widow opened the door for many.

The Last Supper: Transforming Passover (14:12-26)

*12 On the first day of the Festival of Unleavened Bread,
when it was customary to sacrifice the Passover lamb,
Jesus' disciples asked him, "Where do you want us to go
and make preparations for you to eat the Passover?"*

*13 So he sent two of his disciples, telling them, "Go into the
city, and a man carrying a jar of water will meet you. Follow
him. 14 Say to the owner of the house he enters, 'The Teacher
asks: Where is my guest room, where I may eat the Passover
with my disciples?' 15 He will show you a large room upstairs,
furnished and ready. Make preparations for us there."*

*16 The disciples left, went into the city and found things
just as Jesus had told them. So, they prepared the Passover.*

*17 When evening came, Jesus arrived with the Twelve. 18
While they were reclining at the table eating, he said,
"Truly I tell you, one of you will betray me—one who is
eating with me."*

*19 They were saddened, and one by one they said to him,
"Surely you don't mean me?"*

*20 "It is one of the Twelve," he replied, "one who dips bread
into the bowl with me. 21 The Son of Man will go just as it is*

written about him. But woe to that man who betrays the Son of Man! It would be better for him if he had not been born."

22 *While they were eating, Jesus took bread, and when he had given thanks, he broke it and gave it to his disciples, saying, "Take it; this is my body."*

23 *Then he took a cup, and when he had given thanks, he gave it to them, and they all drank from it.*

24 *"This is my blood of the covenant, which is poured out*
for many," he said to them. 25 *"Truly I tell you; I will not*
drink again from the fruit of the vine until that day when I drink it new in the kingdom of God."

26 *When they had sung a hymn, they went out to the Mount of Olives.*

Passover begins with a Seder service focusing on the mercy of God enabling the escape of the Hebrews from slavery in Egypt. As part of the Seder, the host takes a piece of unleavened bread, matzah, and identifies it as "the bread of affliction." It is a reminder of suffering, and it anticipates the need for a quick departure from Pharaoh's dominion lest Pharaoh, after granting freedom, changes his mind as he had done on nine previous occasions, and forbids the Hebrews to leave (see Exodus 7–12). Taking time for bread to rise would take too long. Besides, the Hebrews would soon be in the wilderness where bread made with yeast would grow moldy and need to be thrown out. The matzah would last and would serve as sufficient nutrition for as long as the matzah was available. It is not heavy to carry even if it is not particularly tasty.

Various other foods are eaten during the Seder ceremony, each one with a special reminder of the escape: a roasted meat shank, symbol of the paschal lamb; a roasted egg, symbol of hope and new life; *maror* or bitter herbs, usually horseradish, to remember the pain and suffering of slavery; *haroset*, a mixture of nuts, apples and wine, to symbolize the mortar with which the Hebrews were required to labor; salt water for dipping karpas, usually celery or parsley, to represent the bitter tears. In a sense, this is a meal remembering the gift of life and that life does not always flourish. If you will, this is a meal for the wilderness—hope and life on one hand and pain and suffering on the other. It is not a meal celebrating a flourishing life.

Four glasses of wine are part of the ceremony. The first two are reminders of the divine promise to deliver them from bondage. The deliverance from Egypt itself becomes especially symbolic. Throughout history, the Hebrews found themselves in bondage on many occasions. During the time of Jesus, they were in bondage to Rome. The third cup is the cup of redemption remembering the exodus from Egypt (and in hopes of being delivered from Rome), "So the Lord brought us out of Egypt with a mighty hand and an outstretched arm ..." (Deuteronomy 26:8). The fourth is a cup of joy celebrating the life of freedom (Amos 9:11–15).

Because Passover is a pilgrim festival which required people living nearby to come to Jerusalem for the feast, the chief priests and the teachers of the law had good reason to expect Jesus to be present. The presence of large crowds also meant people familiar with him and supportive of him would be there too. Arresting Jesus would be a challenge for the religious rulers. If a riot breaks out, the religious leaders stood a chance of losing their relative independence and authority under Roman authority. Keeping the crowds in check would be important. Executing Jesus would be a different challenge. Whatever authority the religious rulers had, it did not extend to capital punishment. While Jesus lived, the large crowds gathered around him might threaten the Roman authorities causing them to curtail whatever influence the religious leaders might have had.

This is a short version of the Last Supper, leaving out much of what is reported in the other Gospels. Judas is not confronted by Jesus (Matthew 26:20–25); Jesus' desire to eat this meal with his disciples (Luke 22:14) is not mentioned; the washing of the disciples' feet and the dismissal of Judas (John 13:1–30) are missing. All the Gospels assume familiarity with the Last Supper, known as the Seder meal. Mark simply reports three essential elements in his narrative: a betrayer, the identification of Jesus with the bread, and the fruit of the vine as a new covenant. When the meal is over, they sing a hymn and depart for the Mount of Olives.

Jesus has already made preparation for a room in which to celebrate this Seder meal with his disciples. He has also chosen this moment to mention a betrayer. It is interesting that each of the disciples, though saddened, suspects himself. The betrayer is identified simply as the one who dips the bread into a dish. Presumably, Judas leaves the table at this time for Jesus goes on to identify the broken bread (matzah) with his body.

There is a significance to what Jesus does next. After breaking the bread, Jesus takes the cup. This is the third cup of the Seder meal—that which symbolizes redemption. With this cup, Jesus identifies a new covenant in his blood. The blood is a reference to the lamb's blood splattered on the doorframes of the Hebrews to spare them from the final plague in Egypt (Exodus 12:7). Jesus is transforming the meaning of redemption. No longer is the blood of a spotless animal necessary—the spotless Lamb, Jesus, is soon to be sacrificed for us all.

The Passover commemorates, and celebrates, God's judgment against Pharaoh that results in setting the Hebrews free from their slavery. Jesus' death does more than that. There is another slavery to which all creation is in bondage—a slavery to the one who lives in the wilderness.

God's judgment against Pharaoh resulted in the death of several of God's creatures. Firstborn. Humans. Animals. In many cases, including that of Pharaoh's son, the judgment was carried out against children. God is just. He is holy. He is also compassionate. In this moment, Jesus is taking the place of God's creation. It is he, God, who will die as a result of God's holy judgment. And in so doing, he will free all creation.

There is another significant transformation. The fourth cup is the cup of joy. Jesus announces that he will not drink this cup until he drinks it in the kingdom of God. *Joy comes in the morning* (Psalm 30:5). Jesus has given the disciples (us) a confident hope. He will drink the fourth cup.

Mark concludes this section without reference as to how much the disciples may have understood. It is likely, given how much they have missed, that their understanding will not come until after the crucifixion. They simply sing a hymn and go out to the Mount of Olives. Here, Jesus will make his final preparations to be betrayed and killed.

There may be some interest in trying to figure out which hymn Jesus and his disciples may have sung. It is likely that they sang one or more of the Hallel Psalms (Psalms 113–118). These are Psalms of praise and thanksgiving. Verses below are from these Psalms. I would encourage the reader to examine all of these beautiful hymns in the context of how Jesus transforms Passover. They are hymns about him as the Christ.

Psalm 113

[1] *Praise the Lord. Praise the Lord, you his servants; praise the name of the Lord.*
[2] *Let the name of the Lord be praised,both now and forevermore.*
[3] *From the rising of the sun to the place where it sets, the name of the Lord is to be praised.*

Psalm 114

[1] *When Israel came out of Egypt, Jacob from a people of foreign tongue,*
[2] *Judah became God's sanctuary, Israel his dominion.*

Psalm 115

[14] *May the Lord cause you to flourish, both you and your children.*

[15] May you be blessed by the Lord, the
Maker of heaven and earth.

Psalm 116
[13] I will lift up the cup of salvationand
call on the name of the Lord.
[14] I will fulfill my vows to the Lordin
the presence of all his people.
[15] Precious in the sight of the Lordis the
death of his faithful servants.
[16] Truly I am your servant, Lord;I serve you just as
my mother did;you have freed me from my chains.

Psalm 117
[1] Praise the Lord, all you nations;extol him,
all you peoples.
[2] For great is his love toward us,and the faithfulness
of the Lord endures forever. Praise the Lord.

Psalm 118
[22] The stone the builders rejectedhas
become the cornerstone;
[23] the Lord has done this,and it is marvelous in our eyes.
[24] The Lord has done it this very day;let
us rejoice today and be glad.

Consider also that Mark already referred to Psalm 118 in his telling of the Triumphal Entry.

Psalm 118
[26] Blessed is he who comes in the name of the Lord.
From the house of the Lord we bless you.
[27] The Lord is God, and he has made his light
shine on us.With boughs in hand, join in the
festal procession up to the horns of the altar.

[28] You are my God, and I will praise you;
you are my God, and I will exalt you.
[29] Give thanks to the Lord, for he is
good; his love endures forever.

We have explored various aspects of paradox throughout the text. Understanding Old Testament references as Messianic, or Christocentric, may be among the more significant paradoxes God reveals to us.

There are many ways in which the factual things that happen in our history may be shared. Stories are told. Songs are written. Think of one of your favorite songs. It is amazing that the story of the songwriter somehow seems to fit within your own story. The manner in which our experiences lend themselves to being shared—sometimes across various cultures, and even centuries apart—is part of the universal human experience. There is a reality to which we can all relate.

The *good news* Jesus brings takes that experience further. There is a truthfulness to purpose that is unequaled. His death heals a fracture between God and creation that only God can fill. In that sense, I would encourage you to look at everything within your own experience as it relates to the story of the Christ.

Gethsemane: Thy Will Be Done (14:27-52)

They come to a place called Gethsemane, an area on the lower slopes of the Mount of Olives, where an olive press is used to crush olives with enormous pressure producing cherished olive oil. The pressure on Jesus is unmatched by anything else in his life.

> 27 *"You will all fall away," Jesus told them, "for it is written: 'I will strike the shepherd, and the sheep will be scattered.'*
>
> 28 *But after I have risen, I will go ahead of you into Galilee."*
>
> 29 *Peter declared, "Even if all fall away, I will not."*
>
> 30 *"Truly I tell you," Jesus answered, "today—yes, tonight—before the rooster crows twice you yourself will disown me three times."*
>
> 31 *But Peter insisted emphatically, "Even if I have to die with you, I will never disown you." And all the others said the same.*
>
> 32 *They went to a place called Gethsemane, and Jesus said to his disciples, "Sit here while I pray."* 33 *He took Peter, James and John along with him, and he began to be deeply distressed and troubled.* 34 *"My soul is overwhelmed with*

sorrow to the point of death," he said to them. "Stay here
and keep watch."

35 Going a little farther, he fell to the ground and prayed
that if possible the hour might pass from him. 36 "Abba,
Father," he said, "everything is possible for you. Take this
cup from me. Yet not what I will, but what you will."

37 Then he returned to his disciples and found them sleep-
ing. "Simon," he said to Peter, "are you asleep? Couldn't
you keep watch for one hour? 38 Watch and pray so that
you will not fall into temptation. The spirit is willing, but
the flesh is weak."

39 Once more he went away and prayed the same thing.
40 When he came back, he again found them sleeping,
because their eyes were heavy. They did not know what
to say to him.

41 Returning the third time, he said to them, "Are you still
sleeping and resting? Enough! The hour has come. Look,
the Son of Man is delivered into the hands of sinners. 42
Rise! Let us go! Here comes my betrayer!"

43 Just as he was speaking, Judas, one of the Twelve,
appeared. With him was a crowd armed with swords and
clubs, sent from the chief priests, the teachers of the law,
and the elders.

44 Now the betrayer had arranged a signal with them:
"The one I kiss is the man; arrest him and lead him
away under guard." 45 Going at once to Jesus, Judas said,
"Rabbi!" and kissed him. 46 The men seized Jesus and
arrested him. 47 Then one of those standing near drew his

sword and struck the servant of the high priest, cutting off his ear.

[48] *"Am I leading a rebellion," said Jesus, "that you have come out with swords and clubs to capture me?* [49] *Every day I was with you, teaching in the temple courts, and you did not arrest me. But the Scriptures must be fulfilled."* [50] *Then everyone deserted him and fled.*

[51] *A young man, wearing nothing but a linen garment, was following Jesus. When they seized him,* [52] *he fled naked, leaving his garment behind.*

The Seder meal began sometime after sundown. It was Thursday night. From a Jewish perspective, sundown marks the beginning of the new day. This would be Jesus' final day of his earthly ministry. Indeed, the pressure of all that will happen in the next several hours is closing in upon him. Jesus acknowledges the first of those pressures as he addresses his disciples. This is something he must do alone. Therefore, they will all fall away.

Jesus' abrupt declaration that the disciples will all desert him comes as a surprise to them. Peter protests loudly and all the others do the same. They do not yet comprehend the depth of human weakness and how that weakness is theirs too. Further, they do not recognize the disparity between their declaration of loyalty and their earlier concerns that each one of them could be a betrayer. They want to be loyal; they are unable.

Remember the context for Mark's Gospel. He is telling Peter's story of Jesus. Peter has just been executed by Nero. Even Peter, who rightly identified Jesus as "the Christ" would be unable to keep his oath of loyalty. Jesus goes further, stating that Peter would deny Jesus three times in the next few hours.

Jesus' final preparation for the moment is prayer. Jesus takes three of his disciples with him, and Peter is one of them. He asks them to "watch" while he goes to pray. He begins this deeply personal prayer addressing God as "Abba." Daddy. It is a tender and endearing term of a child. Escaping the hour is at least a thought, but the prevailing thought is the Father's will. The cup will pass, but only by drinking it.

Sadly, the disciples sleep, unable to remain watchful. Only one hour into their professed loyalty, the disciples are already beyond their abilities. Even the warning about falling into temptation does not keep them awake. Their sleep is a precursor to their falling away once the Shepherd is taken captive.

Jesus commands his disciples a second time. "Watch." And he again prays. The result is the same. Jesus feels the pressure increasing. He calls out, "Abba." And he endures what it is to come alone. Jesus knows the time is near.

Judas soon appears with a crowd armed with swords and clubs. Although Judas approaches Jesus with a kiss, he is already known to Jesus as the betrayer.

Jesus accuses Judas, and the crowd with him, of cowardice. If they were arresting Jesus as a matter of principle, they have had opportunity all week. Jesus has not hidden himself. Rather, they come under the cover of darkness, and ready to fight. Perhaps the greater act of cowardice is that of the religious leaders—who are not even present for his arrest.

Some of the disciples were ready to fight. One, whom we know from other Gospel accounts was Peter (John 18:10), cuts off the ear of the high priest's servant. Mark does not tell us who that disciple was (see John 18:10) nor that Jesus restores the ear (see Luke 22:51). Mark calls attention to the offense, not the healing.

The skirmish with the crowds sent by the priests is brief. Jesus does not resist. He submits to the will of the Father. The disciples scatter and Jesus is led away for trial.

The capture, if that is the proper term for Jesus' arrest, ends with a young man in what is likely his night shirt running away. Most people take this to be Mark himself. He would have been about the right age and his family connections would have made it possible for him to know where The Last Supper was held. If it were held in his own house he had opportunity to watch for Jesus coming to the house, and then later to follow Jesus and the disciples into the night. If it is Mark, he testifies that he, too, deserts Jesus.

There are at least three things worthy of additional reflection. These deal with the disciples, the crowds, and our own response.

First, Mark continues the theme about the disciples, especially Peter. Even when they understand who Jesus is (the Christ), and why he is here (to die), they are unable to be faithful. It is noteworthy that they did not even pray with Jesus in Gethsemane. They fell asleep.

Second, throughout the Gospel Mark has used the crowds to help us identify how we are to respond. Initially, they are amazed by how Jesus is able to perform miracles. Near the middle of the Gospel, the crowds become conflicted, with different crowds responding favorably and unfavorably toward Jesus. Now, at the final hour, the crowds are aligned with the chief priests and elders. They are doing the dirty work of the religious leaders, who dare not be present. Mark is suggesting that the crowds bear some responsibility for what happens next. By extension, he is indicting us all.

Finally, especially given the presence of the crowds bearing clubs and swords, there is a cause for introspection. We may find ourselves excusing the crowds. After all, they were following orders from the religious leaders. It is the Pharisees, Sadducees, and Sanhedrin that are more culpable. Still, it is an opportunity through which we recognize that the guilt is our own, and we must find a way to address it.

Despite the unfaithfulness of the disciples, the rioting of the crowds, and our own personal response, Jesus submits to what comes next. He is displaying disciplined power through obedience to the will of his Father. This is *good news*. Jesus is in full control.

Human Judgment (14:53–15:20)

Perception is reality. The truth of this sentence is that judgments are made by each one of us, based upon our own (limited) ability to understand our experiences. By virtue of these experiences, combined with our capacity to reason and make sense of them, we construct a point of view that we each hold to be our reality. These judgments are not themselves representative of what is true. They can't be. For in the very process of perceiving events as they happen, we introduce our experiences into a narrative already constructed in our minds. Therefore, our perception, our reality, is necessarily imperfect.

The next three pericopes each involve an aspect of human judgment, reality in opposition to truth. In each case, there is a predetermined narrative by which events are interpreted. The first and third involve trials of Jesus. First, by the Sanhedrin, the religious leaders who have been seeking to kill Jesus for three years. Ultimately, by Pilate, the political leader who has the authority to condemn Jesus to death. Between these two, there is a social trial involving Peter. This setting, while not formal, is as much a commentary on our own inability to remain faithful as it is about Peter.

RELIGIOUS TRIAL OF JESUS (14:53–65)

> *53 They took Jesus to the high priest, and all the chief priests, the elders and the teachers of the law came together. 54 Peter followed him at a distance, right into the*

courtyard of the high priest. There he sat with the guards and warmed himself at the fire.

55 The chief priests and the whole Sanhedrin were looking for evidence against Jesus so that they could put him to death, but they did not find any. 56 Many testified falsely against him, but their statements did not agree.

57 Then some stood up and gave this false testimony against him: 58 "We heard him say, 'I will destroy this temple made with human hands and in three days will build another, not made with hands.'" 59 Yet even then their testimony did not agree.

60 Then the high priest stood up before them and asked Jesus, "Are you not going to answer? What is this testimony that these men are bringing against you?" 61 But Jesus remained silent and gave no answer.

Again, the high priest asked him, "Are you the Messiah, the Son of the Blessed One?"

62 "I am," said Jesus. "And you will see the Son of Man sitting at the right hand of the Mighty One and coming on the clouds of heaven."

63 The high priest tore his clothes. "Why do we need any more witnesses?" he asked. 64 "You have heard the blasphemy. What do you think?"

They all condemned him as worthy of death. 65 Then some began to spit at him; they blindfolded him, struck him with their fists, and said, "Prophesy!" And the guards took him and beat him.

The injustice and brutality in Jesus' trial are clear. There is no legitimate reason for the arrest and the officials need a fishing expedition to find an accusation they could use. The charge claiming Jesus said, "Destroy this man-made temple," seems ridiculous if one is to be charged with a capital offense.

Jesus is silent. Indeed, there is nothing he can say to this audience that will change their minds. Their narrative has been set for a while. They seek to kill him.

Jesus is then given the one question he chooses to answer. "Are you the Christ?" It is the pivotal question of the Gospel, similar to the question Jesus asked of his disciples: *Who am I?* (Mark 8:27–29). If Jesus gives a clear and unambiguous answer, we will finally learn Jesus' answer to the question he raised with the disciples. He answers, "I am!"

At long last, Mark identifies Jesus clearly. Jesus is the Christ. He puts the confession in Jesus' own words for added clarity. For emphasis and for the sake of truthfulness, Mark records the confession in a courtroom hearing where the truth is presumed to be sacred. Then, for even more clarity, Mark includes Jesus' brief statement about the Son of Man at the right hand of the Mighty One.

The high priest does not miss any of the confession. He heard exactly what Jesus said. He knows the references to the Son of Man and to the right hand of the Mighty One. However, according to the high priest, Jesus utters blasphemy. There would be no further need for other witnesses. He and those with him condemn Jesus to death.

As those present began to spit on Jesus, curse him, and beat him, there is another trial underway. This prosecution is not in the confines of a courtroom. It is outside the home of Caiaphas, the high priest. Peter is warming himself against the chilly night air, attempting to remain close to Jesus. There are charges brought against him. They are not capital offenses, and they are not formal. The first charge simply puts Peter in the presence of Jesus, the second makes him a follower of Jesus and the third calls him a Galilean. The people who judge Peter are not magistrates. They include only a servant girl and a few people standing nearby.

SOCIAL TRIAL OF PETER (14:66–72)

> [66] *While Peter was below in the courtyard, one of the servant girls of the high priest came by.* [67] *When she saw Peter warming himself, she looked closely at him.*
>
> *"You also were with that Nazarene, Jesus," she said.*
>
> [68] *But he denied it. "I don't know or understand what you're talking about," he said, and went out into the entryway.*
>
> [69] *When the servant girl saw him there, she said again to those standing around, "This fellow is one of them."* [70] *Again he denied it.*
>
> *After a little while, those standing near said to Peter, "Surely you are one of them, for you are a Galilean."*
>
> [71] *He began to call down curses, and he swore to them, "I don't know this man you're talking about."*
>
> [72] *Immediately the rooster crowed the second time. Then Peter remembered the word Jesus had spoken to him: "Before the rooster crows twice you will disown me three times." And he broke down and wept.*

Peter's trial stands in stark contrast to Jesus' trial. Peter's protests begin with a simple denial of the charges and conclude with curses on himself and swearing. How very different is this prosecution from that faced by Jesus—different in terms of the truth of the charges, different in the integrity of the accusers, different in terms of the outcome!

When the rooster crows to awaken the morning, Peter breaks down and weeps bitterly. He knows what has just happened. Just as he did not listen to Jesus when they were at Caesarea Philippi, he has not listened again. Although he would truly like to have been a faithful and loyal follower, he wakes up to his failings.

POLITICAL TRIAL OF JESUS (15:1–20)

The political realities of Jerusalem in the first century required the Jewish authorities to appeal to Caesar for the execution. The religious leaders bring Jesus before Pilate, the Roman governor of Judaea, to gain the approval of Rome for his execution.

> **15** *Very early in the morning, the chief priests, with the elders, the teachers of the law and the whole Sanhedrin, made their plans. So, they bound Jesus, led him away and handed him over to Pilate.*
>
> 2 *"Are you the king of the Jews?" asked Pilate.*
>
> *"You have said so," Jesus replied.*
>
> 3 *The chief priests accused him of many things.* 4 *So again Pilate asked him, "Aren't you going to answer? See how many things they are accusing you of."*
>
> 5 *But Jesus still made no reply, and Pilate was amazed.*
>
> 6 *Now it was the custom at the festival to release a prisoner whom the people requested.* 7 *A man called Barabbas was in prison with the insurrectionists who had committed murder in the uprising.* 8 *The crowd came up and asked Pilate to do for them what he usually did.*
>
> 9 *"Do you want me to release to you the king of the Jews?"*

asked Pilate,[10] knowing it was out of self-interest that the chief priests had handed Jesus over to him. [11] But the chief priests stirred up the crowd to have Pilate release Barabbas instead.

[12] "What shall I do, then, with the one you call the king of the Jews?" Pilate asked them.

[13] "Crucify him!" they shouted.

[14] "Why? What crime has he committed?" asked Pilate.

But they shouted all the louder, "Crucify him!"

[15] Wanting to satisfy the crowd, Pilate released Barabbas to them. He had Jesus flogged, and handed him over to be crucified.

[16] The soldiers led Jesus away into the palace (that is, the Praetorium) and called together the whole company of soldiers. [17] They put a purple robe on him, then twisted together a crown of thorns and set it on him.[18] And they began to call out to him, "Hail, king of the Jews!" [19] Again and again they struck him on the head with a staff and spit on him. Falling on their knees, they paid homage to him. [20] And when they had mocked him, they took off the purple robe and put his own clothes on him. Then they led him out to crucify him.

As a trial, this prosecution is no better than the first. Pilate's question of the crowd regarding Jesus, "What crime has he done?" implies Pilate found no fault in him. While Mark does not tell us if Pilate had prior knowledge of Jesus, it is hard to imagine the chief magistrate had not been informed of Jesus' Triumphal Entry into Jerusalem on Palm Sunday. Pilate's responsibility to keep the peace on behalf of Rome would have made him especially attuned to anyone being hailed with hosannas and shouts of the coming kingdom of "our father David."

Pilate is not above showing his displeasure at the religious leaders by taunting them. He knew it was out of envy that they had brought Jesus to him. Hence, he referred to Jesus as their king and even placed a written notice regarding Jesus' crime on the cross above him: "The king of the Jews." His taunting was met with ridicule and mocking from the crowds gathered to support the religious leaders.

Pilate could probably distinguish this crowd accompanying the high priest from the crowd which had followed Jesus at the beginning of the week. The first crowd had intimidated the religious rulers; this one is sponsored by the rulers to intimidate Pilate. The religious leaders learned their strategy the hard way. However, Pilate was able to recognize the envy borne toward Jesus by the Sanhedrin rulers. In the end, it was not justice, but a desire on Pilate's part to satisfy the angry mob that prompted him to convict Jesus.

Satisfying the crowd does not necessarily mean pleasing them. Pilate realizes the situation is such that a major disruption of the Roman peace would likely happen unless he "satisfies" the crowd. Such a disruption would likely cost the lives of many people, Romans and Jews alike, unless he offered an expedient judgment. Pilate also knew he might lose his position in the Roman government if he could not keep the peace.

In a way, Pilate appears to be trapped on the horns of a dilemma. He needs to appease the crowd. He needs to please Caesar. He needs to get along with the religious leaders. And he finds no fault in Jesus, whom they wish to kill.

Pilate attempts to cheat. He takes advantage of a local custom of releasing a prisoner during the celebration of Passover. He offers the crowd a choice between releasing Jesus or Barabbas, a known vile murderer. When the crowd calls for the release of Barabbas, Pilate's trap tightens.

The crowd shouts, “Crucify him!” Pilate condemns Jesus to death. He has Jesus flogged and hands him over to be crucified. Pilate’s actions appear to be prophetic. In his judgment of expediency, better for one to die for all than for all to die, Pilate is hinting at God’s intention. Indeed, it is better that one die. This is *good news*.

Human judgment is flawed. Individually, the flaws are limited by our own capacities: experience, intellectual ability, emotional state, moral character, etc. Corporately, the flaws are sometimes less obvious.

Jesus was tried by the Sanhedrin. At this point in history, this court might be considered the greatest of religious courts. Similarly, he was tried by Pilate, standing in for Caesar and all of Rome. This might represent the best of political courts. Yet, each court condemned Jesus without any evidence of his guilt.

Peter’s situation is a demonstration of peer pressure that is all too familiar for most of us. Despite his proclamation to Jesus just a few hours earlier, Peter denies Jesus three times. Peter is not among the religious or political leaders. He is among the people—called out by a servant girl.

As a pastor, I have often been privileged to hear the private confessions and promises that reveal our best intentions. Everything from a desire to quit an addiction to attending church more faithfully to treating each other with forgiveness and kindness. I confess, I have made my own promises with the best of intentions. Like Peter, we all fall short of keeping those promises.

Peter’s denials of Jesus are not the end of the story. This is the same Peter, *Rock*, about whom Jesus pronounced he would build his church. Neither is our broken promise the end of our story.

We identify with Peter. His perception, his reality, is ours too. It is likely that Peter had shared the importance of this story with Mark many times. It is important because Jesus is not the only person we need to identify in the story. Yes, he is the Christ. We must also identify ourselves, especially in relation to God and his kingdom.

The Christ is obedient to the divine will of God, even to the point of being condemned and dying on a cross. We, like Peter, deny God to preserve an image of ourselves before others. We are in need of the Christ. We live in the limitations of a barren wilderness. Jesus, who is the Christ, brings life to that wilderness.

The story is not just about human judgment. Mark has made a subtle change again, drawing attention to the conclusion of the trials. Notice the way in which he is recording the events. Up to now he has been using a daily calendar, Sunday through Thursday. As we get closer to the Passover, Mark shifts to different times within the same day. He begins with the "evening," (Mark 14:17) the time for the Passover meal. This is followed by the walk to Gethsemane, the prayers, the arrest in the early hours of the night, and the first prosecution later during the "night." When the rooster crows (Mark 14:72), the "night is ended." "Very early the next morning" (Mark 15:1) the Sanhedrin reaches its decision and sends him to Pilate for Pilate to sentence him.

One more observation may be helpful. Mark does not typically give us the names of people. There are a few exceptions such as Legion, Jairus, Barabbas, and in the next few verses Simon, father of Alexander and Rufus. Why are these names provided while other names are left out, like the one who cut off the ear of the high priest's servant, the boy running home without any clothes, and the woman who anointed Jesus?

In the case of the names not given, there may be modesty. For example, the Church at Rome may have had difficulty hearing that their pastor, Peter, was the disciple who cut off the ear of the servant to the high priest. Mark's discretion might be intended to benefit his audience. Another example is speculative. It may be that Mark himself was the young man who ran home without his clothes when Jesus was arrested.

Mark is also using a brilliant, yet subtle, literary technique by not identifying people by name. By keeping anonymity for these characters, Mark is allowing the reader to personally identify with one or more of them. Of course, the readers in his day may have known the identity of some of the unnamed people. Today, we have the ability to project our own experiences upon the religious leaders, crowds, disciples, or unnamed individuals. This gives us the capacity to experience the story.

Earlier in the text Jesus gave the command, "Watch." It is an active task, like a soldier keeping watch. At this point in the Gospel, Jesus is fulfilling his purpose. The enemy is at hand. The religious leaders are near their goal of killing Jesus. The devil believes that by killing Jesus the wilderness will remain barren. As we watch the suffering and death Jesus endures on the cross, we learn it is the very means by which God provides salvation, reclaiming his creation, establishing his kingdom, and bringing a new flourishing life to the wilderness.

Crucifixion: Good News! (15:21–47)

When the soldiers bring Jesus to Golgotha, the place of execution, Mark changes the time referents yet again. The "hour" has come. It is the "third hour" (Mark 15:25). At the "sixth hour" darkness covers the whole land until the "ninth hour" when Jesus "breathed his last" (Mark 15:33–37). With these subtle changes in time referents, Mark draws us into the final moment of Jesus' earthly life. Notice, too, how the most significant event in human history plays out in a matter of just a few hours.

> 21 *A certain man from Cyrene, Simon, the father of Alexander and Rufus, was passing by on his way in from the country, and they forced him to carry the cross.* 22 *They brought Jesus to the place called Golgotha (which means "the place of the skull").* 23 *Then they offered him wine mixed with myrrh, but he did not take it.* 24 *And they crucified him. Dividing up his clothes, they cast lots to see what each would get.*
>
> 25 *It was nine in the morning when they crucified him.* 26 *The written notice of the charge against him read:* THE KING OF THE JEWS.
>
> 27 *They crucified two rebels with him, one on his right and one on his left.* 28, 29 *Those who passed by hurled insults at him, shaking their heads and saying, "So! You who are going to destroy the temple and build it in three days,*

30 come down from the cross and save yourself!" 31 In the
same way the chief priests and the teachers of the law
mocked him among themselves. "He saved others," they
said, "but he can't save himself! 32 Let this Messiah, this
king of Israel, come down now from the cross, that we may
see and believe." Those crucified with him also heaped
insults on him.

33 At noon, darkness came over the whole land until three
in the afternoon. 34 And at three in the afternoon Jesus
cried out in a loud voice, "Eloi, Eloi, lema sabachthani?"
(which means "My God, my God, why have you forsaken me?").

35 When some of those standing near heard this, they said,
"Listen, he's calling Elijah."

36 Someone ran, filled a sponge with wine vinegar, put it
on a staff, and offered it to Jesus to drink. "Now leave him
alone. Let's see if Elijah comes to take him down," he said.

37 With a loud cry, Jesus breathed his last.

38 The curtain of the temple was torn in two from top to
bottom. 39 And when the centurion, who stood there in
front of Jesus, saw how he died, he said, "Surely this man
was the Son of God!"

40 Some women were watching from a distance. Among
them were Mary Magdalene, Mary the mother of James
the younger and of Joseph, and Salome. 41 In Galilee these
women had followed him and cared for his needs. Many
other women who had come up with him to Jerusalem
were also there.

> *[42] It was Preparation Day (that is, the day before the Sabbath). So, as evening approached, [43] Joseph of Arimathea, a prominent member of the Council, who was himself waiting for the kingdom of God, went boldly to Pilate and asked for Jesus' body. [44] Pilate was surprised to hear that he was already dead. Summoning the centurion, he asked him if Jesus had already died. [45] When he learned from the centurion that it was so, he gave the body to Joseph. [46] So Joseph bought some linen cloth, took down the body, wrapped it in the linen, and placed it in a tomb cut out of rock. Then he rolled a stone against the entrance of the tomb. [47] Mary Magdalene and Mary the mother of Joseph saw where he was laid.*

There is little mercy in a crucifixion. It is a form of death intended to be a horrible death and a potent reminder for the crowds witnessing it to respect Roman authority. Stripped of dignity even more than clothing, the crucified is left to die, and to do so very publicly. While someone assisted Jesus by carrying the cross, there is no compassion or comfort hearing the taunts of those passing by while Jesus is nailed to the cross.

Mark describes the scene with brief and poignant detail. He identifies Simon, the Cyrene, as the one who carries the cross for Jesus. Although Mark often does not provide names for people, in this case he even names Simon's sons: Rufus and Alexander. Mark is describing the events well enough for each one of us to imagine ourselves as eyewitnesses. He puts us in the middle of the scene.

We will examine Mark's detailed description of the crucifixion in three sections. The first deals with what happens immediately following the pronounced judgment and prior to the crucifixion. The second section involves the three hours that Jesus is on the cross. The third section details the events in the three hours following his death.

There is an issue that arises from Mark's timeline of events that seems problematic for many scholars. Mark's detail of events has Jesus condemned at 6 a.m., crucified at 9 a.m., darkness coming at noon, and Jesus is dead by 3 p.m. The conflict emerges when this account is compared with John's Gospel, which indicates that Pilate's pronouncement of judgment is not given until noon.

There is agreement from all accounts, both biblical and non-biblical, that the crucifixion occurred, and that darkness fell at noon. I, therefore, will leave the resolution of the conflict to more historical scholars. Remember, Mark's purpose is not to write a history of Jesus. He is sharing *good news*.

We will not, however, ignore the potential conflict. There is value in recognizing that Mark provides more detailed information during these few hours than anywhere else in the text. The events themselves are described in three three-hour segments, as we will examine: Via Dolorosa, Crucifixion, and Darkness. Each of these sections holds significance in revealing who we are as God's fallen creation, who Jesus is as the Christ, and the nature of the kingdom of God.

VIA DOLOROSA

Via Dolorosa: Jesus is on the way of suffering. He was brought to Golgotha, the place of execution. He was offered wine mixed with myrrh, although he did not drink it. He was stripped of his clothes, and those ridiculing him cast lots for his clothing.

Remember the baptism of Jesus. While most *went* to John to be baptized, Jesus *came* to be baptized. Most *went* to repent for their sin. Jesus, who had no sin, *came* to identify with sinners and to affirm the glory of God's creation. Now, at the time of his crucifixion, Jesus is fulfilling the promise of his baptism.

He is brought to Golgotha, the place of the skull. This area is likely just outside the city gate, and near the road most frequently taken into the city. Executions were public. They were a statement. By being brought to Golgotha, Jesus is identifying with those who are condemned—just as he did at his baptism.

He is offered wine mixed with myrrh. This common practice was a means to escape the pains of the crucifixion. The mixed wine dulled the senses. It had an anesthetic value. Jesus does not accept it. He came to endure the pain. He was not about to avoid his purpose.

Jesus is stripped of his clothes. The earliest prophesy about Jesus is found in Genesis 3, shortly after the fall of creation. Adam and Eve, having sinned, found themselves to be naked. They were ashamed (shame being a natural consequence of having sinned) because they knew themselves to be naked. The prophesy says that the serpent will bruise his heal, and that he would crush the head of the serpent. Having been stripped of his clothes, Jesus is naked. He is not ashamed.

Other Gospel accounts identify how the soldiers casting lots for his clothing fulfills prophecy. Mark simply states that they ridiculed him and cast lots for his clothing.

All of these are the way of suffering, the Via Dolorosa. Jesus' suffering does not begin with his being taken to Golgotha. It started with the fall of creation. The fall is what saddened God's heart. The path that Jesus is following from Pilate's condemnation to the cross is a path of victory and strength. God's power is displayed through Jesus' ability to absorb the scourge of others while remaining obedient to his purpose: to give his life as a ransom.

CRUCIFIXION

Jesus was crucified at 9 a.m. The charge was posted above his head: "King of the Jews." By putting this sign above the cross, Pilate is teasing and admonishing the religious rulers, who were envious of Jesus. Pilate realized the religious rulers manipulated the crowds to force the execution of Jesus. These exchanges between competing authorities are symbolic of human life in the wilderness. Treating each other in destructive ways is common, even within religious institutions and in "civil" society.

In truth, there is no value in belittling others; rather, lifting others up is best done through humility. In this case, it is the humble obedience of Jesus, submitting himself to death on the cross, that is the ultimate expression of authority as king.

Mark highlights several other reactions to the crucifixion. Each reaction emerges from a different point of view: from crowds who are passing by, religious leaders, other condemned criminals, and, later on, from women watching at a distance. Yet, each perspective emerges from people in the wilderness. As such, each misses the key fact that this is why Jesus came, to give his life as a ransom.

The city gate is located on a major highway. Those passing by hurled insults at Jesus: "So, you who are going to destroy the temple and build it in three days, come down from the cross and save yourself."

The temptation from all human perspectives is to take care of ourselves. The kingdom of God is different. Jesus had no need to come to earth in order to care for himself. His only purpose was to care for his creation—to die. He had no need for salvation. Indeed, he was not the one perishing. His purpose was to save us—even and especially those who were insulting him as they passed by.

Perspective is essential. Passersby held a perspective that many of us hold also. We understand things in very literal terms. When Jesus claimed that he would rebuild the temple in three days, he was mocked. Now, as he is crucified, people are reminding him of what he said. They are still stuck in the perspective that Jesus was talking about a building of stone.

If you've had the privilege of seeing the remains of the temple mount you know the stone to be massive. One particular stone [1] weighs more than a fully loaded 747. And each stone is mas-

1 The largest stone in the Western Wall of the Temple Mount weighs 570 tons. It is 45 feet long and 11 feet high. Estimates of the depth of the stone are 6 to 8 feet. The estimated weight of a Boeing 747, fully loaded, is 333 tons.

terfully engineered so that the walls are fully supported—each new row offset by a half-inch to ensure structural integrity to the wall.

Jesus had a different perspective. God does not dwell in the stone of buildings built by Herod or anyone else. The temple to which he referred was his own body. Ironically, those casting insults were revealing only their own ignorance—while they witnessed Jesus' prophecy begin to unfold. Yes, Jesus would rebuild the temple, his body, in just three days. This is a prophecy of new life that begins with his resurrection. For now, Jesus endures the criticism of those whom he has come to save.

The chief priests and teachers of the law also mocked Jesus: "He saved others, but he cannot save himself! Let this Messiah, this King of Israel, come down now from the cross, that we may see and believe."

There are a few comments to make regarding the comments attributed to the teachers of the law. First, they share the misperception of the passersby. They do not see the things that are plainly in front of them, and they do not recognize the kingdom of God.

What is perhaps most upsetting is that they do see what Jesus has done. Since the beginning of the Gospel, Mark has identified that the teachers of the law recognize the healing authority of Jesus as he performed many miracles in their presence. Even with this insult the chief priests acknowledge that Jesus saved others. Yet, their response emerges from envy and selfish ambition. There is no appreciation for the good Jesus has done. They are blind to what they have seen.

Thoughtful analysis results in a somewhat humorous observation. "... that we may see and believe." They have seen. They have believed. And they have felt threatened by the power of Jesus. Their belief is not grounded in faith. It is instead rooted in their own pride. These are the ones who go about town in flowing robes to display their value like a male peacock calling his mate. Apart from God, their worth is nothing.

One final comment about the insults from the religious leaders. They call for Jesus, the Messiah, to come down *from* the cross. He came down *to* the cross. His singular purpose is being fulfilled in the moment of the cross.

Those crucified with Jesus add their own voice to that of the passersby and religious leaders. They also heaped insults on him. Mark does not provide an example of the insults that came from others being crucified, only that they also insulted Jesus. They do not recognize Jesus as the Christ. They do not see the kingdom of God.

We know from other Gospel accounts that there is a dialogue Jesus has with one of those crucified with him, one that does acknowledge Jesus as the Son of God. Mark does not include that story. Instead, Mark is focused on how even those who know their own guilt are stuck in a perspective that denies the holiness of God.

How often do we respond in a similar manner? Psychologists identify certain common defenses that people use when they are aware of their own guilt. Projection—attributing their own guilt to others. Denial. Distraction. Our perspectives are those that turn the focus regarding guilt away from ourselves. Jesus has no need for these defenses. He is on the cross to pay a ransom. The guilt belongs to others, even to us.

DARKNESS

At noon, darkness came over the land until 3 a.m.

The text does not say much more than that. However, the silence of the text speaks volumes, especially in consideration of Jesus as the "Light of the World" (John 8:12, 9:5, and 12:46). In each of the verses from John's Gospel, Jesus refers to himself as the light. In chapter 12, he goes further by stating that he has come as a light so that no one who believes will stay in darkness.

For Satan, the darkness coming is an apparent sign of victory. He believes that he is extinguishing the light. There is symbolism well beyond the physical darkness. It is also important to note that non-biblical sources also reference the darkness. [2] For our purposes, we do not need to explore that aspect, although some may wish to investigate further. Rather, for our purposes, it is important to recognize that the darkness seems to be overcoming the light.

Imagine the despair for all who have followed Jesus. Unable to see what is truly happening, they are left to experience the darkness. Perhaps that is true for you, also, as you read the text. Jesus is on the cross. He is there publicly for all to see. He is there to die.

Imagine, also, the response of the religious leaders. Mark does not include it. However, darkness is not a mark of celebration or victory. At best, it is a relief that Jesus' power seems to be dwindling. There is an ominous nature to the darkness that, I believe, yields more a reaction of fear than that of celebration.

Consider also the disciples. Mark notably did not include the disciples' reaction among those in the first three hours. Similarly, Mark says nothing about their reaction during the darkness. As far as we know, the disciples are not present. It is likely they are hiding for fear that they may be next. There is nothing in the text to suggest that they see the coming of the kingdom of God any more than the crowds or religious leaders.

THE KINGDOM OF GOD IS COMING

At the ninth hour (3 p.m.), Jesus cries out "*Eloi, Eloi, lama sabachthani*?" Jesus' suffering was excruciating. Those nearby knew it. When they heard his cry, they assumed he was calling to Elijah for help. At least one person attempts to comfort

---

2 In *The Gospel According to Mark*, Lane refers to some of the non-biblical accounts of the darkness along with a larger discussion of both the historically factual reference to the darkness and the symbolic meaning of darkness that marks the importance of the moment and the significance of he who is being crucified. This is a common marker from both Rabbinic and historic traditions (pages 573–574).

Jesus by offering him wine mixed with vinegar from a sponge attached to a spear so it could be lifted up to him. Others continue to mock him. They wait to see if Elijah answers his cry.

With a loud cry, Jesus breathed his last. His mission is complete. In dying, Jesus has experienced the torturous pain of death. In crying out, "My God, my God, why have you forsaken me?" he has fulfilled the prophecy (Psalm 22:1) and experienced separation from God. He who is God experienced separation from God.

Read the last sentence again. Jesus. God. Experienced separation from God. This is our experience that is the direct result of our sin. When we sin, we put distance between ourselves and God. Rooted in our sin, we are incapable of being restored to God on our own. The Mosaic law is a guide for how we ought to live; yet, not one of us is capable of fulfilling the law.

Remember the rich young man. Jesus did not challenge his assertion that he had kept the law since his youth. Yet, Jesus challenged him to follow further by selling all he has and giving it to the poor. We are incapable of giving up what we have, and we fail to recognize that it is God who has given it to us. So, we go away sad because we think we have much.

Jesus is the one who even the crowds recognize as doing all things well. Even at the time of his trial, Pilate finds no fault in him. He is condemned not because of his actions. Rather, he is condemned for our actions. And he is not so much condemned, as if our judgment held any authority over him, as he is a willing sacrifice. He came with a singular purpose: to die. And now he has.

All creation responds to his death. Mark notes a most significant event: the curtain of the temple is torn from top to bottom. This curtain separates the holy of holies. It has served as the barrier between God's people and God himself. It is not torn from below, as the result of human action. It is torn by God from the top. Jesus death has broken the barrier.

A lone centurion, having watched how Jesus died,

acknowledges, "Surely this man was the Son of God!" It is important for us to be reminded of Mark's primary audience. For the Church in Rome, the observation of the centurion is a comfort. It is an acknowledgement from a Roman authority, a Gentile, that this man, Jesus, is of God.

It is at this point that Mark introduces the women and their reaction to the crucifixion. Three women are identified: Mary Magdalene, Mary the mother of James and Joseph, and Salome. They were there for a purpose: to care for Jesus. Mark states that other women from Galilee were also present, although he does not identify the others.

The suffering and humiliation are over. Jesus is dead.

Once again Mark shifts his reference of time. He no longer uses time in relationship to the events of Passion week nor does he reference time in terms of the final hours of Jesus' life. Instead, he notes that it was Preparation Day, the day before the Sabbath. This is a time when all Jews would make ready for a full day of rest. Having fulfilled his purpose, Jesus, too, will rest on the Sabbath.

The preparation for Jesus' rest falls to the work of the women who were present, and to Joseph of Arimathea. Joseph, who was a prominent member of the Council, is said to boldly approach Pilate to ask for Jesus' body. After confirming that Jesus has indeed died, Pilate grants his wish. Mark describes how Joseph sees to it that Jesus' body is properly clothed and wrapped in linen before being placed in the tomb. And the women watch.

Mark does not specify how Jesus spends the Sabbath. However, there are a few things we can infer. Following the creation, God rested on the seventh day. For this reason, God created the Sabbath. Similarly, Jesus' work on earth is done. As his body is laid to rest, Jesus is fully prepared to rest. The kingdom of God is come—death, as the penalty for sin, has been paid in full. The ransom is paid. This opens the door for a new creation. And that is *good news*!

Transformation: The Empty Tomb (16:1–8)

***16** When the Sabbath was over, Mary Magdalene, Mary the mother of James, and Salome bought spices so that they might go to anoint Jesus' body. [2] Very early on the first day of the week, just after sunrise, they were on their way to the tomb [3] and they asked each other, "Who will roll the stone away from the entrance of the tomb?"*

[4] But when they looked up, they saw that the stone, which was very large, had been rolled away. [5] As they entered the tomb, they saw a young man dressed in a white robe sitting on the right side, and they were alarmed.

[6] "Don't be alarmed," he said. "You are looking for Jesus the Nazarene, who was crucified. He has risen! He is not here. See the place where they laid him. [7] But go, tell his disciples and Peter, 'He is going ahead of you into Galilee. There you will see him, just as he told you.'"

[8] Trembling and bewildered, the women went out and fled from the tomb. They said nothing to anyone, because they were afraid.

THE FIRST DAY OF A NEW WEEK

Mark ends his Gospel with a short story of women fleeing from the tomb, too afraid to say anything to anyone. This is the *good news*?!

Yes, this is good news. To understand why it is good, we will look at the empty tomb from multiple perspectives. First, we will consider the religious and civic authorities that condemned him to death. More importantly, we will consider the authority of God that allowed for those judgments. In doing so, we will reexamine our discussion of the power of God, including creative, coercive, and the suffering context of submissive power.

Next, we will consider the perspectives of those who followed Jesus. This includes the women who flee from the tomb. It also includes the disciples, and especially Peter. There is a special interest in how Mark, Peter's protégé, describes Peter's relationship with Jesus throughout the Gospel.

Finally, we will consider the promise of the empty tomb.

AUTHORITY OF THE CROSS

We begin with the accusers. The overriding issues for the high priest and for the Romans are power and control. Rome is sovereign, requiring the chief priests and the teachers of the law, with their limited power, to solicit approval from Rome to carry out their verdict. Instead of the initial charge of blasphemy, they now charge Jesus with sedition against Rome. They employ a crowd that rejects Jesus as their king, and through the crowd, they threaten Rome with a riot if their request is not granted. "Give us Barabbas!" demands the crowd, "Barabbas, the insurrectionist." The religious authorities know the power of intimidation.

The issues of power and control are important for Jesus, too. Although in his case, he is transforming our understanding of power. Power is not something that requires intimidation of any kind. Power and authority for Jesus are well beyond whatever

Rome could exercise or grant to others. While their power comes from God, who is permitting these things to happen, Jesus knows his fight is with spiritual forces in high places.

In Jesus' response to the high priest, Jesus speaks of Heaven being opened and the Son of Man ascending and descending from above. It is a reference to the dream of the Patriarch Jacob affirming God's sovereignty and identifying ultimate power with God alone (Genesis 28:10–15). With God all things are possible, and the weakness of God is a greater power than any coercive force from Pilate or the high priest. Jesus will win this battle according to the will of God (Mark 14:36).

The real issues for Jesus involve the liberation of the creation to realize its God-given design and purpose. Sin has created a darkness, an evil separation from God. The penalty for this sin is death. And Jesus holds the power to pay that penalty so that sin no longer holds any power to separate creation from the love of God. Political and religious structures that may help us attend to some understanding of God are limited. These institutions are unable to defeat the power of sin. Jesus' power brings new life to the wilderness.

Jesus is the master fisher of men who uses the frailty and helplessness of human life to break the power of evil. In his own body and Spirit, he absorbs the anger and hostility of a world opposed to God and so quenches the evil (Ephesians 6:10–18). By his resurrection he offers new life in a new world for all who repent and believe.

Consider the matter of power another way. In Christian thought there are at least three clearly distinct expressions of power. We may identify them schematically as creative power, coercive power, and redemptive/suffering power. All three are available to Jesus and used by him. He multiplies bread and fish, he demands demons to be silent, commands the wind and the sea to be calm, and here, he suffers the ignorance and abuse from those he came to save.

The divine power of creation brings into being something

ex nihilo, out of nothing. This is the meaning of "created" of the opening words of Genesis, "In the beginning, God created the heavens and the earth." It is affirmed by John in the fourth Gospel (John 1:1–5) and by Paul in a number of places (e.g., Colossians 1:15–20). All creation has its origin from God.

Human beings are given opportunity to participate in the created order in a variety of ways. In the Genesis narrative, they care for a garden and they name the animals. Creativity continues to characterize human beings and human beings look for the creative hand of God to bring healing to the sick, comfort to the bereaved, and direction to the lost.

Coercive power comes when one person, for good or ill, desires to control another. The good uses of coercive power include the nurture and care of children by their parents, the government of society, the employment of people in a workforce, and the proclamation of religious values.

Unfortunately, while coercive power is good, the abuse of this power is evil and appears to require another coercive force to remedy it. Ultimate coercive power belongs to God. In the Scripture, this power is frequently referred to as the exercise of God's right hand. In the words of the song of Moses and Miriam celebrating the exodus, Moses sang, "Your right hand, O Lord, was majestic in power. Your right hand, O Lord, shattered the enemy" (Exodus 15:6). Similarly, the psalmist writes, "Sing unto the Lord a new song, for he has done marvelous things, his right hand and his holy arm have worked salvation for him" (Psalm 98:1).

While the right hand is an expression of power, it is also an expression of honor. "The Lord says to my Lord, 'Sit at my right hand until I make your enemies a footstool for your feet'" (Psalm 110:1).

Jesus gives the right hand of God a new meaning after the resurrection and ascension. When he is seated at the right hand of God, he receives an unparalleled honor (Philippians 2:5–11). He also identifies the right hand of power with his suffering and his suffering is more powerful than any coercive power. It can change lives.

It is the suffering Christ who is victorious over evil. The armies of Heaven do not fight for him. They represent an inferior force. He conquers by redemptive suffering, by absorbing evil and destroying the evil use of coercive power associated with it. In the Epistle to the Ephesians, the Apostle Paul indicates that when Christ is seated at the right hand of God, this is the new expression of divine power (Ephesians 1:18–20).

Years earlier, when Peter had been brought before the Sanhedrin, Peter made the same claims: "The God of our fathers raised Jesus from the dead—whom you had killed by hanging him on a tree. God exalted him to his own right hand as Prince and Savior that he might give repentance and forgiveness of sins to Israel. We are witnesses of these things, and so is the Holy Spirit, whom God has given to those who obey him" (Acts 5:30–32). One cannot give repentance and forgiveness of sins by employing coercive power. Jesus' crucifixion relegates coercive power to the trash heap of human history.

In the letter to the Philippians, Paul uses this "suffering power" as an encouragement to others. It is in the mind of Christ who humbled himself by entering human history even though he could claim equality with God. Hence, Paul writes, "Your attitude should be the same as that of Christ" (Philippians 2:5) who humbled himself even to death on the cross. For this humbling of the Lord Jesus, God has exalted him and given him a name above all others.

Throughout history this type of power has expressed itself more often than one might think, though never with the profound consequence of being seated at the right hand of God. It is the sacrificial love of a parent for a child being threatened, and in the sacrificial service of a soldier for his country. It is in everyone who, out of love, takes the burden of someone else.

Mark clearly emphasizes coercive power in Jesus' death at the hands of others. The religious leaders, the hostile crowd,

Pilate, and the soldiers all flex their muscles. They beat him, spit on him, club him, and mock him. In the end, coercive power kills Jesus without redeeming anything. Coercive power remains and goes on to the next crucifixion, and to the next, and to the next.

Of course, force is sometimes justifiably used to protect someone's interest. In some instances, it promotes good. Jesus, however, who has come to redeem others by giving his life as a ransom, does not appeal to coercive power. He does not "command his angels to fight for him" nor does he come down from the cross.

This redemptive suffering power is a mystery. Mark's two great mentors, the Apostles Peter and Paul, have both proclaimed it. Paul spoke of it in his letter to the Corinthians, "We preach Christ crucified, a stumbling block to the Jews and foolishness to Gentiles" (1 Corinthians 1:23). Peter, speaking at Solomon's colonnade, proclaimed, "The God of our fathers has glorified his [suffering] servant" (Acts 3:13).

The church at Rome would certainly have heard it from both Apostles. In the wilderness where life does not thrive, suffering is an everyday experience. Do not be surprised by it. Learn from the redemptive love of the one who suffered and died for you. This is profound counsel for the Church in Rome suffering oppression and persecution under Nero. Being faithful to the authority of God is sure to result in persecution, from political authorities and even religious authorities who fail to submit to the will of God.

Paul teaches that to suffer with Christ is the prelude to sharing in his glory. Paul writes, "I consider that our present sufferings are not worth comparing with the glory that will be revealed in us" (Romans 8:17–18). "We rejoice in our sufferings," Paul wrote to the church at Rome, "because we know that suffering produces perseverance; perseverance, character; and character, hope. And hope will not disappoint us" (Romans 5:3–5). In the face of suffering, let there be a beacon of hope.

Peter writes, "It is better to suffer for doing good, than for doing evil. For Christ died for sins once for all, the righteous for the unrighteous, to bring you to God." He adds, "Since Christ suffered in his body, arm yourselves also with the same attitude, because he who has suffered in his body is done with sin. As a result, he does not live the rest of his earthly life for evil human desires, but rather for the will of God" (I Peter 3:17–18 and 4:1–2). Suffering is not strange to people living in the wilderness. Those who know the will and power of God rise above the suffering and rejoice when participating in the sufferings of Christ (I Peter: 4:13). For Peter, this amounts to nothing less than a seismic shift in his understanding of Jesus. Peter, you remember, is the one who had said suffering and death would not come to the Messiah.

There is at least one Roman soldier observing the noble suffering of Jesus on the cross who exclaims, "Truly this man is the Son of God." For the casual reader, this may appear a solid identification, but for the observant reader, perhaps not. It has some affinity to the identification of Jesus by demons, hardly helpful for someone from a Hebrew background. While demons are untrustworthy liars and deceivers, the centurion comes from a culture with many gods. As such the comment may reflect less on the identification of Jesus and more on the sentiment of the observer.

Look at the question this way: is the centurion referring to the God of the Hebrews or to one of the gods in the Roman pantheon? The centurion need not identify which god in the pantheon for the focus was on Jesus. Jesus had a dignity and strength beyond what the centurion normally saw at a crucifixion and this "superhuman" quality would make Jesus more than human, namely, divine.

Roman civilization recognized many human beings with noble characteristics and power as people related somehow to the realm of divine beings. Jesus' nobility while being crucified would identify him with that other realm. As the NIV puts in a footnote, "Truly this man was a son of God." From the centurion's perspective, why not include Jesus in the Roman pantheon of gods? In the mind of the soldier, Jesus' death was stunning in comparison to the deaths of so many others.

Even so, the Church in Rome might treat the statement in terms of their own faith. Jesus is the Son of God. Perhaps they would see the centurion like Jesus saw the scribe, not far from the kingdom.

The women who come to the tomb may have had some inkling of the power of suffering in their own lives. What mother hasn't suffered for the betterment of her children? It is a suffering they can honor by anointing the body of the man they loved. And there is much more to the story than what they imagine.

Unfortunately, Mark does not provide us with much more insight into the role the women may have played throughout the Gospel story. It is significant that the text ends with the women being afraid. It is similarly significant that they were instructed to tell people what they have witnessed, and Mark at least indicates that they remain silent because of their fear. We will discuss further why Mark concludes his good news with this story.

Mark is writing during a period of history and in a culture in which gender roles are viewed very differently from the post-modern, post-Christian world in which we live today. That being said, it is noteworthy that he seems to elevate the unexpected role of women: consider the woman who was healed of her bleeding, the woman who gave two copper coins, and the women who are present for the crucifixion and burial.

The theological lesson of how Mark treats these stories goes well beyond any claims of gender equality. He is highlighting something about the kingdom of God. Creation, humanity, and gender are not viewed by social expectations. This holds true today. Rather, God judges the heart.

It is my prayer that by this moment you have already caught

on to the paradox of God's kingdom. Things are not as they seem if judged by human institutions, political or religious. Mark seems to be teaching that God's care is focused on how much we love God, with our whole heart, soul, and mind—and how we care for each other.

Consider now what the crucifixion might mean to Peter. He was the one who protested that Jesus would certainly not die. He saw no power in death. And now that Jesus has been killed (just as Jesus had said), all seemed lost.

Notice how Mark tells Peter's story. Nowhere does Mark include a story in which Peter might boast even though there were many such stories. These stories of Peter are derived from other sources. Matthew calls Peter the "First" of the disciples, not Mark. Peter walks on water (Matthew 14:29), but Mark does not record the story. John and Peter run to the empty tomb, John stops outside the tomb, and Peter is the first to enter it (John 20:3–9). Paul says Jesus appeared to Peter first and then to the other disciples, nothing about this in Mark at all! Indeed, there is nothing in Mark which opens up the slightest possibility of boasting on Peter's behalf, and that includes especially an appearance of the risen Jesus to Peter.

Instead we get Peter's failings. He failed to understand what being the Christ meant, he did not know what to say on the Mount of Transfiguration, he knew the fig tree was cursed but did not comprehend why, he vowed to defend Jesus but failed three times.

These "failures" are what the Apostle Paul would call boasting in our weakness so that the glory of the Lord would shine. It is also a reason to think about Mark as a sermon, specifically as Peter's testimony, rather than a history of Jesus. Like Paul who writes to the Corinthians, "I resolved to know nothing while I was with you except Jesus Christ and him crucified" (1 Corinthians 2:2). Peter appears to do the same thing before the people of Rome whom he loved.

If Peter truly does share the same attitude, then one should not expect a resurrection appearance of Jesus, especially one in which Peter might boast. Instead, expect the sermon to end with a crucified Jesus. This is so "faith might rest, not on human wisdom but on the power of God" (1 Corinthians 2:4–5). One may rely on the Spirit of God to reveal what needs to be revealed.

Hence, the drama not only minimizes the importance of coercive power it also suppresses boasting in anything or anyone other than Jesus crucified to the glory of God. This dependence requires faith, faith in the promises of God. For Peter, his defiance of Jesus' purpose in dying is changed by the resurrection—and that changed him.

When the man dressed in white greets the women, they are frightened by his unexpected appearance. For the reader, his white clothing would be reminiscent of Jesus' clothes in the transfiguration (Mark 9:3). His words, "Don't be alarmed," remind readers of other angelic visitations in which people are greeted with, "Fear not." His encouragement to tell Peter and those with him that Jesus will meet them in Galilee as he promised repeats the message Jesus himself introduced (Mark 9:30; 10:34; 14:28).

However, the women leave trembling and say nothing to anyone. If the message of a resurrection is to succeed, it is without coercion even from angels. It is not without a promise, however, a promise which calls for repentance and faith.

It is interesting that angels play such a small role in the Gospel, smaller than that of Satan it would seem. Yet, it is an important role. In the very beginning of the Gospel, Mark tells of angels ministering to Jesus when he is driven by the Spirit into the wilderness. Now, as Mark closes his account, he lets us know that the angels minister with words of encouragement to the women at the tomb, and by extension, to Peter, to the disciples, and to us while we are in our own wildernesses.

If we may be so bold as to return to the lesson of the fig tree, let us observe that the tree has been replaced in the sowing of a new seed that will come forth from the tomb to the glory of God. Early in the morning when the new day begins, the "seed" that died is reported to be alive and to bring new life into the world, a life that can never perish, spoil, or fade. If we believe this Gospel is Peter's testimony—his sermon—then Mark did not quote from Psalm 118 by chance when Jesus entered Jerusalem on Palm Sunday. The words: "Blessed is he who comes in the name of the Lord" are followed by other words making reference to overcoming death and rejoicing in a new day.

"I will not die but live and will proclaim what the Lord has done. The Lord has chastened me overly, but he has not given me over to death" (Psalm 118:17) and "This is the day the Lord has made; let us rejoice and be glad in it" (Psalm 118:24).

A spiritual reading will rest on a reasonable faith. And faith rests on a promise.

The tomb is empty! This is the *good news!*

PERSPECTIVE

Following the arrest, trials, and execution of Jesus, Joseph of Arimathea asks for the body. He places it in a tomb designed for himself. When people come to the tomb to anoint the body, the tomb is empty. An angel explains, "He has risen! He is not here. See the place where they laid him. But go, tell the disciples and Peter, 'He is going ahead of you to Galilee. There you will see him, just as he told you.'" Trembling and bewildered, the women went out and fled from the tomb. They said nothing to anyone because they were afraid (Mark 16:6b–8). So ends the *Good News*! Brilliant! And, once again, contrary to human expectations.

When we began our study, we made the point that much of what is in the other Gospels is not in Mark. Interpreters often add information from the other Gospels to "fill in" the story of Jesus. This is fine, as long as it does not detract from the point Mark wishes to make. The prologue states that the Spirit of

God is invading the wilderness and guiding Jesus from the very beginning. His story is not about lineage or parentage.

The conclusion is similar. Remember, this Gospel is neither a biography nor a history. It is *Good News*! This is Peter's sermon. It is an evangelistic call to repentance.

Compare the Gospel of Mark to Peter's sermon on Pentecost. Both are a call to repentance, a call to those to whom Peter spoke and a call to those who read the Gospel Mark wrote.

Peter explained: Fellow Israelites, listen to this: Jesus of Nazareth was a man accredited by God to you by miracles, wonders and signs, which God did among you through him, as you yourselves know (Acts 2:22).

This is the outline followed by Mark in the first half of his Gospel. From Peter he knew who witnessed the miracles, wonders, and signs. He knew the various reactions of people to what they saw. He understood why each narrative, or combination of narratives had a role in justifying the claim that Jesus was accredited by God. Peter saw all this firsthand.

The second sentence in Peter's sermon on Pentecost is just as brief as the first.

Peter continues: This man was handed over to you by God's deliberate plan and foreknowledge; and you, with the help of wicked men, put him to death by nailing him to the cross (Acts 2:23).

Mark explains how this happened. Jesus carefully and repeatedly instructed the disciples that he would be killed. He also told them why. Even more importantly, Jesus said this was the point of his mission in the world. This is the *good news*.

The entire Gospel of Mark is summarized by these two excepts from the sermon on Pentecost. The remainder of Peter's sermon describes how God raised him up, making him Lord and Messiah. The people listening ask, what then shall we do? Peter's answer: Repent and be baptized, every one of you, in the name of Jesus who is the Christ (Acts 2:38).

Remember, when Jesus announces his mission, he proclaims:

"The kingdom of God is near. Repent and believe the good news." He did this throughout Galilee. When he comes to the Sea of Galilee, he sees Simon and his brother Andrew. He calls them to follow him promising he would make them fishers of men. Jesus calls two more fishermen and the story begins.

Mark has made the story of Jesus a story about the kingdom of God, repentance, and believing. As such it is appropriate to ask for instances of repentance and faith in connection with the presence of the kingdom.

The first few healing stories—the man with a demon, Peter's mother-in-law, and the many who come for healing—make no mention of either repentance or belief. Jesus heals people and they are thrilled. The next story is of a man with leprosy who understands that if Jesus wishes he could heal the man. This is a story of faith, not of repentance.

The very next story is the healing of a paralytic. Mark calls attention to those who bring the paralytic to Jesus. When he sees their faith, he proceeds to heal the man. Jesus begins by forgiving the man's sin. The teachers of the law take offense at this saying only God can forgive sins. Amazingly, there is no indication of what sin the man had committed and no repentance—just Jesus' responding to the faith of those bringing the paralytic.

Later in Mark's narrative, Jesus meets a second person possessed by a demon who goes by the name Legion. Jesus heals him too. Again, there is no mention of repentance. The following two stories, however, do include faith in Jesus—yet without mention of repentance. First, Jairus has faith that Jesus can heal his daughter. Then, the woman with the health issue believes if she can touch the hem of Jesus' garment she will be healed. To the woman Jesus explains it was not the touch of his garment that healed her. It is her faith. To Jairus, who has learned his daughter is dead, Jesus says comfortingly, "Don't be afraid; just believe."

There are other mentions of faith, primarily regarding the

absence of it. The lack of faith meant Jesus was unable to do many miracles in his hometown. Jesus also chastises his disciple for not having faith when he stills the storm at sea. In the healing of a child possessed by a destructive spirit Mark provides another example. Only the Father had some hope when he said, "I do believe, help me overcome my unbelief." And the disciples sent out were unable to heal as a result of their lack of faith.

The connection of faith with repentance does not come until very late in the narrative. At the Last Supper, the disciples are told they will all fall away. When Peter protests that he will never betray Jesus, that he would die for him, Peter is told he will deny Jesus three times before the rooster crows twice in the coming morning. When Peter hears the cock crow the second time, he knows what he has done and he weeps bitterly. This is a profound and deep repentance. In Jesus' hour of need Peter was not to be found.

To be sure, Peter had spoken against Jesus before this moment. He had rebuked Jesus for saying he would die at the hands of the religious authorities. In turn, Jesus sternly rebuked Peter: "Get behind me Satan! You do not have in mind the things of God, but the things of men." Peter might have repented. He did not. He continued his error up to the end. At that time, it was a foregone conclusion that Jesus would be crucified, and Peter would not have opportunity to ask for forgiveness. Note, this is the only time repentance is part of the story.

For Peter, once Jesus is dead and buried in a tomb, all hope was lost. Jesus had forewarned of his death many times. Peter missed it. Jesus had clearly said "that he must be killed and after three days rise again." Yet, Peter, and all the disciples "did not understand what he meant and were afraid to ask him about it."

Jesus dies on the cross and is buried in a tomb. The tomb does not bear his name. It is the tomb of Joseph of Arimathea—it bears his name. Joseph is described as "one who is waiting for the kingdom of God."

Tombs bear witness to those who were once alive and are now gone. Often, what we know from the tombstone is limited to the name of the dead accompanied by dates of birth and death. The size and quality of the stone is what we believe marks the significance of the life this person led.

Jesus has no such monument. The tomb is empty. We know from other Gospels how Jesus appeared to the disciples. This is not included in Mark's Gospel, yet, his Gospel is telling the *Good News* of Jesus as Peter proclaimed it.

Mark's silence about the conclusion of the story is his brilliance. This is a testimony of faith, giving witness to the kingdom of God. For Peter, the empty tomb is sufficient. This reminds him of Jesus' purpose: he came to die. More than that, it is a reminder that death would not hold him. In three days, Jesus would restore the temple. Jesus is alive. And through his death, he is the first to be resurrected into the kingdom.

Peter is the first to repent. Accordingly, he becomes the foundation for the Church. The proof of his repentance is in the changes that come in Peter's life. His new perception of suffering was the first evidence of that change. Jesus was the suffering Servant of God [3] through whom the kingdom of God would come.

This identification was perhaps the first theological interpretation of Jesus that understood the significance of his life in terms of the kingdom of God. What Peter found most distasteful became the cornerstone of his counsel to others. In his first epistle Peter writes believers "should rejoice when they participate in the sufferings of Christ" (I Peter 4:13).

In the Gospel According to Mark, Peter is the only one whose repentance is emphasized. He wept bitterly! Here is the clue

---

3 See Isaiah 52:13–53:12 and references from Peter's comments found in the book of Acts, in which he uses the word "Servant" to describe Jesus. See Acts 3:13 and 26; 4:27 and 30. F. F. Bruce refers to Peter's identification of Jesus as the Suffering Servant as the earliest Messianic interpretation of Servant in relation to Jesus (*Commentary of the Book of Acts*, page 88).

why there is no reference to Peter seeing the risen Christ. He had boasted throughout his life that he knew better than Jesus. "You will not die." "I will not desert you!" These are among his comments. Realizing how very wrong he was, he would not take any credit for walking on water, or for being the first to see the risen Christ. Even his Gospel is under someone else's name. Peter would speak of his failures, his unbridled pride, and offer his repentance in his final word of conviction. The empty tomb was enough to stir him to faith. His newfound humility would keep him in the background allowing the story to speak for itself.

The Gospel of Mark is pastoral. Peter, pastor to the church at Rome, is sharing his story of coming to faith. The church certainly knew this as Peter's story. They heard him preach about the resurrection of Jesus. They knew of Peter's betrayal on the night Jesus was arrested. His story encouraged the church to endure the brutal suffering, as Jesus had done; as Peter, who asked to be crucified upside down, had now endured. This suffering is powerful and brings God's comfort to the church —a powerful witness to the one who baptizes with the Holy Spirit.

The Gospel is also evangelistic. It is a testimony on how Peter comes to faith. And it is much more. It is a call for everyone who hears the *Good News* to repent, for the kingdom of God is now here. Mark shows great respect for the reader. You are free to hear the story, free to choose whether to believe, and free to answer the call. God's kingdom is come to the wilderness to rescue those who know the voice of the one who is calling.

RESPONDING
TO
GOOD NEWS

Who Do You Say That I Am?

(by David E. Jacobsen, PsyD)

There are many challenges to personal faith in God, even God who, through the incarnation, crucifixion, and resurrection, has become himself the creation and experienced every temptation, emotion, and intellectual struggle with which every human being throughout history has experienced. One such challenge is that very few ever come to know God solely through intellectual pursuits. There are some examples throughout history. Most come to faith through personal struggle, perseverance, and wisdom revealed that defies social expectation. As the scholarly and pastoral reflections of my father have now been shared, I encourage each reader to engage with the Gospel, whether it comes from this book, Mark, or your own personal interaction with God. The Gospel is not a text, nor is it a lecture or a sermon. It is the very *good news* that God loves you. He created you. He prepared everything for you. And, when you, like every human being throughout history, failed in your holy relationship with God, it is he who took your place in death for the penalty of your sin.

My career has in some manner paralleled that of my father. It is not that I was a full-time teacher, nor a full-time pastor. Rather, it is in ways that my personal striving for learning more about God and his creation has been a constant pursuit. I have often described my interests in both theology and psychology as a longing for answers to two questions that have transcended human history: *Who is God? Who is Man?* [1]

During my undergraduate studies, I focused on two majors: psychology and Biblical and theological studies, receiving a bachelor's degree in each from North Park College. I immediately pursued graduate education, studying theology at North Park Theological Seminary. I struggled with the notion of preparing for a life of ministry. Much of that struggle stemmed more from a lack of human experience than understanding. Coupled with watching my peers complete seminary training only to intensely struggle in early pastoral roles confirmed the realization that a prior career would prove invaluable. Hence, I shifted toward graduate education in psychology.

It is amazing how often people from various cultures respond to personal struggles in a similar manner. In child welfare settings, I experienced adolescents asking, "Where is God?" when faced with abuse, neglect, or abandonment. I have witnessed the same question from adolescents in juvenile justice settings, and the same from immigrants, people with disabilities, elderly, and those facing issues of sexual identity, overt racism, poverty, or other oppressions. Similar responses come from those in inner cities, suburbs, and rural areas as well as in Jamaica, Haiti, Guatemala, or anywhere. Individuals who witnessed violence at home, in war, on the streets ask this question as much as those struggling with medical challenges, education, and

---

1 Please note that "Man" in this sense is utilized in a gender-inclusive manner reflective of its usage throughout history. Modern cultural adaptations that might prefer a generic term are subject to missing double entendre that I believe is both theologically and psychologically significant. For example, references to Jesus as the "Son of God" and "Son of Man." The maleness of Jesus is not the issue. It is his humanity. Similarly, this question is not about maleness; rather, it is all-inclusive for humanity throughout history. Changes to this language sometimes interfere with theological perspectives—most obviously seen in references to Psalm 8 in comparison with Jesus' reference to himself as Son of Man, notably in Mark 8:38. A longer study may be worthwhile for some; however, this is not an issue that should rise to the level of being a stumbling block. If the reader prefers, use "Who is Human?"

employment. In fact, those who seem to ignore this question seem rather limited—mostly those who live in what some may refer to as privilege, giving perspective from ivory towers on the trials of life.

This brings me to the first of three key personal stories. Much of my family life has included the mission of the Institute of Holy Land Studies. Located on Mt. Zion, nestled inside the walls of the Old City of Jerusalem, this school has existed amid the socio-religious-political hotbed of the Holy City as a beacon of Evangelical thought. Its mission of providing a distinctively Christian education in the context of the land in which the historically factual events occurred has made an indelible impression on my life, as well as the lives of my children, my siblings and their children, and many Christian brothers and sisters from Wheaton College, North Park College, Westmont College, and churches in Illinois, Arizona, Pennsylvania, and more. This relationship began when I was just four years of age.

That particular year, my father led his first group of students from Wheaton College. My mother and older brother joined him. My sister spent that summer with my maternal aunt and her family, while I spent the summer with Bestamor, my father's mother. It was her personal devotion to Christ Jesus, exemplified through her support for her pastor and missionaries all over the world as well as her leadership with the Ladies' Aid at Calvary Evangelical Free Church in Essex Fells, New Jersey, that first impressed upon me a calling to Christian service. As a four-year-old child, the experience of God was perhaps more clear than the understanding of myself and the sin that lay ahead of me—a sin though within me was nowhere in my consciousness.

Perhaps this is part of why it is easier for a child to express faith. Children are used to relying on others, usually good-enough parents, teachers, or siblings. Relying upon God, therefore, is in some ways a much more natural expression. In reference to Mark, it is this naive nature that allows Simon to follow Christ, and the same ignorance that is part of his identifying Jesus as, "You are the Christ!" Unfortunately, the reality of our own desires overcomes the simplicity of childlike faith.

Each one of us, regardless of our diversity, is unified in our experience of personal sin, failure, and challenges that come from within. Likewise, each of us experiences challenges that come from our experience of others, whether systemic or idiosyncratic. We have professions dedicated to learning disability, justice, social work, and self-help. We have both scientific and alternative medicines for nearly every ailment. There is unity in struggle —even for those who are privileged, even for religious leaders, and even for those blind to their own being.

The good news is Jesus, God, came to see you through those struggles.

The second personal story addresses difficulty. In fourth grade, with a strong desire to be with my friends from school, my parents enrolled me in the local AWANA program at Wheaton Bible Church. This program focused on games, fellowship, and Bible memory. Each year, students would go through a developmentally appropriate book that outlines the Gospel supported by tasks of Bible memory. If the book is completed before the year is finished, the student goes through the same book a second time to reinforce the learning. There are many verses that remain readily available to me as a result; however, it was what happened next that has shaped much of my personal and professional life.

As I finished going through my memory book for the second time, my parent leader encouraged me toward a different task: to memorize the book of James.

> *James, a servant of the Lord Jesus Christ, to the twelve tribes scattered abroad. Consider it pure joy, my brothers (and sisters), whenever you face trials of many kinds, because you know the testing of your faith develops perseverance. Let perseverance finish its work that you may*

be mature and complete, not lacking anything. If anyone lacks wisdom, let him ask God, who gives generously to all, without finding fault, and it will be given to you. But when you ask, you must believe and not doubt, because one who doubts is like a wave of the sea, blown and tossed by the wind. That person should not expect to receive anything form the Lord. Such a person is double-minded and unstable in all his ways (James 1:1–8).

How does James relate to Mark is a legitimate question. Memorizing the entire epistle is not nearly as daunting a task as it might seem. In fact, I have often challenged college and graduate students to memorize it for extra credit—and even challenged congregations to take on the challenge. My love for James is more than personal preference. It flows from an understanding of those two enduring questions. A full explanation is an obligation for a different text. For this text, it is enough to acknowledge that James is written to let believers know how they are to behave. It is what I have come to know as the best psychology ever written.

If you don't know ... ask God. If you think you do know ... check your motivation. Every good gift comes from God—even gifts given to those who deny him. And do not deceive yourself, it is not God who tempts ... for you are tempted by your innermost desires, and when those desires mature they give birth to sin, which, in turn, gives birth to death.

Do not merely listen to the Word ... do what [he] says. Translated ... "Just Do It." Religion that God accepts as pure and blameless is this ... look after orphans and widows in their time of need, and keep oneself from being polluted by the world.

You believe there is one God ... good! Even the demons believe that. Show me your faith without deeds, and I will show you my faith by what I do. Abraham. Rahab ...the prostitute. These are the great exemplars of faith.

Words? They mean nothing. Think of how great a forest is

set on fire by a single spark. This is especially poignant in recent years for people in California, Washington, and Colorado. The tongue is a wicked evil. Humble yourself in the sight of the Lord, and he will life you up. For where there is envy and selfish ambition, there you find every kind of evil.

Finally, if any one of you is sick, pray. In fact, just pray all the time. For it is God who is the source of every good thing. On our own, we are nothing.

Personally, this has been my guiding force professionally. In child welfare, teaching at both college and graduate levels, preaching, working with veterans, people with disabilities, reentry, juvenile justice, Special Education, and access to health care, James has provided both my motivation and my accountability check. It is how my faith is lived, even when I fail.

Failure is difficult. And we really should count it all as joy—for it is in our failure that God shines most brightly. How many times have you failed, only to be a positive example for someone else It does not make sense, yet we all know how it feels.

Rev. Dr. Herbert K. Jacobsen is my dad. Papa. I have discussed this book, as well as at least three not yet written, with him for years. He has lived his faith with both integrity and stewardship as a college professor, pastor, father, grandfather, great-grandfather, and friend. Most everyone who has ever known him understands each role he has played ... he is well-loved.

This leads into the third story. Without any details, it is enough for the reader to know that I have twice failed at marriage. However, the six children who call me Dad all call my father Papa. I have no regrets. In fact, my children have become the next best example of my faith.

In 2017, Papa led yet another trip to Israel. It was my fifth time joining him at what is now known as Jerusalem University College. It was also the second trip for my son, T.J. This time was different. Keli, Ethan, and Lynnea were coming, too. For T.J., it was a second chance. He had enjoyed his first trip, and he fully acknowledges that he did not take it as seriously as he would like. This time, he was determined to learn and grow in faith—and he was equally determined to make sure that his siblings understood the opportunity.

I have several good memories from this trip. I took the approach of thinking it might be the last time I get to Israel with Papa—and I wanted my kids to know what I have known. I did not know at the time that it was Pastor Paul Thompson who would be on the trip for the last time. My kids and I thoroughly enjoyed his pastoral leadership. For the reader, know this: God loves you. There is no greater message from Paul's life. God loves you.

There is no greater privilege in life than watching your children grow in their relationship with the loving God. Watching Keli walk the Snake Path with Papa ... watching T.J. absorb every lecture and vista ... seeing Ethan and Keli holding hands through the Old City ... witnessing Lynnea engage in historical stories of Samson, Saul, David, and Jesus throughout Galilee. Every moment a source of both pride and gratitude as each of them sat at the feet of the master with Papa as their guide. Anyone searching for the meaning of life ... there it is.

Each of these three stories demonstrates my faith in Jesus as the Christ. There is much more to both my failures and my faith. Yet, these are sufficient to identify my own Cephas. For, with enthusiasm, I claim Jesus as my Lord and Savior. And, with shame, I have often found myself awakened by the cock crowing for the third time. This is perhaps the most significant aspect of genuine faith, the paradox of *simul justus et pecataur*.

Papa has taught me a lot about paradox. It is among our favorite subjects—even when watching what some might consider purely secular movie. Even in those, the grace of God is evident for those who pay attention.

So, the time has come for me to introduce the question that guides the epilogue: "Who do you say that I am?" Is Jesus the Son of God? Son of Man? Is he the Christ?

There is one more story to share, although it is not one that belongs to me. Rather, it belongs to my father. In our home we had a wide variety of used furniture. Among the favorites was a pair of rather ugly orange swivel chairs, straight out of 1970s fashion. Papa was sitting in one of these chairs, contemplating the veracity of the Christian faith. In truth, even with a doctorate in theology and serving in a faculty position teaching theology at Wheaton, Dad's faith was highly contemplative. He struggled with the philosophical explanation for the Christian faith, even while teaching apologetics (defense of the Christian faith).

Suddenly, Dad slammed his hands on the arms of the chair. He stood. "It has to be true."

Whether you, the reader, reach this same conclusion is entirely dependent upon your relationship with God. The call to repent is made to all. Follow Jesus. The Jesus who amazed the crowds, befuddled the religious leaders, healed the sick, and privately taught a mismatch of fishermen and tax collectors to advance the *good news* that God loves you.

Epilogue (16:9–20)

9 When Jesus rose early on the first day of the week, he
appeared first to Mary Magdalene, out of whom he had
driven seven demons. 10 She went and told those who had
been with him and who were mourning and weeping. 11
When they heard that Jesus was alive and that she had
seen him, they did not believe it.

12 Afterward Jesus appeared in a different form to two of
them while they were walking in the country. 13 These
returned and reported it to the rest; but they did not
believe them either.

14 Later Jesus appeared to the Eleven as they were eating;
he rebuked them for their lack of faith and their stubborn
refusal to believe those who had seen him after he had risen.

15 He said to them, "Go into all the world and preach
the gospel to all creation. 16 Whoever believes and is bap-
tized will be saved, but whoever does not believe will be
condemned. 17 And these signs will accompany those who
believe: In my name they will drive out demons; they
will speak in new tongues; 18 they will pick up snakes with
their hands; and when they drink deadly poison, it will
not hurt them at all; they will place their hands on sick
people, and they will get well."

> [19] *After the Lord Jesus had spoken to them, he was taken up into heaven and he sat at the right hand of God.* [20] *Then the disciples went out and preached everywhere, and the Lord worked with them and confirmed his word by the signs that accompanied it.*

Most Bibles will indicate that these verses were not included in the original text to the Gospel of Mark. Rather, the text ends with the bewilderment of those at the tomb who found it empty. Mark, quite intentionally I believe, leaves the ending to the response of the reader.

I have shared in my writing both that I know the weakness of my sinful desires and the grace of the forgiveness found in a loving God. For me, responding to the needs of others is a way of showing my faith in Jesus as the Christ.

Mark leaves the text where I now leave it for you. Jesus is the Christ. That is truth. However, you are free to respond as the crowds, Pharisees, Apostles, or even as the demons. Therefore, the question that Jesus has is this: "Who do you say that I am?"

Acknowledgments

When first asked to teach New Testament Survey, it seemed good to present the theme for each work in the New Testament. Only one presented a serious problem: the Gospel according to Mark. Primarily, I was troubled with the ending, as were many others. The explanations offered by scholars was insufficient to explain why there was no appearance of the resurrection of Jesus to someone—especially Peter.

I read many commentaries and was helped virtually by each of them in regard to the outline for Mark's presentation and not by how the conclusion was handled. My appreciation is great for the hundreds of people who have helped me: students, colleagues, seminars, ministerial retreats, camp presentations, family, friends, church groups, and many others to whom this presentation was offered.

In the text there are a few acknowledgments which I leave for you to discover. Here I would merely identify a few who have stood alongside me with their encouragement and expertise.

Who Am I? is the result of my lifelong response to the good news within the Gospel according to Mark. My thanks begin where my journey of faith began, with my family. My parents instilled within me a sense of ministry and relationship with the Lord. My wife, Phyllis, with her reminder for me to seek first the kingdom of God. Our children—Kevin, Cathie, and David—who each in their own way helped clarify the text for others to read.

Several helped provide much-needed scholarly criticism. For their candor and expertise, I am sincerely grateful. Donald Hagner, Hassell Bullock, Morris Inch, and Gilbert Bilizikian have each influenced both my thoughts and my faithful response to Mark's Gospel. Several of my teachers, especially

David Beckman and Keith Yandell, laid the intellectual foundation upon which my thesis is formed. These colleagues are among many who further the good news through academic study and faithful application of the text.

As I have had opportunities to teach the premise of this book in many settings, both academic and pastoral, there are those who have helped with the never-ending task of proofreading. Among them, Rev. J. Paul Thompson, a former student with whom I shared congregational ministry, missions, and study, and one of my closest friends in life. I believe Paul would be proud of this work and how it shares the simple message, "God loves you."

Rev. Paul Wright, Rev. Arthur Barton, Carol Roberts, and several lay readers, provided their own personal responses—both to Mark and to my teaching of the gospel. Their feedback honed this presentation.

I am indebted to my son David, who took it upon himself to clarify for others what his father was trying to say in the language of a college professor giving a lecture instead of the author of a book. Thank you for all you have done.

Most importantly, I want to acknowledge you, the reader. For it is your willingness to engage with this text that is my true purpose in writing it. My days of teaching are mostly behind me, yet God has placed upon my heart the desire to continue to shepherd and serve. For my grandchildren, my great grandchildren, congregations I have served, pastors and colleagues, and the many faculty and students of Christian higher education, this text is intended to engage you further in your relationship with Almighty God. I encourage you to do more than read the book—spend time in thoughtful meditation, prayer, and reflection. Question each premise. Pragmatically apply each lesson. And respond to the prompting of the Holy Spirit with the fullness of God's love.

To God be the glory.

—Dr. Herbert K. Jacobsen

Bibliography

Alter, Robert, and Kermode, Frank, eds. *The Literary Guide to the Bible*. Cambridge: Belknap Press, 1987.

St. Anselm. "Cur Deus Homo" in *St. Anselm Basic Writings*. La Salle, IL: Open Court, 1962.

Aristotle. *On the Art of Poetry*. Edited and translated by Lane Cooper. New York: Cornell University, 1947.

St. Augustine. *The Confessions of St. Augustine*. Translated by John K. Ryan. New York: Image, 2014.

St. Augustine. *The Enchiridion on Faith, Hope, and Love*. Chicago: Henry Regnery Co., 1961.

Babylonian Talmud, *Sanhedrin*. 98 BC.

Barklay, William. *The Gospel of Mark*. Philadelphia: The Westminster Press, 1975.

Barrett, C. K. *The New Testament Background: Selected Documents*. USA: Harper Torchbooks; first printed by S.P.C.K. London, 1956.

Bilezikian, Gilbert G. *The Liberated Gospel*. Grand Rapids: Baker Books, 1977.

Bruce, F. F. *Commentary on the Book of Acts*. Grand Rapids: Wm. B. Eerdmans, 1973.

Brunner, Emil. *Man in Revolt*. Philadelphia: Westminster Press, 1939.

Card, Michael. *Mark: The Gospel of Passion*. Downer's Grove, IL: InterVarsity Press, 2012.

Carson, D. A., and Moo, Douglas. *An Introduction to the New Testament*. Grand Rapids: Zondervan, 2005.

Cole, Alan. *The Gospel according to Mark*. Grand Rapids: Wm. B. Eerdmans, 1975

Cole, R. A. *The Gospel according to St. Mark*. Grand Rapids: Wm. B. Eerdmans, 1961.

Cullman, Oscar. *Peter*. Cleveland and New York: World, 1961.

Edersheim, Alfred. *The Life and Times of Jesus the Messiah*. New York: Longmans, Green, and Co., 1900.

Ferguson, Duncan S. *Biblical Hermeneutics: An Introduction*. Atlanta: John Knox Press, 1986.

Foxe, John. *Foxe's Christian Martyrs of the World*. Chicago: Moody Press, nd.

Garland, David E. *A Theology of Mark's Gospel*. Grand Rapids: Zondervan, 2015.

Gundry, Robert H. *A Survey of the New Testament*. Grand Rapids: Academie Books, 1981.

Hallesby, Ole. *Prayer*. Minneapolis: Augsburg Press, 1961.

Harrington, Wilfrid. *Mark*. Wilmington: Michael Glazier, 1882.

Harrison, Everett F. *Introduction to the New Testament*. Grand Rapids: Wm. B. Eerdmans, 1968.

Healy, Mary. *The Gospel of Mark*. Grand Rapids: Baker Academic, 2008.

Jacobsen, David Schnasa. *Mark*. Minneapolis: Fortress Press, 2014.

Kee, Howard Clark, and Young, Franklin W. *Understanding the New Testament*. Englewood Cliffs: Prentice Hall, 1957.

Ladd, Geoge Elon. *The New Testament and Criticism*. Grand Rapids: William B. Eerdmans Publishing Company, 1967.

Lane, William L. *The Gospel according to Mark*. Grand Rapids: Wm. Eerdmans Publishing Co., 1974.

Luther, Martin. "Lectures on Romans" in *Luther's Works (Volume 25)*, edited by Hilton C. Oswald. St. Louis: Concordia Publishing House, 1972.

Moe, Olaf. *The Apostle Paul*. Minneapolis: Augsburg Press, 1954.

Newbigin, Lesslie. *The Light Has Come*. Grand Rapids: William B. Eerdmans, 1982.

Niebuhr, Reinhold. *Moral Man and Immoral Society*. New York: Charles Scribner's Sons, 1960.

Osborne, Grant. *Mark*. Grand Rapids: Baker Books, 2014.

Otto, Rudolf. *The Idea of the Holy*. Translated by John W. Harvey. New York: Oxford University Press, 1958.

Rollins, Wayne G. *The Gospels Portraits of Christ*. Philadelphia: The Westminster Press, 1964.

Spivey, Robert A., and Smith, D. Moody Jr. *Anatomy of the New Testament*. London: Collier-Macmillan, 1969.

Stein, Robert H. *Mark*. Grand Rapids: Baker Academic, 2008, 23.

Tappart, Theodore G., ed. *Selected Writings of Martin Luther 1517–1520*. Philadelphia: Fortress Press, 1967.

Tenney, Merrill C. *New Testament Survey*. Grand Rapids: Wm. B. Eerdmans Publishing Co., 1961; 16th printing, 1980.

Tenney, Merrill. *New Testament Times*. Grand Rapids: Wm. B. Eerdmans Publishing Co., 1965.

Wright, N. T. *The Resurrection of the Son of God*. Minneapolis: Fortress Press, 2003.

Wright, Paul. *Greatness, Grace, and Glory*. Jerusalem: Carta, 2008.

Follow me בעקבותי

About the Author

Herbert K. Jacobsen was born in Orange, New Jersey, to Norwegian immigrants Kristin and Ingeborg Jacobsen. He was raised within the faith of Calvary Evangelical Free Church, now in Essex Fells, New Jersey, at a time when the majority of services and lessons were primarily in Norwegian. As he reflects upon his childhood, Herb recognizes the importance of congregational faith. Every member of his confirmation class from Calvary has faithfully served in Christian ministry.

Dr. Jacobsen received his doctorate in religious studies with an emphasis on theology from New York University (including study at Biblical Theological Seminary, New York City). He served as Professor of Theology at Wheaton College (Illinois), including tenure as Chair of the Biblical Studies Department, from 1968 to 1989. Following more than ten years on the Board for Associated Schools, during which time he met regularly with the Board for the Institute of Holy Land Studies, Dr. Jacobsen began his service on the Board for Jerusalem University College (formerly Institute of Holy Land Studies, Jerusalem, Israel) in 1986 and was Chair of the Board from 2006 to 2021 and continues to serve as emeritus.

Pastor Herb served as interim minister for the Evangelical Covenant Church for ten years before accepting a call as the Senior Pastor for Northwest Covenant Church (Mt. Prospect, Illinois), where he served for sixteen years. He accepted a new call to the Church at Hemlock Farms (Lords Valley, Pennsylvania) in 2003 where he continues his pastoral ministry.

Christian missions, at home and abroad, have remained a primary interest for Dr. Jacobsen, consistent with his understanding of the great commission. He has led mission work in Ecuador, Jamaica, Romania, Russia (Siberia), Israel, Liberia, Congo, and the Central African Republic. He has led educational trips for college and graduate students as well as parishioners throughout the Holy Land, including Italy, Greece, Turkey, Egypt, and Israel. He has taught theology in college and graduate programs in Jamaica, Romania, Russia, and Israel.

Among his talents is a hobby of painting. Influenced by friends Dwight Walles and Glynn Roberts, his paintings serve as expressions of his faith and the relationship he holds among God and the recipient of his art. Pictured across is a painting to reflect *Who Am I*? Overlooking fishermen in the Sea of Galilee, one might find the relationship of Peter and the Christ as well as the invitation to join them in sharing the good news of God's love.

Printed in the USA
CPSIA information can be obtained
at www.ICGtesting.com
JSHW010929300723
45537JS00011B/2

9 798218 092177